Buru Island

Buru Island

A Prison Memoir

By Hersri Setiawan

Translated by Jennifer Lindsay

This book was originally published in Indonesian as *Memoar Pulau Buru*.

Buru Island: A Prison Memoir
Written by Hersri Setiawan
Translated by Jennifer Lindsay

© Copyright 2020 Jennifer Lindsay
All rights reserved. Apart from any uses permitted by Australia's Copyright Act 1968, no part of this book may be reproduced by any process without prior written permission from the copyright owners. Inquiries should be directed to the publisher.

Monash University Publishing
Matheson Library Annexe
40 Exhibition Walk
Monash University
Clayton, Victoria 3800, Australia
www.publishing.monash.edu

Monash University Publishing brings to the world publications which advance the best traditions of humane and enlightened thought.

Monash University Publishing titles pass through a rigorous process of independent peer review.

ISBN: 9781925835564 (paperback)
ISBN: 9781925835571 (pdf)
ISBN: 9781925835588 (epub)

www.publishing.monash.edu/books/bm-9781925835564.html

Series: Herb Feith Translation Series

Series Editors: Jemma Purdey and Katharine McGregor

Design: Les Thomas

Front cover image: Barbed wire on sunset sky background by kldy. Shutterstock royalty-free stock photo ID: 119311141

Back cover image: Portrait of Hersri Setiawan courtesy of Ken Setiawan

Maps: Robert Cribb

A catalogue record for this book is available from the National Library of Australia.

Printed in Australia by Griffin Press an Accredited ISO AS/NZS 14001:2004 Environmental Management System printer.

The paper this book is printed on is certified against the Forest Stewardship Council ® Standards. Griffin Press holds FSC chain of custody certification SGS-COC-005088. FSC promotes environmentally responsible, socially beneficial and economically viable management of the world's forests.

CONTENTS

Translator's Note vii
Foreword xi
Glossary xx
Introduction: The Tragedy of 30 September 1965 xxxi

PART I: BEFORE BURU 1
1. From Free Citizen to 'ET' 3
2. Operation Keep Your Mouth Shut 8
3. Journey to the 'Isle of Hope' 25
4. Last days in Camp Tangerang 48
5. Freedom Road 59
6. Tangerang versus Salemba 88

PART II: BURU STORIES 95
7. From Sanleko to Bantalareja 97
8. Starting at Namlea 113
9. First Sunset at Bantalareja 124
10. First Night Roll Call 134
11. Firsts at Unit XIV Bantalareja 142
12. Tales of Unit XIV Bantalareja Clusters 153
13. Tap Water Comes to Unit XV Indrapura 179
14. Command Headquarters Band 190
15. The 'Savanajaya Family' 207
16. Salt Tales 218

PART III: BURU PEOPLE 241
17. Heru Santoso 243

PART IV: LIFE AFTER BURU 323
18. The Purgatory Island of Buru Twenty Years Later 325
19. A Birthday Present for My Daughter 360

About the Author 368
About the Translator 368
About the Herb Feith Translation Series 368

To my grandchildren Setia and Raphael

TRANSLATOR'S NOTE

Buru Island by Hersri Setiawan is the last of four books that I have translated for the Herb Feith Translation Series on the bloody aftermath of the 1965 coup. As this is the last, I would like to here commend the Herb Feith Foundation for its initiative in funding the translation and publication of these books, and particularly Dr Kate McGregor and Dr Jemma Purdey for coordinating the series. It was a bold idea. There are many books written about 1965 in English, which tends to give the impression that it is 'foreigners' who are revealing the 'truth'. However, Indonesians have been doing incredibly important and significant work, especially in oral history presenting first-hand accounts. While these accounts are available in hard copy in Indonesia, foreign readers do not have easy access to them. Without translation, foreign readers who do not read Indonesian have no access at all.

However, these accounts are absolutely essential to a nuanced understanding of the cataclysmic events of late 1965-1966 and the following years of terror and imprisonment without trial of thousands of people accused of being communists. The three books already published in the Herb Feith series on 1965; *Truth Will Out* edited by Baskara T. Wardaya; *Breaking the Silence* edited by Putu Oka Sukanta; and *Forbidden Memories* edited by Mery Kolimon (et al), are collections of transcribed oral accounts by various people who suffered or witnessed the violence, imprisonment and killings.

Hersri's book differs in that it is a single person's written account. Like Hersri's fellow Buru prisoner Pramoedya Ananta Toer in his *Nyanyian Seorang Bisu*, which was translated into English as *The*

Mute's Soliloquy, he records the horrors of the forced incarceration on Buru. Both books convey their writers' sense of urgency at bearing witness, yet they have a very different tone. Hersri's writing is more multi-faceted and multi-voiced. Fellow prisoners come fully to life, and he shows that there were many 'us's and 'them's.

Before Hersri was finally arrested in Jakarta in late 1969, he was already somewhat of an outsider to the communist scene, as he had returned to Indonesia in late August 1965 – only one month before the coup of September 30 – after working for four years in Colombo, Sri Lanka (then Ceylon) for the Asia-Africa Writers Bureau. This gives Hersri's memoirs a sharp focus and an observer's distance. His writing has a deeply ironic tone. As the translator of the memoirs, my first challenge was to capture and convey this tone.

Hersri is a vivid, fluent writer. As he explains in the book, before his appointment in Colombo, he was involved in senior management of Lekra, the Institute of People's Culture that had links to the Communist Party. He himself was also a well-known writer, particularly of poetry (in Indonesian). He came from Yogyakarta, central Java, and his mother tongue was Javanese. He was brought up with a strong diet of Javanese oral performance forms like *wayang kulit* and *ketoprak*. His language in the memoirs draws on all these linguistic styles: there is formal Indonesian prose, quotes of his own poetry, and colloquial dialogue often heavily laced with Javanese.

Hersri's Javanese background and his wide interest in language and performance influence his writing. He has a sharp ear for speech and is a born storyteller. He remembers events as fully acted out scenes and recreates them in this way. He hears intonation and dialect, and presents them as an essential part of the character of his fellow prisoners and guards. Dialogue is a huge part of the book. He writes stories of his imprisonment in a novelistic way, reproducing Jakarta Betawi dialect, Javanese, Sundanese and North Sumatran accented Indonesian, and even the Ambon-accented militaristic abuse of the prison guards.

Needless to say, English translation cannot capture the richness of all this, but the translation should not homogenise dialogue. As the translator, I had to find ways to show differences in the ways the various characters speak, and ways their speech reveals their relationships to one another. In Indonesian, terms of address are significant because people use them to avoid the awkward directness of pronouns. An egalitarian term of address for males popular in the independence movement and on the Left was *'Bung'*. The communist term for 'comrade' was *'Kawan'*. Other more traditional terms of address were *Pak* (father) for a senior male, *Dik* for younger brother, and *Bang* or *Mas* for older brother. In the memoir, Hersri shows how among prisoners the non-hierarchical Leftist terms *Bung* and *Kawan* came to be replaced by the more traditional terms. Sometimes Hersri draws attention to this by specifically mentioning how someone addressed him – which gave me as translator an opportunity to highlight the issue. I could not flood the book with foreign terms of address throughout, but occasionally, and at important times, I did include them in the English translation.

Hersri's memory for details of events and voices is phenomenal. I believe that his experience of oral performance traditions allowed for that. He is not only able to remember voices, but he uses them to show the diversity of the political prisoners. They are never one block. There are divisions between them, ideological, cultural and generational, big and small, and this book is extremely important for showing that. Hersri reveals prison life, with torture and forced labour, the tension of being shut off from information, and the prisoners' hopes, fears, suspicions, solidarity and betrayals. But at all times, he remains acutely aware of diversity. He maintains the outsider's sharp eye and ear.

The original Indonesian text of *Buru Island* is longer than this English translation. For various reasons, including funding constraints, we did not translate the whole book. Some stand-alone chapters in the original Indonesian were not directly related to Buru or to Hersri's fellow prisoners in Jakarta or Buru. In making the difficult decision of which chapters to omit in the English version, as translator I made suggestions, choosing to omit those chapters that did not relate closely to the Buru story, and could possibly be published separately at a later time. Ken Setiawan and I discussed this between us, and then with Hersri himself who fully agreed with our choices. I urge readers of Indonesian, however, to look at the whole book for other essays.

I learnt a lot translating this book – not only about the misery of life on Buru for the political prisoners, but about the Indonesian language. I thank Hersri for this, and I also thank him and his wife Ita for their patience in answering all my questions.

Jennifer Lindsay

FOREWORD

In 1935 the Indonesian nationalist Sutan Sjahrir sailed past Buru, the third largest island in the Maluku archipelago, on his way to be exiled in the Dutch prison camp Boven Digoel in Papua. During his journey, Sjahrir kept a diary in which he commented extensively on the natural beauty of the islands he passed. Buru, he wrote, looked like "a fairy tale land". Little did Sjahrir know that just over thirty years later, Buru would be Indonesia's largest site of political detention.

Approximately 12,000 men were held on Buru between 1969 and 1979 without formal charge or trial. These prisoners were all detained in the aftermath of Indonesia's 1965-1966 violence. While there were many detention camps across Indonesia, Buru became particularly notorious because of its remote location, harsh climate and tough conditions of detention. Prisoners were subjected to forced labour and worked long days under constant military supervision. The military regularly inflicted physical and mental torture upon the prisoners, and hundreds of them did not survive imprisonment.

My father Hersri Setiawan survived nine years of arbitrary detention under Soeharto's New Order regime, seven of which were spent on Buru. I was born three years after his release, in a society where people like my father were treated as outcasts. It would have perhaps been easier for my parents to remain silent about his experiences, but they did not. They felt that a child would not be able to love and respect her parents if they were not honest with her. Buru simply became part of our everyday family life. For years, my father continued what my mother once called the "rhythm of the prison". He would wake up early, boil water, and start sweeping the floor. My father would often tell me stories about life on Buru. Some of these were upsetting – for instance, I knew from a very young age that my father was deaf in his left ear as a result of torture. Other memories were more light-hearted. For instance, my father would make me simple toys from the skin of pomelo, "just like the children on Buru".

While Buru's prison camp is an integral part of our family history and everyday life, on the island itself there are very few reminders of the camp. When in 2015 I travelled to Buru for the first time with my father, there were no remnants of the prisoner's barracks – these had been demolished a long time ago. The headstones of graves of former prisoners were worn, their names barely legible. It was as if a prison camp had never existed. Buru's natural beauty once described by Sjahrir – its dense forests, open savannas, dramatic limestone cliffs and bright blue sea – are all silent witnesses to the violence and repression endured by many.

In the opening chapter of *Buru Island*, Hersri writes about ignorance and forgetting, as well as the responsibility of history and justice. These are the main themes that this book seeks to address, through providing a unique and detailed account of mass detention in the aftermath of Indonesia's 1965-1966 violence. *Buru Island* speaks of the horrors of this period, such as disappearance, murder, torture, betrayal and loss. It powerfully describes how individuals were reduced to nothing but objects, no longer identified by their name but instead by their prisoner number. Despite all of this, *Buru Island* is not a call for pity. In telling a story of survival, Hersri makes an appeal for acknowledgement of this dark chapter of Indonesian history. This emphasis on survival is a reflection of Hersri's own belief that he is not a victim of the events of 1965 – but, as he writes, "my past bitter experiences […] are the logical consequence of the position and political stand I took consciously". He continues by saying that "I was aware every moment that I could be captured by the authorities. Being prepared for capture meant being prepared to face all kinds of things that went along with that [...] including electric shock equipment, barbed whips, forced labour, prison, exile and even bullets".

Hersri summarises this acceptance through the Javanese term *sumèlèh*: which does not mean to surrender to fate, but to be aware and calm. This approach can, I believe, not only be explained by his Javanese roots and identity but also reflects his sharp observation of the many social and political events that he witnessed. Hersri was born in Yogyakarta in 1936, in a family that highly valued education, culture and language. His father, the head of a village school, exposed him to literature at an early age with a library that had books in Malay, Javanese and Dutch. Hersri's childhood was marked by historical upheaval, the Japanese occupation (1942-1945) and the Independence War (1945-1949). When Hersri was eight years old, his father passed away, leaving his mother to provide for the couple's seven children. In the 1950s, he studied at Gadjah Mada University and the Academy of Film and Dramatic Arts. He taught at several high schools and together with fellow students founded two senior high schools, in Yogyakarta and Wates – which still exist today.

As a student, Hersri became an active contributor to a wide range of magazines and newspapers and established two literary organisations. In 1958, he joined the Left-wing cultural organisation Lekra (Lembaga Kebudayaan Rakyat, Institute of People's Culture) and served as general secretary of its Central Java branch until 1960. About joining Lekra, Hersri writes: "I did this precisely because I was aware that Lekra was not a place just for artists to hang out and enjoy themselves. Lekra was the organisation for the cultural movement. So, of course, I had ideals and purpose. And what were they? To awaken people to be culturally aware. Further, to make the culture of the people the subject in their own country". In 1961, he became the permanent representative of the Indonesian National Committee to the Asia-Africa Writer's Bureau in Colombo in Ceylon (Sri Lanka). Following the 1965 election of a right-wing government in Ceylon, the authorities prohibited the Bureau. Hersri, and eleven other representatives were given 48 hours to leave the country. He returned to Jakarta on August 24, 1965.

Hersri's life – as that of uncountable others – was fundamentally altered by the events of 30 September, 1965 when six senior military leaders and a lieutenant were killed by the so-called Thirtieth of September Movement. The army attributed the Movement to the PKI (Partai Komunis Indonesia, Indonesian Communist Party), leading to the persecution of party members and sympathisers. On 11 March, 1966 the PKI was banned, implicitly including all associated organisations, such as Lekra.

Due to Hersri's recent absence from Indonesia and his relative anonymity in Jakarta (as his prior activities had been in Central Java), he managed to escape immediate detention: "I was able to spend four more years playing cat and mouse night and day in Jakarta". He bided his time by working for various embassies and by completing further studies at the 17th of August University in Jakarta. However, by December 1969 his luck ran out and he was 'picked up', on his way home from a ceremony to commemorate his mother's passing three years prior. Until 1971, he was held in prisons in Jakarta (Salemba jail and, briefly, Tangerang) and was subsequently transported to Buru, where he remained until he was "returned to society" in December 1978.

For ex-political prisoners such as Hersri, life after incarceration was difficult. Former political prisoners were banned from various types of employment, denied an array of civil rights and often ostracised in their communities. For Hersri, it was difficult to find regular work as a writer or translator. However, he continued to write and only six months after his release, Hersri won a prize from the journal *Prisma* for an article on indigenous children on Buru. This once again allowed him to become a freelance contributor to various media, using pseudonyms to publish his work.

Together with his wife, Dutch-born Jitske Mulder whom he married in 1981, Hersri established a translation bureau that provided work to former political prisoners. In addition, acutely aware of the denial and silencing of history by the authorities, Jitske and Hersri started recording the experiences of other former prisoners, as well as writing their own. My mother Jitske, who in Hersri's words "chose to become one of the millions of pariahs of Indonesian society", wrote an autobiographical account of her experiences as the wife of a former political prisoner, published in English as *Quartering* (1991). Hersri also started writing about his imprisonment, for which he drew heavily on the notes he took while still on Buru. In the camp, he hid these notebooks from the guards by burying them close to banana trees, as these trees would absorb water and therefore protect the books. This material is at the basis of *Buru Island*, which also includes chapters written many years after Hersri's release. Together, his writing provides crucial information about Buru's prison camp and about the long-term legacies of mass detention.

In 1987, Hersri and Jitske decided to leave Indonesia for The Netherlands, because she had been diagnosed with terminal cancer. We departed Jakarta on my sixth birthday. My parents did not leave because they feared the oppression of the Soeharto regime. Hersri says, 'as an ex-Buru island prisoner who had experienced everything except death, I was not in the least worried […] Nor was my late wife […] she was fully aware of the consequences of her choice: to live in Indonesia under the military boot, and to become the wife on an ex-Buru prisoner whose life was difficult indeed'. But, he continues, 'we had a daughter. And we could not let her become the victim of people taking law into their own hands'. In 1989, my mother passed away in The Netherlands, when I was seven years old. My father faced a new challenge in his life: to raise a child alone, in a country that was completely new to him. He was a very present father, who placed great emphasis on education. He nourished my knowledge of the Indonesian language, by always speaking this at home, as well as culture and history. He did so because he, and my mother, strongly believed that this would foster my awareness of the world around me. And as my mother wrote in her memoirs, this was important because people 'who stand firm on their feet, [who have] a strong sense of reality can usually survive'.

Hersri also continued working in The Netherlands, initially as a translator and editor at Leiden University. He was a vocal opponent of the Soeharto regime, often speaking at rallies and other public events about his experiences as a political prisoner. In the 1990s, he commenced a project to record the oral histories of Indonesian political exiles in Europe, China and Vietnam. These interviews were deposited primarily at the International Institute for Social History in Amsterdam, while a smaller number of recordings is held at Kunci Cultural Studies Centre in Yogyakarta. The audiofiles and transcripts of these interviews are important because they contain unique data on the history of the Leftist movement in Indonesia before 1965 and the diaspora of the Indonesian Left.

Following the fall of the Soeharto regime in 1998, Hersri returned to Indonesia in 2004. By that time, I had completed a Master's degree. My father told me he could return, not only because the authoritarian regime had ended, but most of all because I had finished my studies, and he had fulfilled the promise made to my mother. In Indonesia, he married women's rights activist Ita F. Nadia, whom he had known for many years before. After his return to Indonesia, Hersri published various autobiographical accounts, most notably *Memoar Pulau Buru* (2004, 2016), *Aku Eks Tapol* (2003) and *Diburu di Pulau Buru* (2006), as well as the poetry collection *Inilah Pamflet Itu* (2007). He continued recording the oral histories of former political prisoners and worked as a translator, predominantly of works that he felt were crucial to the understanding of the history of the Indonesian Left, such as Harry A. Poeze's biography of Tan Malaka. Together with Ita, and in collaboration with family and friends in Yogyakarta, Hersri established Sekolah Budaya mBrosot, in the place where his parental home – and his father's library – once stood. Intended to be an alternative learning space, this illustrates Hersri's continuing commitment to the development of cultural awareness.

Hersri's life and actions show that he deeply recognises the relevance of personal history to our understanding of political change and power structures. It is this that explains the detail found in *Buru Island*, a book that is so much more than a recount of Hersri's individual experience. Instead, he writes at length about other prisoners, including extensive detail on their life and activities before they were incarcerated. Many of those sent to Buru were members of Indonesia's intelligentsia, such as the well-known actor and film director Basuki Effendy. By including them, Hersri compels us to understand how the New Order regime simply discarded them and calls for their work to be acknowledged and remembered.

But it is not only these members of the elite that Hersri writes about. About the 500 men in his unit, Hersri records 'only seven had tertiary education […] the great majority were just ordinary members of mass organisations'. He mentions some of the teenagers sent to Buru, who were only around 15 years old when they were 'picked up'. Hersri also writes about the wives and children who, by and large, were coerced to come to Buru to join their imprisoned husbands and fathers and made their home in the 'village of tapol families', Savanajaya. He narrates, with ethnographic detail, encounters with the indigenous population on Buru who on many occasions helped the political prisoners. For instance, he recounts the story of a man called Mahele, who teaches 'city boys' Hersri and his friend Heru, a former leader of the Indonesian Student Movement Concentration (CGMI) in East Java, how to harvest "white gold": sago, crucial for the prisoners to supplement the meagre rations they received from the camp authorities. In telling stories of so many different people, Hersri's memoirs show how '1965' came to permeate all levels of Indonesian society, beyond the organisational confines of the Indonesian Left.

In such a context, what possibilities were there to resist? *Buru Island* shows that even in the most unlikely circumstances, there are always ways to do so. Perhaps the most powerful example of that is when Hersri recounts how he, alongside two others, was tortured after an escape attempt of three prisoners including his friend Heru. The men were made to lie in a gutter for hours, with water coming up to their mouths and guards pointing bayonets at them. Hersri did not ask them to stop: 'I shut up because of my own sense of pride about self-worth. [...] I would not stoop to call out or beg from those low, arrogant tyrants, drunk on power. I just wanted to survive'.

It is this inner control and Hersri's refusal to give in that explains the choices that he made after his release from Buru. Hersri may have been unable to participate in most aspects of political life, as political prisoners were denied the right to vote, but he found ways to resist. He acted in the smallest, and perhaps only, space available to him at the time: his family. Hersri always had a close attachment to his family and particularly his mother. In fact, he has often said that the spiritual presence of his mother – who passed away in 1966, very much aware that her son's life was in danger – helped him through his imprisonment. This awareness of the strength of familial ties meant that he made no secret of his past on Buru. At home, in a similar fashion to his narration in *Buru Island*, he told stories without emotion or drama, but simply as they were. To me, my father's imprisonment became a symbol of injustice and inhumanity. In sharing his experiences with his family, Hersri defied New Order propaganda and history-writing, denying the regime further control over his life.

In 2015, I stood with my father on Buru's Sanleko beach. This was the place where he first set foot on Buru. At the time, the commander told him and the other prisoners to 'take a good look. This is where you all are going to live and work. Forever, until you die, one by one'. But, in Hersri's words, 'they miscalculated'. He survived, and since then has consistently worked to demand attention for a largely forgotten part of Indonesian history. We did not speak much when we stood on that beach, but words were not necessary. There and then, I understood that resistance does not need many words, only an unwavering commitment.

Ken Setiawan

GLOSSARY

1926 Era	refers to the abortive revolt by the Indonesian Communist Party (PKI) in 1926.
3 July 1946 Incident	the kidnapping of Prime Minister Sutan Sjahrir by factions within the army opposing the Republic of Indonesia's negotiations with the Dutch.
Affandi	an Indonesian artist (1907-1990), one of the founders of Pelukis Rakyat (see Pelukis Rakyat).
Agus Djaja	an Indonesian artist (1913-1994), one of the founders of PERSAGI (Persatuan Ahli-ahli Gambar Indonesia, Union of Indonesian Painters).
Aki	(Sundanese) Grandfather.
Alhamdulillah	praise be to God.
ASRI	Akademi Seni Rupa Indonesia, the Academy of Fine Arts.
Astagfirullah al-azim, or Astagfirullah	(lit. 'I seek forgiveness from God, Allah') a short prayer of redemption, or an expression of shame or regret.
Bapak (Pak)	Mr., father.
Bapreru	Badan Pelaksana Ressetlemment dan Rehabilitasi Buru, Body for Administration of Buru Resettlement and Rehabilitation.
Basuka	Barisan Sukarno, Sukarno Front.
Bersih lingkungan	(lit. clean environment) 'clean' of involvement and association with the 30 September Movement (see G30S/PKI).
BKS Bumil	Badan Kerja Sama Buruh dan Militer, Military Body for Cooperation with Workers.

Glossary

BKSPM	Badan Kerja Sama Pemuda Militer, Military Body for Cooperation with Youth.
BPH	Badan Pemerintah Harian, Body for Daily Government (of Indonesian Communist Party).
BTI	Barisan Tani Indonesia, Indonesian Peasants' Front.
Bung	Brother, comrade (see Kawan).
Cak	(East Java) brother.
Camat	sub-district head.
CDB	Comite Daerah Besar, Regional Committee of Indonesian Communist Party.
Ceylon	now Sri Lanka.
CGMI	Consentrasi Gerakan Mahasiswa Indonesia, Indonesian Student Movement Concentration.
Chairil Anwar	an Indonesian poet (1922-1949).
CPM	Corps Polisi Militer, Military Police Corps.
Dewan Revolusi	Indonesian Revolutionary Council, declared on October 1, 1965 by Lieutenant Colonel Untung Syamsuri, composed of civilian and military personnel to support the 30 September Movement.
Digul	shortened from Boven Digul, an upstream swampland in southern Papua, Indonesia. In the 1920s it hosted a penal colony. As a result of the abortive 1926 revolt by the Indonesian Communist Party (PKI), the Dutch exiled hundreds of the most troublesome revolutionaries in Digul (see 1926 Era).
Digul group	group of 823 accused revolutionaries who were exiled in Digul after the 1926 revolt by the Indonesian Communist Party (PKI) (see Digul, 1926 Era).
Dik	younger brother or sister.
Diponegoro	Javanese prince who opposed the Dutch colonial rule and played an important role in the Java War between 1825 and 1830.

DPRD	Dewan Perwakilan Rakyat Daerah, People's Representative Council local assemblies.
Drs	Doctorandus, a Dutch academic title from the pre-Bachelor–Master system.
Dua-Tinggi	(lit. Two-High) 'high in ideology' and 'high in aesthetics', a Lekra motto, introduced at the 1960 National Congress of Lekra (see Lekra).
Dwikora	Dwi Komando Rakyat, People's Dual Command, operations against the formation of Malaysia, especially in north Kalimantan, 1964-1965.
ET	Eks Tapol, ex-political detainee (see Tapol).
FDR	Front Demokrasi Rakyat, People's Democracy Front, a coalition of Left-wing parties (Indonesian Communist Party, Indonesian Labor Party, Socialist Party, and Socialist Youth), established in January 1948 following the fall of the Amir Sjarifuddin government (see Pesindo).
G30S/PKI	Gerakan 30 September/Partai Komunis Indonesia, The 30 September Movement/Indonesian Communist Party. G30S (also called Gestok, for Gerakan Satu Oktober, The First of October Movement) was a self-proclaimed organisation of Indonesian National Armed Forces members who, in the early hours of 1 October 1965, captured and murdered six Army generals in an abortive coup attempt. The army leadership blamed the coup attempt on the Indonesian Communist Party (PKI), that led to the imprisonment and death of real or supposed Communists Party members and sympathisers. Under the New Order, the movement was usually referred to as G30S/PKI by those wanting to associate it with the PKI (see New Order).
Gatutkaca	a character in the Mahabharata epic, the son of Bima, one of the five Pandawa brothers (see Pandawa).

Glossary

Gerwani	Gerakan Wanita Indonesia, Indonesian Women's Movement, a women's organisation, founded in 1950 as Gerwis (Gerakan Wanita Indonesia Sedar, Movement of Aware Indonesian Women), primarily to lobby for women's interests in the government. In 1954 it took the name Gerwani and became increasingly close to, though never formally affiliated with, the Indonesian Communist Party.
Gestok	Gerakan Satu Oktober, the First of October Movement (see G30S/PKI).
Golkar	Golongan Karya, Functional Groups, Indonesian ruling group from 1971 (the first post-1965 legislative election) to 1999, which Soeharto created as the parliamentary rubber stamp for his 32-year rule. In 1999, forced by the new election law, Golkar reformed itself as a political party.
HIS	Himpunan Sarjana Indonesia, Association of Indonesian Graduates.
HW	Hisbul Wathan, the Muhammadiyah scout organisation (see Muhammadiyah).
ibu (bu)	Mother, Mrs.
Inrehab	Instalasi Rehabilitasi, 'Rehabilitation Installation', Detention Camp.
IPPI	Ikatan Pemuda Pelajar Indonesia, the League of Indonesian Youth and High School Students.
Irama Melayu	Indonesian popular music that combines local music traditions, Indian and Malaysian music and Western rock.
isha	Muslim evening prayer.
ITB	Institut Teknologi Bandung, Bandung Institute of Technology.
Kalimasada	the holy heirloom of Yudhishthira of the Pandawa brothers in the Mahabharata epic (see Pandawa).

KAMI	Kesatuan Aksi Mahasiswa Indonesia, Indonesian Student Action Union.
KAPPI	Kesatuan Aksi Pemuda dan Pelajar Indonesia, Indonesian Youth and School Students Action Union.
Kartosuwiryo	leader of the Darul Islam rebellion against the Indonesian government from 1949 to 1962, which aimed to establish an Islamic State of Indonesia based on sharia law.
Kawan	Comrade, friend (see Bung).
Keimin Bunka Shidosho	Institute for the People's Education and Cultural Guidance, established in 1943 by the Japanese Military Administration in Java.
Keroncong	an Indonesian music genre inspired by 16th-century Portuguese sailor songs. Keroncong music is usually played with ukulele, cello, guitar, bass, violin and flute.
Ketoprak	a Javanese form of costume drama, featuring actors who may also dance and sing to the accompaniment of gamelan (Javanese traditional music ensemble).
Ki	(Javanese) male title of respect, shortened form of kyai.
Ki Ageng Suryamentaraman	a Javanese prince and philosopher (1892-1962).
Ki Hadjar Dewantara	a leading Indonesian nationalist activist and pioneer of education for native Indonesians in Dutch colonial times, founder of Taman Siswa (see Taman Siswa).
KNIL	Koninklijk Nederlandsch Indisch Leger, Royal Netherlands Indies Army.
Kodam	Komando Daerah Militer, Regional Military Command.
Kodim	Komando Distrik Militer, Military District Command.

Koramil	Komando Rayon Militer, Military Sub-District Command.
Kostrad	Komando Strategis Angkatan Darat, Army Strategic Command.
KRIS	Kebaktian Rakyat Indonesia Sulawesi, Sulawesi Devotion of the People Brigade.
KSSR	Konferensi Seni dan Sastra Revolusioner, the Conference of Revolutionary Art and Literature.
Langendriyan	traditional Javanese narrative dance with dancers singing poetry.
Lekra	Lembaga Kebudayaan Rakyat, Institute of People's Culture, founded in 1950.
lenong	traditional theatre of the Betawi people of Jakarta.
LIPI	Lembaga Ilmu Pengetahuan Indonesia, Indonesian Institute of Sciences.
LKMD	Lembaga Keamanan Masyarakat Desa, Institute for Village Community Resilience.
Lubang Buaya	(lit. Crocodile Hole), name of the suburb in the south-east of Jakarta which is also the site of the murder of seven Indonesian army officers during the 30 September Movement. It is located on the outskirts of Jakarta near Halim Perdanakusuma Air Force Base (see G30S/PKI).
ludruk	East Javanese traditional theatre. The dialogue or monologue is mostly comedic, and intersperses dance and songs with gamelan accompaniment.
lurah	village head.
Madiun Incident	uprising by sections of the Indonesian Communist Party in Madiun, East Java, in September and October 1948.
Maghrib	Muslim prayer, undertaken just after sunset.
Mako	Markas Komando, Command Headquarters.
mang	older brother (Sundanese),
Marhaenist	an adherent of Marhaenism, a socialist political ideology developed by Sukarno.

Mas	(Javanese) older brother.
Mbakyu	(Javanese) older sister.
MPRS	Majelis Permusyawaratan Rakyat Sementara, Provisional People's Deliberative Assembly.
Muhammadiyah	Islamic organisation, founded in 1912.
MV	Motor Vessel.
Nasakom	Nasionalisme, Agama, dan Komunisme, Nationalism, Religion and Communism, a political doctrine, introduced by Sukarno in 1956, as a rejection of the ideological and religious divisions of the nationalist movement in Indonesia.
New Order	Orde Baru or Orba in Indonesian, a general term for the political system in force after the accession of Soeharto to power in 1966 until his fall in May 1998.
NKB	Ngudi Kawarasaning Badan, (lit. Maintain Physical Health) local football club in Yogyakarta.
Ny	Nyonya, Mrs.
Pancasila	The five principles of state ideology: belief in the one supreme God; just and civilised humanitarianism; Indonesian unity; popular sovereignty governed by wise policies arrived at through deliberation and consensus; social justice for the entire Indonesian people.
Pandawa	the five brothers from the Mahabharata epic: Yudistira; Bima; Arjuna; Nakula and Sadewa.
Pangkopkamtib	Panglima Komando Pemulihan Keamanan dan Ketertiban, Commander for the Restoration of Security and Order Operations.
Parmusi	Partai Muslimin Indonesia, Indonesian Muslims' Party.
Paskoarma	Pasukan Komando Armada, Armada Command Brigade.
PDI	Partai Demokrasi Indonesia, Indonesian Democratic Party.

Glossary

Peci	black fez-like cap for men that become an emblem of the nationalist movement and is now official Indonesian attire for men.
Pelni	Pelayaran Nasional Indonesia, Indonesian National Lines, the national shipping company of Indonesia.
Pelukis Rakyat	People's Artists, an artists' collective, founded in 1947.
Pemuda Rakyat	People's Youth, youth organisation affiliated with the Indonesian Communist Party, formed in 1950 to replace Pesindo (Pemuda Sosialis Indonesia, Indonesian Socialist Youth) (see Pesindo).
Perjuta	perjuangan bersenjata, armed struggle program of the Indonesian Communist Party.
Pesindo	Pemuda Sosialis Indonesia, Indonesian Socialist Youth, the armed youth wing of the PS (Partai Sosialis, Socialist Party), founded in 1945. In 1950 it affiliated with the Indonesian Communist Party and changed its name to Pemuda Rakyat (People's Youth) (see Pemuda Rakyat).
Petera	Penghibur Tentara dan Rakyat, Entertainers of the Army and the People.
PGRI	Persatuan Guru Republik Indonesia, Indonesian Teachers Association.
PKI	Partai Komunis Indonesia, Indonesian Communist Party.
PKI Malam	PKI Malam, Night PKI, the underground section of the Indonesian Communist Party.
PNI	Partai Nasional Indonesia, Indonesian National Party.
PPP	Partai Persatuan Pembangunan, Unity Development Party.
PSIM	Persatuan Sepakbola Indonesia Mataram, Mataram Indonesian Football Association, local football club in Yogyakarta.

PWI	Persatuan Wartawan Indonesia, Indonesian Journalists' Union.
Radio Peking	now China Radio International (CRI), a state-owned international radio broadcaster of the People's Republic of China.
Reog	East Javanese traditional dance.
Resopim	Revolusi, Sosialisme, dan Pemimpin Nasional, Revolution, Socialism and National Leader.
RPKAD	Resimen Pasukan Komando Angkatan Darat, Army Paracommando Regiment.
RRI	Radio Republik Indonesia, Indonesian National Radio.
RT	Rukun Tetangga, administrative division below the village level.
RUTAP	Rumah Tangga Partai, the Indonesian Communist Party internal affairs.
S. Sudjojono	an Indonesian artist (1913-1985), one of the founders of PERSAGI (Persatuan Ahli-ahli Gambar Indonesia, Union of Indonesian Painters) and SIM (see SIM).
Sanggar	Workshop or studio, artists collective.
Sarbupri	Sarekat Buruh Perkebunan Republik Indonesia, Plantation Workers Union of the Republic of Indonesia.
Saudara	brother, you.
SBIRBA	Serikat Buruh Industri Ringan dan Bangunan, Small Industry and Construction Workers Union.
SBKB	Serikat Buruh Kendaraan Bermotor, Motor Vehicle Workers Union.
SBPP	Serikat Buruh Pelabuhan dan Pelayaran, Dock Workers Union.
Sendenbu	Japanese propaganda and information department, established in August 1942 by the Japanese Military Administration in Java.

Glossary

Serbaud	Serikat Buruh Angkatan Udara, Air Force Workers Union.
Serma	Sersan Mayor, Sergeant Major.
SH	Sarjana Hukum, Bachelor of Law.
Silat	traditional martial arts.
SIM	Seniman Indonesia Muda, Young Artists of Indonesia, an artists' collective, founded in 1946.
Sitpol	situasi politik, political situation.
SOBSI	Sentral Organisasi Buruh Seluruh Indonesia, All Indonesia Trade Union Federation.
Supriyadi	leader of the rebellion against the Japanese in Blitar, East Java, in February 1945.
Taman Dewasa	junior high school of Taman Siswa (see Taman Siswa).
Taman Siswa	educational movement and school system founded in Yogyakarta in 1922 by Ki Hadjar Dewantara (see Ki Hadjar Dewantara).
Tapol	Tahanan Politik, political detainee.
Tefaat	Tempat pemanfaatan, utilisation location, official euphemism referring to Buru island as a location to 'utilise' political detainees.
TP	Tentara Peladjar, High School Student Army.
Tripanji Partai	Three Flames of the Party, post-G30S 1965 Indonesian Communist Party program consisting of 1) Freedom from political opportunism and revisionism, 2) Armed agrarian revolution under the working class' leadership, and 3) National united front based on the peasants and the working class' alliance.
Tsanawiyah	Islamic junior high school.
UNRA	Universitas Rakyat, People's University.

Wayang (Wayang kulit)	Javanese traditional shadow-puppet theatre, wherein a single puppetmaster (dalang) tells a dramatic story using leather puppets accompanied by gamelan (Javanese traditional music ensemble). Wayang refers to the entire dramatic show. Sometimes the leather puppets are referred to as wayang. The dramatic stories primarily depict episodes from the Ramayana and particularly the Mahabharata epics.
Wayang orang	or wayang wong (lit. human wayang), a Javanese theatrical performance wherein human characters imitate movements of wayang kulit in dance form and, in the commercial form, the dancers speak their own dialogue.

INTRODUCTION: THE TRAGEDY OF 30 SEPTEMBER 1965

There are at least three things that people often ask me about my life. First, what was my most painful experience from the tragedy of 30 September 1965, which scarred myself and my family most deeply? Second, how did I handle the bitter realities at that time and in the times following the tragic event? Thirdly, what lessons can I pass on to today's generation from my personal experiences?

I am going to try to respond to those queries, not point by point, but in a series of narratives. This is firstly so that these narratives do not become long-winded, because there were so many bitter experiences that my family and I suffered, which we had to bear and suppress. Secondly, so that from these narratives will emerge a figure 'I myself', and from that, it will become evident how we faced and managed the bitter reality, and what can be drawn as a bridge and tool for reflection. It is not, or not yet, necessary for this to be a lesson, but rather will suffice as a mirror.

At the end of 1987, my family and I – my wife, my daughter and me – left Indonesia for The Netherlands. We were leaving Indonesia, the beautiful land that we loved. Why? As an ex-Buru island prisoner who had experienced everything except death, I was not in the least worried about facing the oppression and humiliation of the Soeharto regime. Nor was my late wife. As a Dutch woman, she was fully aware of the consequences of her choice: to live in Indonesia under the military boot, and to become the wife of an ex-Buru prisoner whose life was difficult indeed. But we had a daughter. And we could not let her become the victim of people taking law into their own hands, a manifestation of the 'culture' of 'weeding' that is totally uncultured and accepted, as long as those affected were people 'polluted' by what was called 'G30S/PKI' (The 30 September Movement/Indonesian Communist Party).

My wife really loved Indonesia. But Indonesia allowed no place or opportunity, even for love. She wanted to die in Indonesia and be buried in her mother-in-law's grave, but she had to surrender this wish. One year before she died, she returned to the country of her birth. But she was able to fulfil her desire to complete her writing before she died. Twenty days before she died, on April 2, 1989 at Kockengen, she wrote the last words of her story: 'Farewell Indonesia, I send to you my hopes, my tears and my love.'

Is there any other country on this planet in this so-called modern era that a person has no liberty even to die? But this is truly what happened in a country called Indonesia, and not only for a fictional heroine like Ruth Havelaar. This was just Jitske Mulder. An ordinary person among countless oppressed. Perhaps I need to remind readers of an event towards the end of Bung Karno's life. People know that Indonesia's greatest hero wanted to be laid to rest as the mouthpiece of the people in the Priangan highlands of West Java where he had met the farmer called Marhaen. But the Siliwangi district military commander said, 'Siliwangi soil is too sacred to receive Soekarno's corpse!' Can you imagine! Even someone of the stature of Bung Karno had no right to choose a place to die.

This is why I wrote a short story titled *Rat*. There was a rat hiding in the drain in the kitchen of our house at Tebet in South Jakarta. My wife, who saw this big fat rat, remembered my stories about life as a political prisoner on Buru. For us there, rat was a delicious delicacy. So she called me over to see the rat, and told me to bring something to hit it with to kill it. And I was getting ready to do just that. I raised the stick high, while my wife watched from the kitchen doorway. But what happened next was not a strike to the rat's head. My hand shook. I saw that the rat was not moving. Not making any noise. Just its blinking eyes were talking. Maybe because it was sick, or old, or both. The stick fell from my hand. I picked up the rat by its tail. Not to thrash it against the tiles, but I took it outside and let it go on an empty lot. Let it die without torture. Let it die without having its love confiscated. Let it die in liberty.

To me, this – the limiting and confiscating of love, life and death – not only caused a profound wounding of the spirit. It was more than that. It was the essence of the naked face of savagery, which one can only lament, and further, if one wants, oppose through the long road of a process of awareness. Just as the age of the Enlightenment brought light to the Dark Ages, or the path of the Prophet Muhammad awakened the Arabian Peninsula that was buried in barbarism.

To this day I still often dream about the time of oppression in Java and the time of slavery on Buru. All of us crowded naked around a single well to bathe, our roof the sky, the wind our walls; watching a fellow prisoner being beaten; being hunted for capture; even being tied to the execution pole before a firing squad. Strangely, when I have these dreams, at the very last moment before the bullet hits, I am aware that I am actually asleep. In order not to be shot dead, I then try to wake.

When I told a friend of mine about this dream, meaning well, he took me to see a psychologist. The psychologist advised me to let the dream run its course to the end. That way, she said, I would be freed from the traumatic dream. I listened to her advice, but I did not take it, because I do not agree with the 'trauma theory' she used as the basis of her advice. Why? Because I do not feel that I suffer trauma as a result of my past bitter experiences. Why not? Because for me, all of my bitter experiences are the logical consequence of the position and political stand I took consciously. How should dreams about that bitterness be explained? Perhaps indeed through Freudian and Jungian theory. But that is not my field, and nor is it the purpose of my writing here.

In 1958, I began my involvement with, and passion for building up the Yogyakarta branch of Lekra (Lembaga Kebudayaan Rakyat, Institute of People's Culture). I did this precisely because I was aware that Lekra was not a place just for artists to hang out and enjoy themselves. Lekra was the organisation for the cultural movement. Movement. So, of course, I had ideals and purpose. And what were they? To awaken people to be culturally aware and to make the culture of the people a subject in their own country. In this, Lekra was the organisation of a cultural movement that was political and at the same time, a political organisation that moved specifically in the field of culture. So this was where I stood, and it was from there that I viewed and took a stand on all matters and experiences.

The incident that came to be called G30S, or which Bung Karno called Gestok (Gerakan Satu Oktober, the First of October Movement), was obviously a political incident. As a political incident, it should rightly be viewed with a political approach, and assessed or weighed up using political scales. In political life, it is normal for there to be various different and even opposing interests. The consequence is that each of those interests supports power, and with that power each competes strategically or in political steps for its own victory.

Introduction

This reality – namely that the 30th September incident – was a political event. It is a fact of life that politics always contains various different interests. One must put aside personal likes and dislikes, whether one is pro or contra; accepts or rejects the fact of conflicting interests. We can only offer our personal perspective about the individual programs of different political interests, and how they carried them out.

I was keenly aware of my own position, attitude and opinions, and understood and accepted the bloody tragedy of 30 September as the political event it was. So it was that I was not surprised when one day I was arrested by the authorities – one of the political forces had indeed won. The 30 September Movement had brought truly terrible consequences. But I both understood and approved of Bung Karno's response to it. In the midst of the chaos of the Unilateral Action undertaken by the Army Strategic Special Command (Kostrad) and the Army Elite Forces (RPKAD), Bung Karno calmly explained that the September 30 Movement was just a ripple in the ocean. Nevertheless, this was a phrase Bung Karno's enemies could superficially take to mean that he both sympathised with the Revolutionary Council, and trivialised the deaths of six generals in the dead of night.

When the newly elected government of Ceylon made me *persona-non-grata* and gave me 48 hours to leave Ceylon – the island that in times long past had been a place of exile for rebels from Java – I returned to Jakarta arriving on August 24, 1965. I had been away not quite five years, but on my return, I could barely recognise the Communist Party in its strength and I felt how chic Lekra had become. Yet just ten days after 1 October, 1965 the building housing the Central Secretariat of Lekra at Jalan Cidurian 19 in Jakarta had turned into a place of danger. From then on I was aware. Friends had been captured. Some were said to have disappeared or been murdered. My turn, then, was just a matter of time. I was aware at every moment that I could be captured by the authorities. Being prepared for capture meant being prepared to face all kinds of things that went along with that. I was also aware that all state powers had all kinds of equipment of force, including electric shock equipment, barbed whips, forced labour, prison, exile and even bullets.

And so with this awareness, all the consequences that I could (and subsequently did) endure, I faced with a spirit of resignation, or what in Javanese we call *sumèlèh*. This was not fatalism, or just surrendering to fate, but being aware and calm. I experienced life in isolation as a time of retreat. Those were the times that gave the most opportunity for what we political prisoners called 'film show'. This meant, more or less, introspection. Reflecting on every step one had taken in the past; which was right and which was wrong. But all the while not questioning one's political stand and opinions, because these are matters of an individual's beliefs in the truth of the ideology and politics he holds. With this understanding, one's heart could become calm and resigned. *Sumèlèh*. With this understanding, one could accept that one had been thrown into prison or exiled as a political prisoner. Imprisonment and exile were completely separate from matters of morals and ethics, or right and wrong. With this awareness, even though being a political prisoner or ex-political prisoner meant society made you a pariah, there was no need for that to become a mental and physical burden which could destroy one's self.

The September 30 incident was a tragedy. But even more tragic was the series of events that followed. The New Order, built and defended by sanctioning the methods of Soeharto and his ilk, was a barbarous order. And what can a barbarous order produce other than barbarity? The apple never falls far from the tree, as the saying goes. To me the evil of Soeharto and his clique was not merely the cronyism, the siphoning of the money off the people to the tune of billions, the murder of people in countless numbers (if we take the epilogue of 3 September alone, according to Sarwo Edhie at least three and a half million (yes, three and a half million), compared to one rat held in my hand!). No, apart from all that, there is still one other thing even more evil; Soeharto and co made Indonesia into a nation that (to use Bung Karno's word) has the spirit of a balloon frog, a *kintel*. The balloon frog is small and grey in colour, and when you touch it, it puffs itself up as camouflage. A balloon frog nation is one that is stupid and lacking in courage.

When she returned home after a five-week visit to Indonesia my daughter Ken Setiawan wrote an article. It was a small article, but large on the Richter scale in the way it rocked my thinking. The story begins with her being handed a pamphlet by a Muhammadiyah student in Jakarta. It was just a small pamphlet. But it certainly caused large-scale shocks in Ken's conscience about the responsibility of history and justice. The pamphlet listed Soeharto's sins, but, strangely, there was not a single word about Buru. The students distributing the pamphlet were probably about the same age as Ken. They were not even born when the September 30 tragedy occurred, but the explanation that they did not know, or had forgotten, is just as barbarous as their ignorance and forgetting. This is a clear example of the symptom of national balloon-frogging, something the New Order managed to achieve atop the lake of blood and tears of civilisation.

I have a good friend in a town in Java. He is the head of an NGO and a writer (from the 1980s generation, if I may say so) who has published many books. After reading my article about the songs '*Genjer Genjer*' and '*Hidup di Bui*' (Life in Prison), he made a comment. Not about the basic issues, namely the two songs, but about the socio-historical context when the two songs were composed. His words: I do not know what exactly happened back then. What I remember to this day are just the stories about terrifying cruelty.

Does not know, or has forgotten? If he does not know, this means there is on one side, a process whereby facts as messages are blackened; and on the other, a process whereby facts are falsified. Forgetting means there is a process when social memory has been corrupted in an organised way. When the situation of the physical and spiritual life of society has been so conditioned that it becomes totally dependent on authority, and it permits anything to happen, then of course, there has been a process. Because the New Order was essentially Golkar. Because Golkar was essentially the army, and so on ... Because Pancasila was essentially anti-opposition. Because opposition was essentially communist. Because communists were essentially to be completely wiped out, and so on.

It was not just the Muhammadiyah students Ken met or my friend the young writer and NGO leader who did not know. Indeed, did not know, did not want to know, pretended not to know, or – and this is what is tragic – were afraid to know. It was also the case with many in academic and scientific circles, and most tragically, those academics from activist circles making such a fuss about human rights. It is only recently that there have been one or two of them who have begun to have the courage to speak up.

Why have they kept their mouths shut all this time? Is it because those who were murdered and oppressed were 'communists'? It reminds me of a story about the late Father Y.B. Mangunwijaya when he was interrogated by the Diponegoro V Military Command about the protests against the construction of the Kedungombo dam. Father

Mangunwijaya was reminded that those behind the protesters were this and that, in short, people who did not have 'a card of clean association' (*bersih lingkungan*). Father Mangunwijaya replied with a rhetorical question; 'If you see someone sprawled in the middle of the road because they have been hit by a car, before you extend your hand to help them, do you have to ask first, 'do you have a card of clean association or not?'

Clean association! This was one of the New Order's constructions that was fake morally, ethically, socially and politically; constructed on the foundation of the first principle of Pancasila, which is also fake. It is 'Pancasila' according to a single interpretation along the lines determined by the Body for Development, Education, Implementation, Guiding, Understanding and Experience of Panca Sila, which is worthless.

The 30 September event was a political event. It had tremendous consequences for every aspect of national life. But the most tragic of all, even more tragic than the event itself, was the effect in the field of culture. The proclamation of independence in 1945 was not only a call for political emancipation. It was also a call for cultural emancipation. Emancipation from ignorance. Emancipation from fear.

The road of political reformation is long and difficult. But even longer and more difficult is the path of cultural reform. But history does not repeat, let alone retreat. And so we do not need to ask: *Quo vadis*?

PACIFIC OCEAN
MALAYSIA
Medan
SUMATRA
KALIMANTAN
SULAWESI
Buru
Makasar
IRIAN JAYA
MALUKU
Jakarta
JAVA
Surabaya
Yogyakarta
INDIAN OCEAN
TIMOR
N
© Robert Cribb

Buru Island (detail)
Airfield
Political prisoner settlements
Sawah (irrigated rice fields)
Namlea
Savanajaya
Bantalreja
Ancol
Indrapura
Kajeli Bay
Indrakarya
Wanapura
Wanareja
Adhipura
Wanakerta
Wanayasa
Wanawangi
Argabhakti
Birawa
Wanajaya
Wanasurya
Wanakencana
Wanamulya
Giripura
Wanadharma
The Javanese word *wana*, meaning forest, was used in the names of many of the settlements to reflect the work of the prisoners in clearing jungle.
RBC

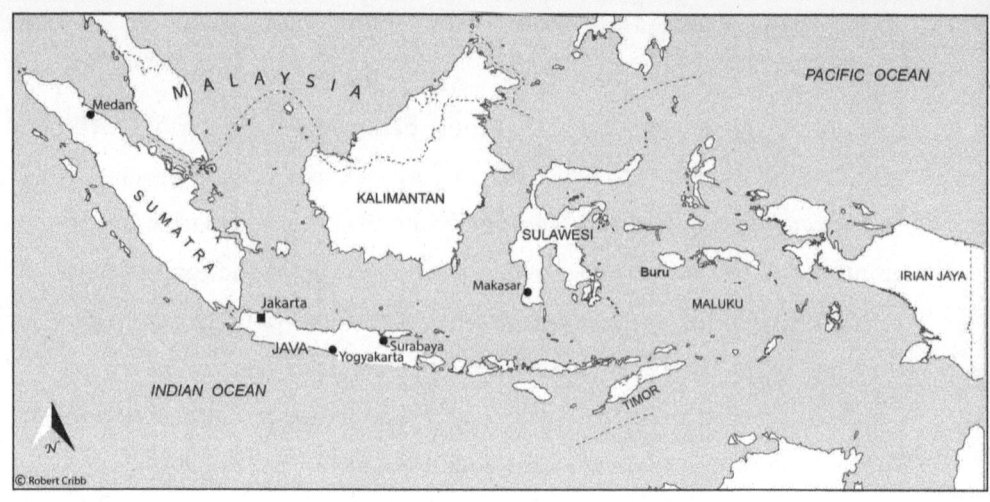

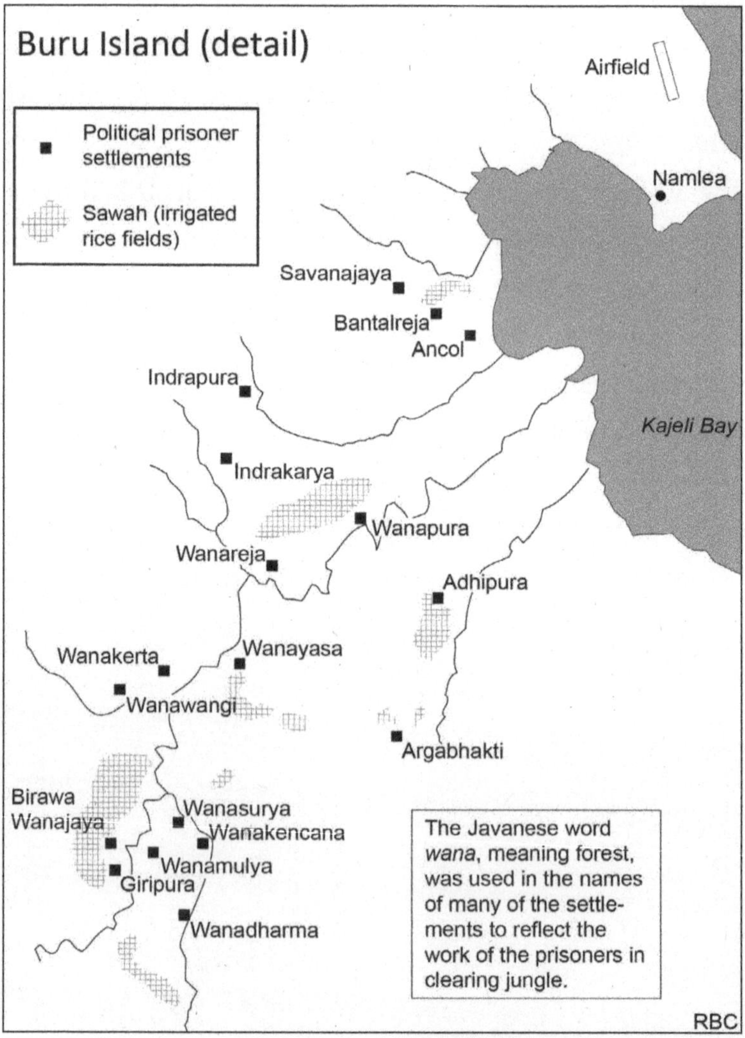

Part I

Before Buru

Chapter 1

FROM FREE CITIZEN TO 'ET'

In August 1965 I returned to my native land, having worked as the representative of Indonesian writers at the Asia-Africa Writers Bureau in Colombo, Sri Lanka. At the end of 1969 I was 'picked up', a euphemism for captured, by two army Intelligence men. Needless to say, there was no arrest warrant because in their words I was being taken in because they wanted 'information'. It was clear what they intended: examination and interrogation, which in practice meant being forced to admit whatever it was they wanted.

They 'asked me for information' for five days and nights. Three nights were without any sleep – 'watching a *wayang* shadow-puppet performance', they called it. Over all this time, I was not allowed to have any contact with anyone, except for the three interrogators who took turns. When the examination was over, I was allowed to send news to my family and ask them to send me some basic necessities: toothbrush, clothes, sandals (closed shoes were not allowed), a mat (mattress and pillow not allowed), tin plate and mug, medicine. Writing utensils, radios, anything sharp (including nail clippers) and belts were prohibited.

During the day I was usually given work to do, which they called *'corvée'*. For instance, repairing roads, making, fixing and cleaning drains and clearing the yard of grass.

In 1970, I was moved to the Salemba jail in Jakarta. Here the words 'do this' and 'don't do that', which we referred to in our prison jargon with one word, '*konsiyes*', were more frequent and more strident. This included not being allowed to talk or laugh loudly, and we were forced to adopt one of the state-sanctioned religions. For instance, we were not allowed to say our religion was Confucianism, Judaism, non-orthodox Islam, and so on.

We were put into cells measuring 2 x 2.5 metres square, with windowless concrete walls and an iron door with bars as thick as thumbs. Every cell housed at least five people, often seven or even nine. In this situation, we had to sleep at night sitting up or top and tail, five people facing one way and four the other.

Every day at six in the morning we would get a small kettle of drinking water for the whole day. Midday and evening we would be given a ration of food; rice mixed with cracked wheat, which is usually fed to animals. The ration was about seven to nine spoonsful. The food was slipped under the cell door, served on prison-issue aluminium plates, which were slimy and stinking because they were never washed with soap or any cleaning agent.

Apart from that, we got a cup of 'soup', which was basically warm salted water. The political prisoners called this 'head soup' because all you could see in the soup was the reflection of your own face, and this was a play on words from 'goat head soup'. Sometimes they called it 'nipple vegetables' because there might be one or two tiny bits of spinach that looked like the nipple valve-stopper on a bicycle tyre.

The door of the cell was opened once or twice a day, morning and evening, for thirty minutes to bathe (behind the cell block there was one well with no bathroom), to defecate (there were four or five latrines in each block) and to breathe a bit of fresh air while walking around the yard, or do a bit of exercise. Every evening, before the cell door was closed, every prisoner prepared plastic bags as containers for pee and shit during the night. When they were filled, they were hung on the bars of the cell door, waiting for the morning when the door would be opened and their owners could empty them in the latrines. If during the night there was someone seriously ill in the cell, or someone died, the person with the loudest voice would yell: 'Block X Guard!' (saying the name of the block). 'Someone is sick (or dead).' The yell would then be relayed from cell to cell, block to block, until it reached the ears of the guards at the front door. They would then come, taking their time, cursing all the way, and take the sick person to the policlinic, or the dead one to the morgue.

Between 1969–71 and 1974–76, more than 12,000 political prisoners were deported from Java to exile on the island of Buru. In the area of South Buru, there were 21 units for exiled political prisoners, each one housing between 500–1000 prisoners, with the distance between units around 4-5 kilometres the closest, and 30-40 kilometres the furthest. In these units, the political prisoners had to work every day under armed guard, from dawn to dusk. In the first five years, they often had to work from four in the morning until midnight, under the light of pressure lamps.

The requirement that we had to work to produce our own sustenance, meant that our status changed from political prisoners to slaves in the purest sense of the word. We had not a single right left, and all obligations were foisted upon us. Political prisoners had to produce food not only so their existence would not be a burden to the state, but also to support the welfare of the unit guards and for the development of the area. Because of this, for every unit housing 500 prisoners, there was allotted between 80-120 hectares of wet ricefields, between 60-100 hectares of other land for farming, between 10-20 chainsaws, 20 or more sago crushers, 4-6 eucalyptus oil distillers, and other necessary equipment.

Meanwhile, our food rations were fixed. If the harvest was good, the maximum was 750 grams per person per day. That was just rice, nothing else. Political prisoners were given clothing once only, on the day they departed for Buru from Salemba: one pair of trousers, one khaki shirt clearly marked with the prisoner's deportation number on the chest and backside and one conical bamboo coolie hat. The second day after arriving in Buru, they received one aluminium spoon and plate, one 10-litre plastic bucket, and a postcard. Over ten years, postcards were distributed no more than ten times in all.

In 1978, having signed a statement with 1001 musts and 1001 must-nots, I was 'returned to society'. This was not just a euphemism. Political prisoners were indeed not freed, but merely returned to society from where they had previously been 'picked up'. Because of this, the party who received the returning political prisoner, whether that be family or the neighbourhood head from the place where he was going to live, had to sign a statement from the military authority that they were prepared to receive the ex-political prisoner and be guarantor for their actions. The ex-prisoner now became labelled 'ET', from *eks-tapol* (tapol being the acronym of *ta*hanan *pol*itik, political detainee).

When political prisoners were 'returned to society' they were issued an identity card, just like other citizens. However, there was one difference. After the number, the code 'ET' was written. This code had an incredible impact on their lives, both practically and mentally. They were bound by particular regulations: for instance, they had to report to military authorities at regular intervals; carry out *corvée* labour, working as cleaners and as watchmen; and undergo 'direction' courses or other courses called *'santiaji'* (which was a euphemism for indoctrination or brainwashing). If they left their homes for more than 24 hours they had to carry a travel document issued by the military and upon arrival at a place report to military authorities there. They were not permitted to work as civil servants or work in the private sector in 'vital' areas. If assessed to be loyal they were given the right to vote, but not the right to be voted for themselves. If they changed their address they had to first get permission from military and civil authorities both in the original place and in the place of destination; and many other regulations besides.

As an institution, the authoritarian, militaristic New Order government may have collapsed in May 1998, but all the social and political issues that became the norm for more than a generation did not suddenly disappear along with it. Because, in general, issues become issues, or become bigger issues, not because of the issue itself but through the way that people view them. Therefore, when people are prepared to change the paradigm or their own viewpoint, then as a logical consequence, their understanding and approach will change too.

Chapter 2

OPERATION KEEP YOUR MOUTH SHUT

Whenever I wanted to take the bus from Cawang I would walk there from home. It was not all that far. Maybe two kilometres at the most. It was even easier if I was going in the direction of Grogol or Blok M Kebayoran. All I had to do was stand and wait for one of the many kinds of public transport that travelled along Jalan Gatot Subroto, over the Jakarta-Bogor railway bridge. The bridge was maybe just a hundred metres from our house. It was the same when I returned home. I would walk back from that bridge or from Cawang. Apart from not having much money, back then I also often wondered why the people who lived in real brick houses in Jakarta rode *becaks* (pedicabs) even for short rides. I thought it must be for reasons of show rather than anything to do with their feet or the heat.

In the early 1960s, there were not many buildings on either side of the Gatot Subroto bypass. There was still a lot of vacant land filled with weeds and shrubs, among which, here and there, were a few fruit trees. On the large plot of land across from the Air Force headquarters building grew a special kind of grass that was supposed to be good for dairy cows. Every day farmers from Setia Budi, Pasar Minggu and Cililitan came by bicycle, cut the grass and carried it home.

There were one or two shacks alongside the bypass, which had been thrown together perhaps by the landowner, or someone who had business there. These shacks were used as a place to rest or seek shade by kids herding their animals or labourers. The labourers were casual workers who would roam from place to place carrying a hoe and large dustpan basket hoping to pick up some work. They were called '*sindang* workers' because most of them were farmers from the village of Sindang in West Java, who, during the dry season sought labouring work in Jakarta.

It was past the evening prayer time and near sundown. There were not many cars on the road. I could see only one or two pedestrians, one far ahead of me and one far behind. I had got off the bus at Cawang intending to go straight home and was walking towards the Dirgantara statue. Most people called it the Hanuman statue because the figure of 'man in space' standing tall in the middle of the Jalan Pancoran crossroad did indeed look more like a statue of a monkey. The sculptor was Edhi Sunarso together with his fellow artists from the Sanggar Pelukis Rakyat (People's Workshop of Artists) in Yogyakarta. In my opinion however, compared to Edhi Sunarso's other statues, like the Liberation statue in Banteng Square for instance, the Dirgantara statue was a failure.

As I got between the two bridges, the rail bridge and the bridge over Ciliwung River, I heard a sound.

'Ssst …!'

I turned. Sitting cross-legged on a low bamboo bench in the shack in the field was a man. He was wearing a straw hat and sandals. I knew that smile and face. 'It's Musayid', I said to myself. What is expected of me this time? I thought. Since my mother's death and the recent incident when I had rejected the call of the 'courier' sent to make contact with me, I had built my own circle of friends. It was an entirely new circle made up of the students from 17 August University, and people in East Tebet.

Without looking left or right, I went down from the bypass, answering his wave. We embraced each other.

'Ah, finally! I can't tell you how many times I have hung out here …' he said.

'How would I know? Why did you wait until now to signal me?'

'Now, how could I possibly just rush straight up to you? You have to size things up, have to be sure. Wouldn't want to make a mistake …' I heard his old familiar laugh.

'How did you know that I come this way?'

'Operation Keep Your Mouth Shut doesn't mean you have to remain completely deaf and dumb to everyone', he replied. 'Take us, for instance …'

'But who told you? May I know?'

'No need to know. Right?'

I shut up. I knew that in this climate of K-M-S (keep your mouth shut) and what we called 'frog larva network', questions like this, apart from being unnecessary, were also stupid. But I remembered the recent visit of Abu Chaer who had appeared totally out of the blue. He had come just once and never again. Was he a courier? Or was he a blabbermouth who had mentioned me when chatting while on night watch duty? Or was he an Intelligence informant, who had been given the task of tracing someone's 'frog larva network'?

'Have you been here long?' I asked, changing the subject.

'About one and a half years. I live in the neighbourhood just behind here.'

The houses in the neighbourhood behind were still sparse, almost hidden behind trees and thick bushes. One night, when it was my turn to join the neighbourhood watch, a thief had entered our neighbourhood. When the five of us on the watch had chased him, he had disappeared into this neighbourhood of Kebon Baru.

'Are your wife and children here too?'

'Yes. But we do not live together. We have to limit risk. Who knows? I also am too conspicuous with my large family. I have six kids. You remember, right? And we have no help in the house.'

I was silent. Isn't it actually the other way around? I wondered. Isn't it more strange and conspicuous if an outsider from Java, a man of his age, lives without a wife and has no relatives nearby? That was not the case with me. At that time I was of an age at which it was considered fairly normal to still be a bachelor. I had also come to live with my younger brother's family, whom the neighbours all knew well. Our mother also lived with us. To a Javanese, parents are highly revered. To live close to them is the right thing to do. Just as people do in the densely-populated neighbourhoods near the palaces in Yogyakarta and Solo.

'But what about you', I asked. 'Do you feel safe?'

'Oh, sure!' he answered confidently.

He pulled out his identity card from his shirt pocket. His shirt was white tetron, transparent. It was as though he was deliberately showing anyone curious, 'You see? Here's my identity card! I'm not on the run.'

I read it fleetingly. The name on the card was Pradjasudiardjo, retired, and it had the stamp and signature of the head of Kebon Baru Neighbourhood. I don't know what the exact date of our meeting was. I didn't note it. But it was in December 1966. That I remember well because it was the month and year that my mother died, and the whole family accompanied her to her final resting place in Yogyakarta.

Musayid had been elected as neighbourhood head (RT) about a year earlier. He was known as Pak (Mr) Dardjo or Pak Sudarjo, and he claimed to be a retired official from a village in the area of Demak. And so, he told me every month at the time when retired government officials collect their pensions, he would act out a play. Collecting his pension! On the day of his performance, towards evening he would return home carrying various household necessities. Rice, oil, sugar, coffee, soap and so on. He would share them with his closest neighbours, to ensure good relations with them and also as a shield should the time come when he would need it.

But even to get the tiny sum of a pension was impossible for people living in those difficult times. And so, he said, he had to create another part of the performance, namely to earn some money by helping his friend who traded batik cloth. This friend would come and go from Solo in Central Java once a month.

'What!' I interrupted his story. 'There are wandering traders who go in and out of city neighbourhoods where I live too, in Tebet, but they nearly always come from Sumedang in West Java. But a trader like that from Central Java – isn't that odd?'

He seemed shocked to hear my question. 'Well, what else can I do?' he asked. 'Apart from needing some money to live, I also need some kind of umbrella.'

Now it was my turn to keep quiet. For people like Musayid, this was indeed an inevitable consequence and was part of the heavy responsibility on him as a husband and father. His wife, as I had known her, was the type of well-born housewife who had been raised to that position in order to prove the truth of the story that woman was created from man's rib. She had no experience at all in earning her own money. And her husband, or let's say the man, seemed to accept that as being the nature and destiny of woman. She had no experience of life, or her husband ensured she had none, and on top of that she had the burden of caring for numerous children. Because children, in the view of Javanese families, are blessings.

'Are you suggesting I should do some illegal land deals like the local Betawi guys do?' he asked. 'It's not that I don't want to or that I couldn't do it. What's so hard in that? But it would mean having to meet lots of people I do not know. And I want to avoid that. And anyway, it's like the lottery. If you get a good deal, you get a lot. But then you have to share it with lots of people. And you never know when that lucky break will come, or even if it will ever come.'

'Yes, you're right. So, who is your batik trader friend, Yik?'

'Don't call me Yik. Call me Husin', he interrupted. 'It's Zus Ranti. Do you remember her?'

'Mbak Rantiyem? The one who worked as an assistant for Pak Kasbun in Labuhan?' Kasbun was a PKI figure of the 'Digul group', and Labuhan was the name of the street in East Semarang where the headquarters of the Central Java Committee (Comite Daerah Besar) was. Pak Kasbun was the staff member for the Communist Party internal affairs (RUTAP: Rumah Tangga Partai) and Mbak Rantiyem was his assistant.

Yes, she's at Setiabudi now.

'Setiabudi? But on the Intelligence's map, that is red territory. Surely you know that?

'Yes, and so does Ranti', he said. The important thing is to keep on your guard and your mouth shut. That's why we never visit each other's place. We always make an appointment to meet somewhere else. This time here, next time there. Like we all do now.

Ah, this is the 'frog's larva network' of Semarang or Central Java, I thought to myself. Making a living and a shield at the same time. Both of them were doing it. Rantiyem and Musayid.

As for me, I had no other thought but to go on living and not betray the commitment I had decided upon. I believed that the Musayid there in front of me was still the old Musayid I had known. All the time we had been apart, I had never seen or heard anything extraordinary about him. Even as recently as early September 1965, not long before the Incident occurred, I met him in Semarang when I went there as a special guest to watch the dance-drama *'Jayalah Partai dan Neg'ri'* (Glorious Party and Nation).

I was being given the red carpet treatment. I was the former first head of Lekra for Central Java, and had left Semarang to take up a position for Asia-Africa only to be sent back by the rightist regime in Sri Lanka as an unwanted person. Pak Kasbun, a senior PKI figure in the Central Java CDB (Comite Daerah Besar; Regional Committee), greeted me at the door, hugged me, cried, and led me to sit between the Governor Mochtar and Musayid. The Governor was warm and greeted me in a fatherly way, just as I remembered him from when I was his assistant as the Central Java Regional Secretary for the National Front (Sekretaris Pengurus Daerah Front Nasional) of which he was head. The 'top civilian' for Central Java called Musayid, was the old Yik I had known; the clever conversationalist who was always well-dressed. I did not know any other stories about him. But if there were any, time was too short and I was too busy to hear them.

My meetings with Musayid in the shack in the field continued regularly; sometimes there and sometimes at a different place but always at the same time. We would work out the details at the end of our meeting. Sometimes it would be ten days before we met again, sometimes two weeks or three weeks, but deliberately not too often and never more than a month apart.

When I met him under Ciliwung Bridge, I had been out of contact, or more correctly, been 'cut off' from all my old networks. As I mentioned earlier, this was the case since the afternoon of December 19, 1966, when my friend the courier visited. He was a young man whom I had not met before. He was clean-shaven, with an educated look about him, and a crew cut. His hair cut was clearly a camouflage. To look like the military.

I met him on the front verandah. Inside, in the front room behind the closed window, my dead mother was laid out. She had died that morning at ten o'clock from a heart attack. We had already fixed the normal sign of a death in the house – a yellow flag – to the front gate. My tears were not yet dry. But this courier was not only a young man with a heart of steel, but like a robot who depressed me greatly. He uttered a word or two of condolence, although said without feeling. But I did not even hear. What I heard was the order from the leadership that I had to take part in a long march (*longmars*) to South Blitar.

'You can think me a traitor if you like. You can shoot me if you like. Just don't shoot me in the back. Come on, facing each other!' I challenged him.

Actually, I did have a pistol back then, but I had never learnt how to use it. An artist friend of mine, A. Rachmad, not long after the Incident, in those terrifying days of uncertainty, had given me the pistol one night at the end of Jalan Pasar Minggu. In those days, at the end of what is now Jalan Piere Tendean, there was a house that the Pelukis Rakyat artists had turned into a studio.

'Don't be like that', I could hear him backing off. 'I am only passing on the decision of the leadership.'

'Well, you tell that to the leadership from me. I do-not-want-to-do-it. Get it? Do-not-want-to-do-it. Is that clear?'

'And your reason?' he asked, in a commanding tone of voice.

'You need a reason too?' I chuckled, deliberately mocking. 'Alright then. Listen carefully to what I have to say. This is not for you alone, but I want you to pass it on to those leaders. One. I am sure you also listen to the broadcasts of Radio Peking. It would be strange if you didn't. And how many times a day does that radio antennae blast out news about the base in South Blitar? One little spark burns a whole field, it says! What kind of bluster is this? Revolution, revolt, or escapade?

Reason number two, learn from history. Diponegoro in Central Java managed to hold out for five years. Kartosuwiryo in West Java, for years and years. And Supriyadi – how many days? In East Java, and also in Blitar! Hasn't it been written, and hasn't the Party school taught that over the whole of Java there is nowhere the army cannot enter? So why is Radio Peking joining in and rallying for a long march to South Blitar?

'So you go and tell the leaders. If I was asked to go to Irian or to Kalimantan, without all the hoo-ha, I might think about it. But a long march to South Blitar? Are they trying to look tough with the words "Long March?" Not me. I don't want any part of it. And reason number three I hardly need to spell out. Do you have eyes or not? What does the coffin behind us mean? You might say that my mother has no meaning compared to the Great Revolution. But I see it the other way around. Mother is above everything, including your revolution!'

Perhaps he could find no words to respond. Or maybe he had them but was embarrassed to speak loudly in front of my mother's dead body.

'That's enough', I said. 'I have nothing more to say to you. Go now, and don't come back again until after the 40-day ceremony for my mother.'

And I showed him out. He left without saying a word, and without even looking up. And after that, he never came back again. Nor did any new courier sent by the leadership to contact me. There were two possible reasons for this. First, that everyone had left on the Long March to South Blitar; and second, they had cut me out of the network of their political movement. But I did not care. I remembered my father's words to me, during the Japanese occupation, three days before he died. 'Don't be afraid of life without me. You were born alone, and you will also die alone. We must have the courage to face life alone. Help your mother by becoming a brave boy.'

But I was sure that Musayid was still in a regular network. Even though he might have no links within Jakarta, at least with Central Java through Rantiyem. After the outbreak of the G30S incident at the end of September 1965, the monolithic nature of the party organisation, which had been such an item of pride, was also broken. Apart from the Central Committee, there were the regional committees (CDB) in each of the large areas of Java, which competed for authority. This was probably one of the main reasons that 'cockroaches' (our name for spies) sprang up from within the party and the mass organisations and why the 'cockroaches' were more prevalent among the upper echelons than among the lower cadres. 'South Blitar' seemed to also be something of a therapeutic way out rather than a real offensive step.

Aware of just how many 'cockroaches' there were within the body of the organisation, I wondered who exactly Abu Chaer was and what his position among them was. I did not find out from Musayid. Meanwhile, I received a whisper from Sardjono to be careful of him.

He gave no further explanation. But just that single word 'careful' was pregnant with meaning. Especially because Sardjono and I had known each other for a long time. He was a former member of the Lekra leadership in Yogyakarta who became a student of Saptopriyo at the Yogya College of Music (Sekolah Musik Yogya) and had then moved to Jakarta to become a member of the Air Force music corps at Halim Perdanakusuma.

One day, Musayid was not at the shack at the appointed time for our meeting. He was waiting instead on top of the rail bridge. Something was not quite right, I thought. He then asked me to go to Pancoran, and from there we took a public van to Ragunan Zoo in Pasar Minggu.

'I'm in trouble, Brother', he said, opening the conversation.

We sat on the grass. Back then, Ragunan Zoo was very quiet, not like now. Especially during the week, which was when we were there. The view in front of us, the habitat made for the tigers, was like the Gembira Loka Zoo in Yogyakarta or zoos in Sri Lanka, a wide piece of open land with a steep bank and iron fences. The tigers were not kept in iron cages (with no yard) like in the zoos during the Dutch time. The wild animals were cared for in this habitat, which was good for them and for those who visited the zoo.

So, I was right. Something was not right with Husin, alias Yik.

'Three days ago I was called into the military sub-district command (Koramil). The summons came via the village head, so he was the one who took me there. It was really for *'verhoor'* [questioning] because after asking me to fill in forms, they began to question me on what I had written. After the question and answer session, they gave me coffee and cigarettes, chatted politely and let me go home, but I felt uneasy, and still do. What do you think? Should I run or not?'

'What was the reason for calling you in?' I asked.

'That's exactly what's troubling me now. Do you remember when there was a "pick up" in Kebon Baru and Wisnu Suryono was taken?'

'Yes, but what has that got to do with you being called in?'

'Well, back then they were looking for Supardjo or Sudardjo, or Supardjo and Sudardjo. My name on my identity card is Pradjasudardjo, as you know. And they were also searching for Musayid. I didn't hear this direct from the officer at the Military Command, but from the neighbourhood head when we went back home.'

'So, actually, they had already hinted, but were keeping it secret. Even the neighbourhood head. Is that what you mean?'

'Yes, whether Pradjasudardjo is Sudardjo, and what is the connection with the name Musayid.'

'Well the name Supardjo is not important here', I interrupted.

'You're wrong! Because according to them, he was the Commander of the Volunteer Brigade at Lubang Buaya.'

I did not reply. The sound of the gibbons calling to each other echoed throughout the zoo, answered by all the birds screeching in fright.

'There's no way they don't already have a photo of Musayid.'

'Exactly', he said. 'I thought of that too. That's why I said I'm in trouble. If I move, it just attracts attention. If I don't move, it means I make myself a sitting duck.'

'If it were me, I would move. But not right away. And you have to create a new scenario first.'

'Like?'

'Well, a relative or a family could arrive. After staying with you for one or two days, you could go with them.'

But he did not seem to pay attention to what I said. Even though I gave him my opinion because he asked for it. His eyes gazed to the distance, following his thoughts.

'If I am arrested, I just hope they don't take me to Central Java.'

I was startled by his words that changed the direction of the conversation. It seemed as though he no longer needed anyone's advice. He only wanted to hear what other people thought if they had to face the problem he faced. Maybe he felt like a boxer cornered in the ring. He couldn't get out, or no longer wanted to get out. All his colleagues, all the cadres beneath him, had been killed, had died while being hunted or thrown into the ravine at Gunungkidul, or were in prison. Whereas he, who had been the person in charge of the region, was still alive and kicking. Even with all the limitations.

'Is that what you want?'

'I'll go mad if they take me there.'

'Why's that?'

'The youth from Pemuda Rakyat and Gerwani, bearing whatever weapons they could find, were all ready to intercept – all along the road into Kartasura from Semarang and Klaten, but they were wiped out by soldiers "arriving out of the blue".'

'How could that have happened?'

'Following orders. Stop armed contact and avoid bloodshed.'

'That was the order Bung Karno made on the 5th of October. And did you forward that order to the rank and file as Party instruction?'

'Are you nuts?' He snapped. 'It was not my order. From 1 October, the Party Committee had ceased to function. Leadership was now more in the hands of the Special Bureau.'

That was my last meeting with Musayid alias Pradjasudardjo alias Husin. When I went to our prearranged meeting three weeks later, he did not turn up. I did not know why, and I could not have found out. In the frog-larvae way of networking, there was never a third person who acted as a go-between for person 1 and person 2. Once the connection was cut, without knowing why, the connection had to be completely severed, until such a time when it was necessary to restore it.

After waiting for him for some time and when I was sure that he was not going to come, I left our meeting place. With an acute sense of alert, I began to walk home. Who knows, our rendezvous spots might have been under surveillance all along. When I got to the top of the railway bridge it was already past sunset. I heard a teenage girl calling my name, with no sense of unease.

'Uncle Hersri!'

I turned to her. I vaguely recollected her face, but I did not recognise her.

'Who are you?'

'Have you forgotten me, Uncle? It's Wiwien, the daughter … from Jalan Bergota.' She did not want to say the name of her father or mother, and so said the name of the street of the house where she lived. While deliberately concealing her parents, she was at the same time jogging my memory.

'Wiwien!' I cried, and I embraced the eldest of Musayid's children. 'Why are you here when it's dark like this?'

'It's Dad, Uncle …' she said while sobbing on my chest.

'What's happened to your Dad?'

She did not answer. I could still feel her sobbing on my chest. Actually, there was no need for me to ask 'what's happened'. I had already been through this three times before. With Ajoeb, with Rivai Apin, and also Anantaguna. And now, Musayid! When someone did not appear at the appointed time, you had to conclude they had been arrested. This was also a sign for me that I had to hide and lay low for a while.

'Dad…' her voice was faint.

'I understand, Wiwien. We'll talk later. Right now let yourself cry. Then we will get away from here. It is not good to stay here long. Especially as it is getting dark.'

She released her embrace.

'You've grown up, Wiwien!' I said, rocking her shoulders, to change the mood. 'What class are you in now?'

'Third year of junior high school'.

'And how are your brothers and sisters?'

'Wawan is sick'

'Wawan? Which one is he?'

'He's the youngest, Oom. When you left Semarang, Mama was still pregnant, do you remember?'

Oh yes, I remembered everything. Jalan Bergota number 5, Semarang. It used to be the address of the Communist Party's Regional Office for Central Java before it moved to 19 Jalan Labuhan. But at Bergota there was also a huge cemetery with crowded gravestones and lots of white and red frangipani trees. Like the Krapyak public cemetery in Yogyakarta, it had a scary, haunted feel about it.

That's right. Musayid's wife had been pregnant back then. She was like Wiwien, short in stature and her skin quite fair. But also pale. All the time I knew her, she was never well. And her skin had scabs that never healed. Probably she typified the wife of a Javanese activist at the time: lots of children, sitting around the house, only moving as far as the market, and never speaking unless asked a question.

I continued chatting as I walked with Wiwien. We walked in the direction of the Hanuman statue, towards Pancoran pharmacy on the corner of the crossroads of Gatot Subroto and Pasar Minggu. There, Musayid's wife was waiting for us, while picking up some medicine for the little one.

'*Mbakyu!*' I cried, answering the embrace of an older sister, so full of longing and trust.

'It's my husband', she said, in a semi-whisper as she held back the tears.

'Yes, I heard from Wiwien. Let's talk more later at home.'

As we travelled by public van, all along the Pancoran-Ragunan road we did not talk much. Keeping quiet was also one of the easy ways to conceal identity. Under the dim street lights and inside the van, I stole a glance at Musayid's wife. I sighed with relief. Sitting across from me was not the Mbakyu Musayid from Bergota back then, with her hair in a neat Javanese bun and wearing Javanese cloth and blouse, but the current Mbakyu Sunarsih from Ragunan, with shoulder-length hair and wearing a dress. In this harsh capital city and in the midst of a political climate of terror, she was now supporting her six children, alone. Her face was no longer the pale face of a lady in silent self-control, patiently waiting, but now that of a woman who was independent and liberated.

Musayid had been picked up two weeks previously. Abu Chaer had not brought any news, even though he also lived in Kebon Baru and Musayid was a figure of more importance than Wisnu Suryono. My suspicion of Abu Chaer intensified. After four or five days of questioning in Jakarta, Musayid had been sent directly to Semarang. The very thing he feared. He was afraid of going mad, he said. But perhaps he was also afraid of his own shadow. It transpired that he acted out a drama not only among the kampung dwellers in Kebon Baru, but also with his wife and children and probably also with his comrades and cadres in the regions. He escaped to Jakarta, along with not only his wife and six children, whom I had known well for a long time, but also with an unofficial wife, who I will call Endah, a beautiful young activist from a mass organisation from a town in central Java. Her father was also a comrade and professional mass organisation activist in the same town.

Mbakyu Sunarsih ended her story. She let out all her cares in one, long heartfelt sigh.

'So, that is what your friend was like these last few years.' Her voice sounded sad.

'Do Wiwien and the other children all know?'

'All except the two youngest. I told them on purpose. So they would not hold out too many hopes for their father.'

'And what about you?'

'I ...' the words did not come.

She once again exhaled a deep sigh. In the dim light of the 40 watt light bulb, I caught a fleeting glimpse of her eyes, wet. I regretted my question.

'I am resigned to things as they are. Actually, I have always been like that ...' her sighs were stifled by the palms of her hands holding her face.

Outside there was the sound of the jackfruit buds and night insects greeting each other. Ragunan felt very cold and lonely.

Chapter 3

JOURNEY TO THE 'ISLE OF HOPE'

Camp Salemba. A few months before August 1971. The Camp Commander First Lieutenant CPM Mardjuki ordered us to study Pancasila, the nation's five principles. Not just to memorise everything as handed down from above, but he wanted us to come up with a fresh concept about Pancasila. A concept that was not tainted with Ruslan Abdulgani's old political slogans or showing the influence of the thinking of Muhammad Yamin and Bung Karno.

Political prisoners from all the cell blocks at Salemba prison, namely from A block to R block and including the hospital block, were gathered into study and discussion groups. The activities were organised along the same lines as the cadre schools had been in the past. So from this time on, the political prisoners' daily activities increased: study Pancasila! Our daily routine was: morning exercise in each block; cleaning duty in each block, like sweeping, scrubbing toilets and bathrooms; waiting for the distribution of drinking water three times a day; waiting for the food ration at midday and in the evening; for those whose religion had been recorded as Islam, observing prayer time five times a day, and studying to chant and read the Qur'an; for Catholics and other Christian denominations, attending service once a week; for Hindus and Buddhists, attending services every now and then. Alongside all of this was the activity that both delighted us and made us tense, namely the family visits three times a week. This was the case for those who had family members visiting them once, twice or three times a week, or just occasionally, and also for those who never ever had anyone visit them.

I don't know where the order came from. 'One day' (and 'one day' was a frequent phrase) the news went around that Major Sani Gonjo, the Commander of Tangerang Camp, was coming to Salemba jail. This news spread swiftly, mouth to mouth, like a spirit's hiss in martial arts' tales. And with numbing fear, all the Pancasila study groups and discussion groups suddenly disbanded. The different groups pretended to do other things. There were various kinds of odd activities. Some of them quickly opened the Qur'an and started chanting, some turned their Bible back and forth, and some got busy with handicraft, using the plastic string saved from the wrapping of packages brought by families on visiting day, or plastic bags, to weave or to use as thread to make labels. They also made pipes out of coconut shells and all kinds of other things. But there were also some who just lay staring at the prison ceilings, weaving their own dreams.

The hiss of the spirit not only sent word about the impending visit of the Tangerang Camp Commander Sani Gonjo, but also about warnings and orders: immediately disband study groups of any kind whatsoever! The Salemba Camp Commander, First Lieutenant Mardjuki did not want to be responsible if Sani Gonjo saw there were such activities going on. And especially that there were pencils and notepaper lying around! He had to take personal responsibility for the aforementioned political prisoners.

Strange: I actually did not understand. How could one ship have two captains? Mardjuki ordered one thing, and Sani Gonjo another. But I did not feel it was necessary to try to understand. Just a waste of energy. However, some fellow political prisoners whose hobby it was to be political observers, with their stock of theory from when the national ideology of Nasakom reigned supreme, came up with two theoretical models; for-the-people and against-the-people. Sani Gonjo was placed as anti-the-people, and Mardjuki as with-the-people. And what was the point of all this? Not a single person among all those political prisoner theorists or politicians would explain this to me.

* * *

It was a few weeks before August 1971. There was news of release going around. It was said that the source of the news was an utterly reliable one, none other than the Camp Commander himself, First Lieutenant Mardjuki. In the days leading up to Indonesia's Independence Day of August 17, the mood was extraordinary. Busy and full of mystery. Certain political prisoners, those who could be said to be young, were called 'forward'. To the Interrogation Room. There was more interrogation, blood tests, smallpox vaccinations, and photos taken from every side: front, behind, left and right – except for top and bottom! After each one of us was photographed, we were told the number of our photo. I was one of those who was called 'forward'.

'What's the number of your photo?' asked someone who looked as though he was the most powerful in the room. Apart from the photographers, there were a few army guards there.

I replied with my six-digit photo number.

'Correct. Don't you forget it!' he yelled.

I was reminded of when I was at junior high school. I can't remember the precise year, but it was not long after the end of WWII. There was a film titled, if I am not wrong, *Achter de wolken*, Beyond the Clouds. It was showing at the Indra cinema near the Beringhardjo central market in Yogyakarta. The whole school, one group at a time, was taken to see the film. There was one scene that stayed with me, namely when the political prisoners were gathered in the yard of the Nazi concentration camp. They were all wearing striped uniforms, like the striped cloth we use for blankets. One by one they were called using only numbers. No names. The prisoners no longer had names. Because names are things that humans possess. In Javanese, the word for name is *jeneng*. And *jeneng* is subject. Political prisoners are not subjects!

The closer that 'liberation day' of August 17, 1971 approached, the more people began to doubt all the rumours of release. Their reason was quite simple. The only ones called forward were those who, on the whole, were under 40 years of age and who were healthy. How was it possible that they would be the ones released while the elderly and sick would be left huddled in their cells? I myself was sure that this was preparation for the third wave of prisoners to be sent to Buru. My reason was also simple. When I was called up for the interrogation, I saw the manila folder and on it, in the top right-hand corner was written the letter C. This letter had been crossed out in red felt pen, and beneath it was written B2, and beneath this was written 'night communist (PKI Malam).' So, I am a night communist, I thought. Now, why would a 'night communist' be called forward, be vaccinated and have his blood tested, then be ordered to memorise the number of his photo ... only to be released?

Meanwhile, something else interesting happened, which did not support the rumours of freedom. Dozens of political prisoners from Tangerang prison were moved to Salemba prison. Almost all of them were young, under 30. All of them were put in D Block in complete isolation. The news went around that they had been involved in the murder of a prisoner called Silitonga, who was well known as an informer – we called them cockroaches.

People said they had been moved to Salemba for interrogation and investigation. Those responsible would have to go to court. And just what sort of court would that be? Political prisoners who had already been held in prison without due process taken to court for the murder of a fellow prisoner?

Probably it was not investigation but confusion that the authorities wanted. And sure enough! The news about the murder of Silitonga circulated at the same time as even more incredible news, namely that a communist network cell had been discovered in Tangerang Camp. Among the dozens of young prisoners who were moved to Salemba were the two ringleaders, Slamet Wijaya and Sabar Santoso Pangarso. The rumour was that the two of them were going to be taken to court. Spreading words like 'instigate' and 'instigator' was one way of instigating confusion. And instigating confusion was one part of the work of Intelligence.

That was probably early 1971. While stories circulated inside the prison of forthcoming releases on Independence Day, outside people were being forced to celebrate the 'fiesta of democracy', or general election. It was the last days of the campaign period for the Indonesian Democratic Party, Partai Demokrasi Indonesia or PDI. I don't know what date it was, because all the time I was in camp remembering the date was just a useless waste of energy. From the early morning, a loudspeaker had been blasting away, coming from the basketball field outside the camp. Nonstop. Guntur Sukarnoputra (Sukarno's son) was going to give a speech. At 4 pm.

The Camp Commander, First Lieutenant Mardjuki, lost no time in hitting back. That morning the heads of each cell block were called up.

Soon after the end of Islamic religious class, which took place every day from around 10-11 am, the cell block leaders returned to their separate blocks with an announcement. Today there was going to be a volleyball and handball competition between cell blocks. It would run from 3-6 pm that is before the distribution of drinking water and the sounding of the call to evening prayer. Every prisoner, without exception, had to come out to the yard to watch and cheer on their team. Even the prisoners in isolation were ordered out to participate in this compulsory duty of cheering and clapping.

> Competition is everywhere
> One must win
> And the others must lose

This is part of a poem by Ho Chi Minh, I can't remember the title, but I had read it once a long time ago.

And so it was with us. Just as long as we played. One had to win and the others had to lose. The one who won was, of course, First Lieutenant Mardjuki, and the losers were us, the prisoners. The Salemba prison yard that afternoon was full of cheering and applause. But actually, it was not the obligatory sport that we were playing and watching, but rather the Camp Commander's own Intelligence operation so that the sound of Guntur campaigning outside the camp would not reach our ears. Even so, many of the prisoners were duped by this ruse, and came to their own conclusions. 'The day of liberation is near! We are allowed to play sport! See, even the isolation blocks have been opened!' They were the prisoners who, for all kinds of different reasons, had ties with the past that were too strong, so that they were not aware of what was going on in the present, and certainly could not see the future that awaited them.

1 August 1971. Group by group, truck by truck, the prisoners were moved. The ones from Salemba went to Tangerang, and the ones from Tangerang to Salemba. And because their scenario was fully developed, their interpretation of this move followed suit. They were all being prepared to be released, and this was going to happen from Tangerang prison. It seemed that the Camp Commander was completely aware of the full-blown dreams of many of the prisoners. Over those days, he deliberately stirred things up in the camp. He did roll call a few times a day for each block. Some prisoners were moved from one block to another, some were called forward to be photographed, and others were told to gather their belongings together, to run to the yard at once and to march out towards the awaiting trucks, engines rolling.

All that day, you could hear First Lieutenant Mardjuki yelling abuse and the slap of his hand.

'Idiot! Moron! So you like it here? You don't want to be let out? You want to stay in your cell forever? Pig! Buffalo! ... and all kinds of other abuse that a person with power uses with powerless detainees.

My turn arrived on 3 August. A few of my friends embraced me and smiled. One of them was Pracoyo, a senior official in the Department of Marine Communications. After the event of 30 September, in the midst of the tussle of power between those who were pro and contra Sukarno, he became one of the leaders of the Sukarno Front (Barisan Sukarno or Basuka). Basuka was formed in late 1965 with the aim of supporting President Sukarno after the mass power of the Communist Party (PKI) and the National Party of Ali and Surakhman (PNI) supporters was paralysed. The highest ranking leader of this semi-official front was Lieutenant General Amir Machmud.

'Ah, Hersri! So you got your turn first ...' The dream of release was glowing from his eyes,

'Good luck!' Pak Sudadi said.

Pak Sudadi was my cellmate and my bridge partner. Later, when I was at Buru, he shared a unit with me: Unit XIV Bantalareja. He loved to talk about how he was the son of the headman in a village in Bantul, Yogyakarta, who had family links to Pak Harto (President Soeharto) who came from Kemusuk.

At the time of the revolution (for Indonesia's independence), he was a member of the Pesindo (Pemuda Sosialis Indonesia, Indonesian Socialist Youth) squad. Then he moved to the central leadership of the Indonesian Plantation Workers Union (Sarbupri), and became the top person for the All Indonesia Trade Union Federation (SOBSI) for the Jakarta district. When the army formed the Military Unit for Cooperation with Youth (Badan Kerja Sama Pemuda Militer, BKSPM), which later became the BKS Bumil (Military Body for Cooperation with Workers) he sat as the representative of SOBSI. Later he was fired from his position as regional representative of SOBSI and from the Jakarta regional committee of the Communist Party because of abuse of various facilities he had obtained from his position at BKS Bumil.

'Take care, son', he said in a fatherly tone. 'I ask for just one thing. Send news to my family.'

He slipped into my pocket some tightly folded pieces of paper on which he had written the addresses of his family in Jakarta. It seemed that he had forgotten that, in a jail for political prisoners, paper was a banned product. Or maybe he remembered, but thought it did not matter because in just a moment I would be out there, in the free world. And the free world did not know banned products.

'Farewell! He said. With a face bright with conviction, he shook my hand strongly. As did other friends who flanked the prison gate.

'Until we meet again outside!' they called.

'Yes, until then!' I replied, with warmth matching theirs. But I deliberately did not copy their word, 'outside'. Dreams indeed have no limits. Sometimes they even know no shame. Whether that be a dream while one is asleep, or a dream while awake. Whether it is a dream of a free person or the dream of a person who has been imprisoned for years.

***

So it was that I left my cell and block at the cold, damp Salemba prison. I went out the door of I Block holding my rolled-up mat under my armpit, and passed the walls of Blocks G, F, E and D. I went through the double iron gates that divided the internal blocks with the outside blocks A, B and C.

As I was walking along, before I reached the last iron door where lots of guards were standing, I chewed up the scraps of paper from my shirt pocket as best as I could. Then I spat them out along the hedge. I was absolutely sure that we were not heading for freedom. We were being moved. Maybe to Tangerang, or Nusakambangan, or Buru island, like the two groups who had already left. And so I was thinking of just one thing: I had not been able to send news to my family.

Actually, that very day was 'visiting day'. The Indonesian word for this was *besukan*, from the Dutch word *bezoek*, meaning to visit. But in prison, the word '*besukan*' had a special meaning, namely something that the family sent you. That was usually food of course, because anything else was forbidden. But sometimes it might be money, sent by 'special delivery' and outside of real visiting days. This could happen because the guard had received a bribe from the family, apart from the 'customs duty' that would also be charged to the prisoner himself. This charge was a cut of a certain percentage of the goods or money sent by the family, taken without the knowledge of the prisoner recipient. Certain necessities could be ordered from families at certain times, for instance, light bulbs, buckets, rope for the well and paint for the walls.

There were three visiting days a week at Salemba jail; Monday, Wednesday and Friday. At that time, families who could afford it and were brave enough would line up before the prison post at the first gate, waiting their turn to hand over their '*besukan*' parcels. How 'fat' or 'thin' the parcel was, and how 'high' or 'low' the quality of the contents were, was of course determined by the family's situation. So too the 'frequency' of the parcels, for instance, whether they came once or three times a week, once or twice a month, or just occasionally. The words 'fat', 'thin', 'high' and 'low' were the Salemba and Tangerang prisoners' jargon.

On this particular day, the visiting day had coincided with extraordinary activity going on inside and between the camps, the moving of prisoners from Salemba to Tangerang and the other way around, and from one block to another within Salemba. The hour of opening the post for the visitors was delayed until all the prisoners who had to be moved had departed.

I left Salemba prison with just the clothes on my back. A shirt with 1001 patches, so that you could no longer tell what the original colour and cloth of the shirt was. Prisoners called shirts like this '*antakusuma*' shirts, referring to the magical multicoloured garment worn by Gatutkaca who, when he put it on, was able to fly even though he did not have wings. My long trousers were moss green in colour, given to me by Pracoyo. Some of the clothes that I had with me when I first entered Salemba one and a half years earlier had been stolen by the criminals inside who were thugs under the head of the block, Johny Ayal, a military criminal prisoner (not a political prisoner) who had been arrested for holding up a gold shop in Mayestik, Kebayoran Baru. That was when I was still being held in isolation for about eight months in the military criminal block: Block E2.

My possessions amounted to two mats which my younger brother or older sister had sent me when I was still in Cilandak prison in South Jakarta, some nail clippers, and a toothbrush which had broken a number of times and I had rejoined by burning it.

It turned out that it was not trucks waiting for us, but black prison buses, with iron doors complete with chains and large padlocks. Two guards sat to the left and right of the door holding carbines with naked bayonet blades. Through the super-thick glass, you could see yet another soldier sitting beside the driver. Thirty-five prisoners and their possessions were shoved into each bus.

***

We slowly passed through the gates of Salemba prison. The line of buses crawled along, rumbling. From the glass windows with bars as thick as fingers, I could see the women and children thronging. Some had come specifically to look, searching for a possible glimpse of their loved one in one of those black buses, and others were just there by chance because it was a visiting day. Becak drivers, passers-by, meatball soup sellers and roadside coffee sellers, all stopped stock still and did not even blink as they looked at the buses. Yes, their gaze pushed through the gaps between the metal bars. And so did ours from within the bus. Everyone was searching among the crowd in the yard and the road in front of the prison. But there was no waving of hands. There was just a sense of compassion shining from their faces. Some could not hold back the tears rolling down their cheeks, catching the midday sunlight.

We looked at them, our jaws locked. There were no tears. Our tears had run out long ago. Our source of tears was dead, burnt by the sting of electric shocks, or crushed by the kick of a boot, or destroyed by the blows of a barbed whip or one of General Soeharto's soldier's holsters. No. There were none among us with tears. Sad, maybe. But who could this sadness be expressed to? We were all quiet. Because that was all we could do. In that silence, we could each individually speak to our own hearts. What more did we have to experience? We had had the electric shocks. We had had the kickings with the boots. We had had the chairs thrown at us. We had had the blows of the holsters and barbed whips. What else?

As we entered the yard of Tangerang prison, the sun had descended the wall of sky. One by one we were ordered to jump down from the bus. My knees were shaking. Maybe it was from fear. But it was certainly from hunger. Since morning we had not had one sip of water. The water distributed in the morning had still been hot when we had suddenly got the call to get ready and go immediately to the yard. Officers were already there waiting for us. Some were in army uniforms, some looked like security guards, some were prison officials, and some were from the student regiment.

We went towards the prison yard. One by one we were frisked, then another officer opened our pathetic possessions and rummaged through them. He took the nail clippers from my shirt pocket and threw them aside. My eyes flared in protest. I wanted to run and pick them up. But Alibasah, a prisoner who had been in the leadership of the Air Force Workers Union (Serbaud, Serikat Buruh Angkatan

Udara) in West Irian, and who had been imprisoned for a long time, shunted back and forth between Salemba and Tangerang, held me back by the arm. His eyes flashed his protest at me.

'Clippers are in the forbidden category here', he whispered, after the guards had finished their examination of us, and we had walked off a little way.

'Has anyone ever died from nail clippers?'

'No need even to ask!'

Then we had to line up and stand to attention. We had to listen carefully as they were calling out names, one by one. We were divided into different groups. The groups were the blocks we were to join. As in Salemba jail, each block had a few large rooms where prisoners were all together, but there were also rows of cells each measuring 2 x 4 metres that housed between 5 and 7 prisoners each.

As I went through the door to the block, my chest seemed to hiss, the nape of my neck sensed a cold rush of air and my eyes suddenly went dark. Just for a moment. I always feel like that when I face something new that startles me. When I felt the musty, cold air in the cell, smelt the sour stink of the rust on the door and the iron bars, when I saw all the torture implements on the interrogators' table, and even when I faced the lunch ration at Salemba jail.

That was back when I was first moved from the operational detention centre Paskoarma (Pasukan Komando Armada, Armada Command Brigade) II in Cilandak to Salemba jail. As a political prisoner of the navy, I was better treated than army prisoners. This is also what my interrogator, Command Corps Captain Sutarno Muchali told me. Navy political prisoners were given the same food rations as navy prisoners arrested for discipline offences. Apart from rice and side dishes, once a week we were given green lentil soup or milk.

After briefly calling at the Military Police headquarters in Jalan Guntur, the six of us were moved from Salemba. There were two women who were sent to the Bukit Duri prison, and the four men – myself, Slamet Parto (the uncle of Command Corps Commander Hartono, Hadisuwarno, a bicycle repairman from Klaten), and Suprapto, a member of the Klaten branch of the League of Indonesian Youth and Students (IPPI, Ikatan Pemuda Pelajar Indonesia) – were taken to Salemba. My three friends were escorted off separately while I was put alone into a cell. The door was shut and locked. It was around midday, the time for the distribution of the lunch ration.

'This really is prison', I said to myself.

I remembered the song 'Life Inside' which I had once heard Command Corps Sergeant Sugiarto sing when I was still at Paskoarma II in Cilandak. People said that some anonymous prisoner at Tangerang had composed the song, which I ended up being able to sing. It went like this:

> Life inside is like a bird
> Breakfast just a few grains of maize
> Sleep on the cold floor with thoughts confused
> Helpless and powerless my body caged
>
> Wake up now it's morning call
> Queue for quota of morning mush
> Want to wash but no soap at all
> Want to smoke but only butts
>
> Friend, listen to this song, oh do
> Prison life is torture and dread
> Never let this happen to you
> Your body alive but feeling dead

> Especially at Tangerang jail
> Go in fat, go home just bones
> Forced labour never fails
> Young and old in ricefields toil

My new cell was narrower and lower than my cell at Paskoarma, and the floor was concrete, not tiles. The window was an iron grill, just enough for air to come in, just beneath the ceiling. The whitewash on the walls no longer had any colour, they were covered with smears of blood from squashed bedbugs and mosquitoes. The stink of urine mixed with the sour smell of the rusty iron and the floor. I spread out my mat. I put my roll of clothes at the head as a pillow. I was tired and felt lonely.

'Brother', I heard from the cell beside mine. 'That's you, isn't it, from Tebet?'

'Who are you?' I asked, holding the bars of the cell door.

'Your neighbour. Naryo from the Air Force. I have been here for about three months already. That head of your neighbourhood, Hadi Brengos, is a bastard ...'

'And welcome from me too', came a voice from the cell on my right. I'm Saleh, from the Semarang branch of Lekra ...'

'Oh, what's the news of Yohed and Harno?'

'No idea. I haven't been to Semarang for ages. I was in Jakarta at the Union of Motor Vehicle Workers (SBKB, Serikat Buruh Kendaraan Bermotor).'

'How long have you been in here?'

'About three years. I've been moved around from one block to another. Mardjuki has been searching for you for ages ...'

Our conversation stopped. We could hear the door to the cell block open. The prisoners on food trolley duty were going around with the prison guards. The atmosphere went quiet instantly. I understood. Talking was one of the most forbidden things.

'Food!' I heard, but my cell door did not open.

My ration was pushed through a gap between the door and the floor. It was an indescribable aluminium plate, filthy, torn and smashed. There was no spoon. On the plate were five or six spoons of rice in clear green water with one or two spinach leaves.

When I picked up the plate, wanting to put it in the corner of my cell, my fingers felt slimy. I lifted the plate and put it close to my nose. The vile stink made me retch. The plate had probably not been washed for years. I vomited. For three days after that, I lay on my back with a fever and an empty stomach. I could not eat.

'Brother', it was the prisoner on duty standing outside my door. 'Here is some palm sugar from the block next door'.

'Thank you.'

Two pieces of palm sugar sent by someone from the block next door. This was because they had heard I was sick. It was a simple gesture of solidarity, or whatever you want to call it. A statement of true fellowship, 'a friend in need is a friend indeed' as the saying goes.

The cell block door closed. You could hear the padlock and chain.

'How are you, Brother? Any better?' came the voice from the cell next door. 'You must eat, so you can get well.'

'That's the problem. I have no appetite …'

'Don't eat with appetite. Eat with your head!' he advised. 'Appetite is for when you have a choice. Not here. But then what? We have to survive.'

'Just put it in your mouth and swallow', came the voice from the cell on the other side. 'I was the same as you. If you have to, close your nose.'

Compared to Salemba, Camp Tangerang was worse. The cell blocks were narrower, but there were more prisoners. So it felt even more crowded and filthy. Especially because at that time, Tangerang had just come to the end of an enforced eight-month period of heavy isolation. Only a few prisoners had any flesh on their bones. Most looked like living skeletons. Quite a few were paralysed and sprawled in cells here and there. Just like the prisoners in Hitler's Nazi concentration camps before they were sent off to the 'showers' and then thrown into the ovens.

According to Alibasah, the story went like this: Around the same time as the incident of the murder of the informer Silitonga, there was the discovery of an underground Communist Party movement at Camp Tangerang. Some documents listing the leadership and members of the organisation together with training material were confiscated. The recriminations were felt not only by those underground Communist Party political prisoners, but by every single political prisoner in the camp. All were dished out harsh and cruel treatment. They were tortured with all kinds of equipment, and for three months Camp Tangerang was put in total lockdown. The doors of all cells were locked, except for certain times for a few minutes; all visiting was forbidden; all camp agricultural projects ceased and the political prisoners involved in them were taken back to the camp.

Before this incident, the political prisoners at Tangerang had been divided into two groups. One group lived inside and the others lived outside the camp. Those who lived outside were usually those who were young and healthy. Their labour was needed to work on various projects run by Jaya District Military Command (Kodam) V (now Kodam VII), especially their ricefield and agricultural field projects outside of Tangerang.

Meanwhile, in the middle of all this fuss and widespread tension, there was rumour. But of course, in prison life, and particularly in the life of political prisoners, all news is rumour.

It went like this. By now there were already 6000 political prisoners on the island of Buru. And now, in 1971, that number was to be increased to 10,000. And so there came to be a kind of trade in prisoners. Every person was said to be worth 10,000 rupiah. As to who was doing the buying and who the selling, the rumour left you to fill that in for yourself. But because the spirit of anti-military dictatorship and anti-imperialism, especially American imperialism, was generally high among the political prisoners from the September 30 incident, the guesswork was predictable. The seller was the Soeharto regime, and the buyer was the United States, the global enemy of the people. This is a rough summary of the gossip going around. The more subtle essence of it was that the project of 'utilisation' of political prisoner labour at Buru came about because of foreign aid.

However, the acronym itself, *'Tefaat'* for *'tempat pemanfaatan'* or 'utilisation location' reveals what was really going on. As an agency, the Buru 'utilisation location' was a vessel for political prisoner labour. As political prisoners, they were of the caste of useless 'new pariah'. But as labourers, they had a potential power to be 'utilised' as much as possible, namely to work on any project at all that would support the government's development plan.

* * *

The mood in the camp, August 3-5, 1971. No action. There was only the order to be on full alert to respond to the summons of the guards from time to time. At least three times a day we had to move from one cell to another, or change groups or cells.

The cells or groups actually functioned as the smallest unit in the management of the political prisoners in the camp. One group was usually made up of five to seven people. But sometimes there were also groups of nine or even eleven people. This happened whenever there had been a series of 'pick up' raids. The groups were necessary for organising work squads – for cleaning the block, distributing drinking water and so on – but also to equalise 'welfare'. This was because the 'visiting parcels' that visitors received differed in their contents and quality. So the units were named *'corvée* groups' or 'sharing groups'.

The rumours about imminent releases also turned out to be raging at Tangerang Camp. In fact, raging even stronger and in more detail. Inmates said that their constant regroupings were part of the organising of groupings for our release. They said the whole problem of the September 30 Movement political prisoners had to be settled by August 17, 1971! The mass release would take place on the square in front of Jakarta City Hall, or in the Ikada Square led by the then Governor of Jakarta, Ali Sadikin.

On 5 August, the riddle that was causing such tension was explained. Explained by the authorities, those holding power over the fate of so many political prisoners and even the fate of the republic. The brief dream that the prisoners had that August 17 would be their day of release turned out to be completely wrong. It was true they were going to be taken out of prison. Not to be released, but to be exiled to the island of Buru. The idea that over there the prisoners would be free to do business, farm, grow crops and so on (as some prisoners said, including Bambang Sasmoyo), was contradicted even by the name of the place: *tefaat*, short for *tempat pemanfaatan*, utilisation location.

This was the place where prisoners were to be 'utilised', exploited, rather than letting them go to waste. This was particularly so in what the New Order called the era of 'development'.

Two days after I entered Tangerang, the visitors' mail was reopened. I was one of the prisoners who received a package. I had no idea how my family had found out that I had been moved. Moreover, it seemed as though they already knew that I was going to be 'Burued'. Apart from the rice and dishes, cracked wheat and palm sugar, there was also a new woven grass mat, wooden sandals and … tucked inside the label on the box two Rp 200 notes!

To receive this parcel at just the right time made me want to weep. The visiting post had already closed so it was too late to return the bag containing the package. I regretted this deeply; that I was not able to signal to my loved ones about my pending departure to the island of exile. I remembered stories my mother had told me about the Javanese rebels who were exiled to Ceylon, and now here was one of her own children being added to those stories of exile.

I could have replaced the money in its hiding place under the label with a note with a few words: 'I am one of those to be Ceyloned', but I was too late. Yet again, political prisoners did not own time. This might have been the last time we would have contact, albeit not face-to-face. Who knows, maybe I would never be with them again? When I thought of this worst-case scenario, my emotions went crazy.

Two years earlier, I had received the news. My younger brother, who had been visiting me regularly and who was a major in the Indonesian navy, was arrested, interrogated, detailed and fired from his position. This was because, before I was taken in, I had stayed with him and his family at their home. As a navy officer, he was accused of having protected and supported a September 30 Movement entity. The political powers-that-be did not care that my mother, our mother, also lived in that house, as well as one of our older sisters; that I had no other place of my own to live; that Javanese people live in extended families, and that Javanese live by the saying *mangan ora mangan waton kumpul*, meaning that the first priority is to be together, and only then to worry about food.

In this atmosphere, the Tangerang prison felt completely different to Salemba. There were no group sessions to study Pancasila. There were not even any group sessions studying the Qur'an. Religious activities were restricted to fulfilling basic requirements: prayer times for the Muslim prisoners, and worship for the Christians and Buddhists. The terms of address that were common to us from being involved in the Party, terms like 'Bung' (brother) and 'Kawan' (comrade), which to the ears at Salemba were thought dangerous, were here at Tangerang used just as they had been outside prison. This was obviously because there was less danger of informers here because the cadres had stamped them out. It was the same with 'solidarity', a word that had at Salemba become bland and greeted with yells of cynicism, at Tangerang it was still a meaty word.

Compared to the Salemba prisoners, who were controlled by the upper-middle cadres, the Tangerang prisoners were controlled by the middle cadres. This was probably why the leaders at Tangerang, if there were any, did not have space. Surely they knew what was happening with the extraordinary goings-on in the days leading up to Independence Day. There would be hundreds of political prisoners sent off to the island of Buru like those who had gone before them. That was certain. But when exactly, and who exactly would be sent, that was something prisoners did not know.

In Tangerang, there were no bright faces weaving dreams of freedom busy writing letters to be entrusted to friends to send to their families. You could see here and there small discussion groups, but they were not discussing Pancasila! They were determining the leaders of teams for the journey and on the ship; how to help their comrades who were paralysed; how to rehabilitate them so they would be healthy and strong; whose duty it would be to pilfer some of the requisitions once on the ship. And all kinds of other things to prepare for the worst.

Meanwhile, some of the other prisoners who had craft skills were also busy. With coloured 'thread' that they had unravelled from cloth, they were making labels to put on bags and knapsacks in various shapes and sizes. The knapsacks were made from gunnysack, a few from flour sacks, and some from burlap from old fertiliser sacks. They made them not only for themselves and their close friends, but also for others who were not quite as dexterous. One knapsack was worth one piece of palm sugar, or 25 rupiah.

Suripto, a young man from Solo who had been a member of the Gembira choir led by Subronto K. Atmodjo, one day brought us a song written out with cipher notation. This was not just to motivate his fellow prisoners who were about to be 'Burued', but also to preserve this event for posterity in a song. It seemed that he had been influenced by his choirmaster, Subronto, who always used to record historical events in song, especially President Sukarno's speeches every year on 17 August. Songs like *'Nasakom bersatu'* (Nasakom unite), *'Resopim'* (Revolusi-Socialisme Pemimpin Nasional, Socialist Revolution National Leader), and *'Sukarelawan'* (Volunteer). It was a 'pity' that Suripto himself did not get sent to Buru, and to this day I have no idea where he is.

I was asked to write a poem for the march he had composed, and we agreed that it would be called 'burlap knapsack' (Ransel Goni). The song's first singers, apart from Suripto and myself, were Suwardi Penjol and Bambang Irawan who had been one of the leaders of the League of Indonesian Youth and Students (IPPI), and Heru Santoso, a former leader of the East Java branch of the Indonesian Student Movement Concentration (CGMI). The last verse of the song went like this:

> Pick up your burlap knapsack
> and your determination too
> Hold your head up high
> It's off to Buru Isle for you

Chapter 4

LAST DAYS IN CAMP TANGERANG

All the inmates of Camp Tangerang had just been released from strict isolation. This was not because of some twinge of conscience on the part of the authorities, but for at least two reasons. The first was – how could they hide their faces when every day around ten political prisoners died from hunger – as happened over 1967-68. The second was the frantic activity of the authorities in drawing up the scenario of 'Buru, the Isle of Hope', which was like a double-edged sword. On one side was the exile and slow killing of political prisoners far from the centre of power, and on the other was the 'generous' exploitation of labour to support the 'national development program' in the east of Indonesia. An analogy from the world of the Javanese shadow-puppet play is when the Pandawa are 'given hospitality' to become sacrificial lambs for the prosperity of the Astina kingdom.

From this perspective, the so-called 'Tangerang incident', from the murder of the political prisoner Silitonga to the unravelling of Slamet Wijaya's underground Communist Party plot, filled merely one or two scenes in the overall scenario of 'Buru, the Isle of Hope' that the authorities were currently writing.

Over those days, the mood at the camp also changed. There were no more Qur'an reading activities or Pancasila study groups. I filled the time meeting friends I had previously known – those within the same block of course – and listening to their stories of their experiences, especially the agricultural project run by the Jaya V district Military Command (Kodam V), the labour for which was provided by the political prisoners in Tangerang. And during this hiatus, there were a few, probably those of Slamet Wijaya's cadres who had escaped the 'cleansing', who got us talking about what we should do when we were on the boat, how we could organise to help those prisoners who were old or frail, from when we landed until we got to the unit and so on. And, of course, another important thing was how to 'rehab' those prisoners who were paralysed or as thin as skeletons, as a result of the severe isolation over many months at Tangerang.

Those with craft skills were busy doing other things. They offered their services making backpacks from gunnysack, calico, old fertiliser bags or wheat sacks. I have no idea where they managed to get all that. It had to be through bargaining, for instance with palm sugar, tobacco, boiled cassava, or a little money, between ten and twenty-five rupiah. In short, with whatever they could. Others made stylish labels with coloured 'thread' pulled from rags. And there were those who wove bags from bits of plastic string, which they then sold for between ten and fifteen rupiah. The fact that I mention money here should cause no surprise. Even when I was at Salemba, I had known about the circulation of money among the prisoners who had already been there for years. The division between 'rich' and 'poor' political prisoners was actually set even before that, when they were still in temporary places of detention before they were moved to the prisons in Salemba, Bukitduri or Tangerang.

Our prison ration of one mug of hot water and one piece of boiled cassava had already been distributed, along with the leftovers from our friends' visitor parcels from yesterday. It was unusually early for breakfast. We were driven by the mood of increased uncertainty and haste. 'Take every opportunity you can!' had become our motto. Also as far as food was concerned, it was 'get it in your mouth and swallow' while you could.

It often happened that you were just sitting cross-legged with your food-sharing group, sharing out the proceeds of the parcels, when suddenly, before you had put the spoon in your mouth, a guard would appear outside the door yelling out names. The ones called had to stand at once and 'face forward'. And 'facing forward' could mean all kinds of things. Yet another interrogation with complementary abuse and torture; moving cells; moving blocks; moving camps or being 'disappeared'. And being 'disappeared' could end in the worst of all, being killed, which in prison-slang we called being *'mangkubumi'*-ed, which was a pun on the name of one of Java's cruellest tyrants in history, Mangkubumi, and also the word itself, namely being 'embraced' *(mangku)* by the earth *(bumi)*. This was why prisoners lost no time at all in eating. Unless they were too sick.

'Even your own food ration, until it gets into your stomach, is not actually yours', Siswondo used to grumble.

Another young prisoner called Karta bin Deris, who was always cheery, would chime in.

'Keep your grumbling until you've finished. Whether war then breaks out or you're struck by lightning … at least you will have eaten.'

That morning was like that. We had not yet finished drinking our water or eating our boiled cassava when suddenly a guard appeared at the door to the block.

'Attention!' He ordered. 'Be prepared to be called forward.'

Sure enough. From the yard came the squeal and shrill squeaks of the loudspeaker cranking up. Then the microphone being tapped: 'One-two-three, one-two-three, testing, one …'.

All at once the Tangerang sky seemed to close in. The loudspeaker, the megaphone, the roar of dozens of trucks. Not to mention the yelled orders of the guards from cell to cell, the hurling of abuse, the slaps and the screams of prisoners who were on the other end of fists or boots.

I was ready. Since I had moved to Tangerang from Salemba I was always ready. I even wore my shirt and trousers to sleep so that when I was called all I would have to do is roll up my mat. And be ready.

The prisoners' names were called out, one by one, their full names together with the name of their parents, together with their registration number and their photograph number, all yelled out in sequence through the megaphone. It was around ten when my name was called. I immediately went and joined the line of prisoners walking very slowly, one by one, past the fence of guards. The din was like a night fair.

Way over in the corner were some guards. We had to open up everything we were carrying and show them, one by one. The only things we were allowed to take were clothing, toothbrush and soap. Mats, blankets, pillows and mattresses – now, that surprised me! Some of the prisoners owned pillows and mattresses! – and eating utensils, all were forbidden. The ransackers, (alias guards), just chucked these forbidden items to the edge of the yard.

Wasga, a friend from Indramayu, tried to hide his plate and cup.

'Throw them out!' ordered the guard, his eyes threatening.

'But they're new, Pak!' Wasga said. 'My family sent them. Just yesterday …'

'Moron! Chuck them!' And he kicked Wasga's hand. The plate and cup in his hand went flying and fell in pieces.

'You moron! Where you're going you'll get fancy porcelain plates and cups from those Communist Chinks. Your favourites!' Another guard chipped in. 'And mattresses, pillows and mattresses. All of you. Chuck out those disgusting old ones. We'll burn the lot.'

It was incredible how many guards and officers there were on that day. Judging from their uniforms, they came from various places: security guards, prison and justice staff, but most of all, of course, the army.

Once all the ransacking was done, we were marched off one by one to a different place. There, a guard yelled out our names, which we had to respond to with a yell of no less volume: our registration number and photo number. After giving a bow of respect, another guard gave us our reward: a khaki short-sleeved shirt, brown and green long trousers, and a hand-made Tangerang hat. A bamboo hat. It reminded me of my primary school when I was in first grade. My geography teacher, Pak Bei Harjautama, told us that Tangerang had been known for its bamboo craft since Dutch colonial times.

'The number of your shirt is (x)', the guard said while writing on a wide sheet of paper. 'Memorise it. And don't forget it!' he ordered.

'Watch out if you forget!' another chirped in.

Oh, my poor head! Here was another series of numbers I had to memorise. A brain that was nourished every day with ten spoonsful of rice and one mug of water had to remember so many numbers.

Then we were herded to another corner of the yard, joining the others who were already there. We had to strip naked (and that was a strange sight! There were so many guards, but not a single female guard or officer. This country seemed to be a country of male-only soldiers, it seemed!). We all had to change out of the clothes we were wearing into the set given to us by the 'New Order government under the leadership of the kind General Soeharto'. I don't know how many times we heard those words in every speech that morning, as we moved from one line to the next.

True. On the chest of my shirt was a number emblazoned large in black: 438. It was on the seat of my pants as well. It reminded me of once rafting past the abattoirs beside the Gajah Wong River in Yogyakarta. The cattle about to be slaughtered had all been branded with numbers, on their left and right flanks. If those cattle had worn trousers and shirts, they would not have had to suffer the burning of the hot branding iron. So we political prisoners had it better than cattle. Oh Yes. Soeharto and his New Order were kind indeed. Thank you, Pak!

Without being given any time to rest, and don't even mention food or drink, we had to wait until all the arrangements were completed.

The hand on the clock of the old wall above the prison gate pointed to two. We were ordered to leave the yard, marching towards the open trucks that were there waiting for us, lined up in the yard and road in front of the prison. Every truck was loaded with fifty prisoners according to the numbers on our shirts. These groups and the order of the numbers were to remain fixed during the journey on the ship and when we arrived and entered our units.

Almost all the prisoners carried a gunnysack rucksack. One or two of the rich prisoners carried rucksacks made out of more expensive material – fertiliser bag or flour sack. Some had very light loads, but there were many carrying huge loads – heaven knows what on earth they had inside! Probably old rags and junk, like old people collect. (Javanese people say that when old people start making their nests like that, it is a sign they have accepted their end is near). Most carried just one rucksack or carried a small package, but there were also a lot who really gave themselves problems by carrying too much stuff. Like people leaving on transmigration programs.

I was on the truck. One more requirement done. My tenseness began to lessen. My eyes had the opportunity to look at those around me.

Strange, I thought. After more than five years in prison, there were still some who were not ill at ease wearing a watch and shoes (instead of sandals like the rest of us). And how had they been able to hide those things from the eyes of the guards? As for me, I had not even been able to stop them confiscating my nail clippers!

Back when I had been moved from the Navy Corps Command in Pasar Minggu to the Salemba prison, I too still wore shoes and a watch. So back when I was still a detainee scooped up in 'Operation Whale', not all my rights had been taken away.

'Leave your watch and your shoes here!' ordered a sergeant who accepted me at Salemba that day. 'We put everything in the storeroom. When you are released you can collect them', without saying when that 'when' would be.

I followed his order. Why not? Not only shoes and watches were banned, it turned out nail clippers were too. I just had no energy or desire to ask. What is the point of one feeble person's question before power?

Yes, my dialogue could only be with myself.

Actually, what is the crime in a political prisoner, or even a criminal, wearing shoes or a watch? I suddenly remembered the photo in Bung Karno's book *Under the Banner of Revolution*. He was on the gangway to the ship that was taking him into exile at Ende. He stood tall and proud. He was wearing the black *peci* fez-like hat, long white trousers, a long-sleeved white shirt and shiny black shoes. He was surely wearing a watch. And behind him were those accompanying him, particularly his wife Ibu Inggit. So back then, you were even allowed to take your wife. But Bung Karno was a political prisoner in the 1930s, and we were political prisoners in the 1970s. Bung Karno was a prisoner of the colonial Dutch East Indies government, whereas we were prisoners of the military government of the independent Republic of Indonesia.

Can you imagine Bung Karno and his wife being issued with khaki uniforms emblazoned with huge numbers on their chests and their backsides, and carrying gunnysack rucksacks!

And with thoughts like this running around in my head, I took a deep breath. I just hoped, that no matter what, this group – like Bung Karno and his colleagues – were leaving to face their future with their heads held high and their chests puffed out.

The day still had long to go. The story had not finished yet. In fact, it was just beginning. Becoming an exiled political prisoner meant becoming someone who had lost absolutely everything. Even one's name was gone. For political prisoners, in this state, even opportunities to try to prolong one's own life became rare. You had to steal opportunities when they arose. I had to learn a lot from the younger prisoners from Tangerang. Learn how to steal, most of all. The word they used for this was '*membebed*', literally meaning to cut, clear, or pilfer. You 'pilfered' your right to live. Their skills in pilfering agricultural produce, which was, of course, the produce of their own sweat and toil, was no more than a declaration of the endeavour to seize opportunities to survive.

The trucks that took us were painted dark green. They were army trucks, but looked brand new. Beside the driver sat a guard with the rank of corporal. He held a carbine, fixed with a bayonet. Two Military Police with pistols on their belts rode motorbikes on either side of each truck. Each truck had 50 prisoners, counted according to the number on their shirt. The truck that I rode in had prisoners from number 401 to 450. There were no seats on the back of the truck. We all had to stand, clinging to each other. Three of the prisoners were paralysed after being so long in solitary isolation, so we had to carry them, namely Pak Ruslan (Purwokerto), Pak Aminta Kemo (Indramayu) and Mang Jumsa bin Ebed (Jakarta).

Heru Santoso, a young prisoner who had formerly been the leader of the Surabaya branch of CGMI (Consentrasi Gerakan Mahasiswa Indonesia (Indonesian Student Movement Concentration) was shirt number 436. Just two numbers below mine. The one with the number immediately below mine was Syamsudin Gobel, from the Pemuda Rakyat (People's Youth), who had been a member of the guard of Njoto, the Deputy Head II of the Communist Party. After being a political prisoner for quite some time at Unit XV at Indrapura Buru, one day he was circumcised. Somehow, it seems the Unit Commander found out that he was not circumcised, even though his religion was recorded as Islam. Maybe because he had yellow-hued skin and his eyes were rather slanting, like Chinese, his Islamic faith was questioned. Or maybe it was because other prisoners ganged up on him that he was 'raided'.

Number 441, Slamet Karyadi, had been a member of the security guard at the offices of the Central Committee of the Communist Party at Jalan Kramat Raya 81 in Jakarta. We called him 'Slamet Kondor' (*kondor* meaning hernia), and he accepted that nickname. Because of his hernia, his testicle swelled as large as a coconut shell, as a result of the torture he had undergone during interrogation in Jakarta.

'Pak Her', Heru said to me, while looking back, leaning forward on the truck cabin.

I stared at him with my chest beating. I was afraid he was going to get us all to carry out an 'act of rebellion'.

'The minute we get beyond the gate, we'll all sing.'

'Sing what?'

'Anything. It is going to pass from the truck at the front down to the one right at the back.'

The convoy of trucks began to move. One by one they left the front yard of Tangerang prison. And then there echoed a choir from all those trucks, one song after another reverberating, 'The Internationale', along with other revolutionary favourites including *'Halo-Halo Bandung'*, *'Sorak-Sorak Bergembira'*, *'Drah Rakyat'* and *'Dua Belas November'*. The Jakarta afternoon heat got hotter still.

The choir on the back of those moving trucks continued to resound. My attention was drawn to the Tangerang-Jakarta road that I had not known before. I had no appetite for song. I don't know why all those valiant songs just sounded bland. Like the song *'Bangunlah Kaum'* (Rise up) for instance. Just twenty years earlier this song had brought me to tears. That was when I, with a group of students from the People's University (UNRA, Universitas Rakyat) in Yogyakarta had gone on a pilgrimage to the Ngalihan grave in Madiun. The grave is in the corner of ricefields in a small village, and that is where lie buried the bodies of the figures of the People's Democracy Front (FDR, Front Demokrasi Rakyat), Amir Sjarifuddin, Maruto Darusman, Jokosuyono, Oei Gee Hwat, Suripno, and the others – eleven of them in all. Standing there beside their grave we solemnly sang 'The Internationale'.

My thoughts flew to a childhood memory.

One day in 1948, the newspapers in Yogyakarta, which was then the capital of the Republic, published a photo of the eleven FDR figures just before they were executed. The photo was not very clear. But the face and build of Amir Sjarifuddin, who was so often in my dreams, I recognised at once. His glasses, his curly hair – but in this photo without the long pipe he usually smoked. He, like the other ten, stood up straight facing the front. They all had their hands behind their backs – tied of course. And in the background of the photo, you could see one mass grave, as long as the row of them standing. The news that went with the photo said that Bung Amir – for that was what we called him – asked for time to sing two songs: Indonesia's national anthem, *'Indonesia Raya'* and 'The Internationale'. And the Ngalihan sky sang, still moist with morning dew, accompanying eleven Indonesian communist figures, ending the journey of their part in history.

The choirs still echoed. The soldiers guarding us seemed to pay no attention. This was certainly not because they couldn't hear us, or had forgotten those songs. Of course, they remembered, and songs like *'Genjer Genjer'* and *'Blanja Wurung'* had even been now been banned. Not to mention these 'red' songs these few hundred prisoners were singing so enthusiastically that day. Maybe the one in command of the convoy was thinking the same as the commander of the firing squad who took the lives of the eleven FDR figures thirty years previously. Let them sing, in a moment they will be lost from view.

Chapter 5

FREEDOM ROAD

forti et fideli nihil difficile

The trucks we boarded were all painted green, army trucks that looked brand new. The open tray of each truck was filled with 50 prisoners, and in the cabin sat two people, a driver and an army corporal fully armed with carbine and bayonet. To the left and right of every truck were two Military Police with pistols on their belts, riding motorbikes.

That day 850 prisoners were moved. The truck I was on was around the middle of the convoy. In that long convoy, in the midst of the roar of the engines of the speeding vehicles, the clamour of the choir actually just added to the cacophony. It was more directed to the singers themselves than to anyone else. And anyway, the roads we were driving on were completely empty. It was the same when we entered Jakarta via the Grogol bypass – Gatot Subroto-Ahmad Yani in the direction of Tanjung Priok. On that day the roads on the outskirts of Jakarta had been kept especially for us. We did not come across a single other vehicle, nor were there any behind us. Nor were there any crowds of people where one would normally expect them, or people on the roadside who would witness this interesting convoy. Occasionally you would see one or two people standing at quite a distance from the road. Probably they had been forbidden to look, or they were afraid of what they were seeing, because along the bypass, left and right at intervals of every 50 metres were armed soldiers standing with their backs to the road. Back then it was still only bushes and scrub alongside the bypass, except for the eastern bypass.

The convoy had passed the Jalan Yos Sudarso turn-off and entered the port area. It was only then that our rowdy choir stopped its singing. They were all exhausted. Our eyes and focus were scrutinising what crushing blow was coming next. At the turn-off, there were many people beside the road. Their mouths gaped, and their glances were unfathomable. They surely knew who we were and where we were being taken.

Truck after truck entered the dockyard. The soldiers ordered us to jump down. Then we had to immediately squat in groups of 5 x 5 according to the numbers on our shirts and the truck we had come on. We each had to link our hands and hold them behind our necks. It was an anticlimax after the raucous revolutionary song during the journey. We could see lots of soldiers, probably outnumbering the prisoners, which we knew from looking at their shoes and the edges of their green-grey-and ochre-coloured trousers.

When we heard the order to move forward, we remained in the crouching positions with our hands behind our necks, and then all waddled like ducks. One by one. A soldier on the right was holding a rubber club and a soldier on the left had a pencil and notebook. When we got in front of the one holding the club, he thumped the club on our head, which we had to respond to by yelling out the number on our shirt, and the note-taking soldier wrote it down.

Then we were allowed to go towards the gangway, still in the duck-waddle position. It was only when we were actually in front of the gangway that we could stand. As we walked between a barrier of soldiers, the numbers on our shirts were checked and cross-checked with the notebook. Still in our groups of 50, we went to yet another group of soldiers. There we were issued with one small rectangular dish, one mug, and one spoon, all aluminium. No Chinese porcelain to be seen!

In front of us was an old ship, like a black monster, blocking the view. The writing on its side said *Tokala*. It was a ship owned by the state shipping company, Pelni, which the Attorney General had apparently chartered to carry us to Buru. Those prisoners who knew a thing or two were relieved. And this relief spread to us. Just as well, they said, we did not have to board an army ship – of any kind! One such wreck had been used to transport the group of prisoners before us. It had not even managed to get back to Jakarta. It sank on the return journey after taking the first lot of political prisoners.

We were quickly herded in, still in our groups of 50, and entered the hold. There waiting for us were piles of pillows and straw mats. A soldier guarded the door to the hold. Other officials of army bearing but in civilian attire were wandering around. Two of us were appointed as head and deputy head of the hold. They had to assist the officers, including doing roll call three times a day, morning, noon and before sleep.

At six in the evening, the *Tokala* raised anchor. Eight hundred and fifty people were leaving Jakarta. With no waving, with no tears, with no revolutionary songs. The shore of Jakarta Bay was visible only by its blinking lights. But we had to stay there in the hold. And even had we not been forbidden to move, what beauty would there be in the view of Jakarta Bay in such an atmosphere that evening?

For the entire day we had had nothing to fill our stomachs, except for those who had brought along something of their own, palm sugar or boiled cassava from the visiting day the day before. After about an hour at sea, the prisoner appointed on kitchen duty called the 'food and drink *corvée*'. We queued for the kitchen in our groups of fifty. What a feast! Our noses could already smell the aroma as we walked down the stairs to the kitchen. And this was after so many years eating rations of a hundred corn kernels or seven spoons of rice or cracked wheat with watery greens.

We were handed back our dishes full of fragrant steamed white rice, vegetables in creamy coconut sauce of unbelievable aroma, together with a whole egg and a piece of meat, and a mug of hot sweet tea! While we were eating, we heard a racket in the kitchen. It was Daryono, one of the 'central-level' prisoners, being 'disciplined' by the officer because he was found taking two portions, and hiding one under his jacket. The old Javanese saying is true, 'like a beggar invited to a party'. He forgot everything except his own stomach.

A soldier-guard then made an announcement that night roll call would be at 8 pm and after that, we were permitted to hang out with our co-prisoners in other holds until 10 pm. During that time we could talk about anything we liked, and read anything we liked. There was various reading matter on the ship, like the magazines *Keluarga*, *Varia* and *Selecta*.

But I was too exhausted to enjoy this atmosphere of freedom given us within this limited time and space. It was our first night at sea, after a whole day of exhaustion and tension. We all went to sleep early after the roll call. Each of us was carrying his own fantasies, intertwining them as we were rocked by the waves. I was unable to fight off tiredness and fell into a deep sleep.

***

The mood of the first and second days at sea was still like people departing on a cruise. Many comrades, meaning 'comrades' in fate, not comrades in ideology, wandered in and out of the holds or up and down the decks. They would catch up with old friends or enjoy the view of the open sea. Fishing boats bobbed like coconut shells floating on the waves. Fish would leap and dive, jumping as though in a competition in the rolling waves. You could see the flash of lightning far in the distance, like arrows fired by gods in the heavens stabbing the horizon.

There were virtually no sad faces to be seen. Bright faces were lit up by smiles. And why not? On the ship we had no need to whisper to one another or to play 'Keep-Your-Mouth-Shut'. We could talk about anything, with anyone, even with the crew and the guards!

Catching up and chatting with old friends, and finding new friends, no-one was stopping it. And so we were busy. Some were just doing it for sheer enjoyment, while others had 'long-term plans'. They were gathering together long-separated 'bones' and rebuilding broken 'bricks'. Meaning, of course, the bones and bricks of the foundations of organisational structures.

The MV *Tokala* was not the Salemba or Tangerang prison. On this ship, we could laugh as much as we wanted without having to hide behind the wall of the latrine, and we did not have to fear the imposition of all kinds of arbitrary prohibitions. On the *Tokala* we did not have to sit cross-legged for hours chanting the Qur'an, or go to pray five times a day through fear of being noted as missing prayer time. We did not have to act serious in circles discussing Pancasila in the style of Captain Mardjuki, the Commander of Salemba. We could play dominoes as long as we liked while exploding with laughter, with no fear of reproach and threats from the furious looking head of the cell block. We did not even have to wait with anticipation for the visiting day food parcels with dashed hopes, because all that got through to us was an empty bag with a flapping label bringing greetings from the family. Because on board this ship food and drink always arrived three times a day, and right on time. One plate full of steamed white rice as smooth as silk, covered tightly with delicious, aromatic spicy meat, a whole boiled egg that did not have to be cut up and divided into six or eight as usually happened in prison. And it did not stop with this luxurious food! We still got what in intellectual prison-slang in Salemba was called '*extra voeding*', and in common Tangerang prison-slang was called '*rehab*', namely: sweet tea, milk, and mung bean porridge. And there was still more that should be mentioned. Here, on this ship, it was not just the bell for roll call, the beat of the drum calling to prayer, and other calls exhorting us to do this and that which we heard, but the sweet music of *keroncong* songs and soothing entertainment.

Incredible! From the prison where every day the only thing we awaited with certainty was the daily quota of torture and abuse, here we were almost spoiled and treated like real people again. Was this a kind of last meal that is given to the prisoner before execution? A kind of Last Supper shared between the Redeemer and the Twelve Apostles? Or was it just a part, a kind of introduction to the large scenario they called 'The New Order Humanitarian Project'? So we prisoners of the so-called 'G30S-PKI' were deliberately being placed in an atmosphere, as the Javanese proverb goes, where we are like 'a beggar invited to a celebration'; like putting on a show for international viewing. Meanwhile, the New Order seemed to shine with kindness and generosity.

Probably, consciously or unconsciously, we all nevertheless felt the return of our own human dignity. But because this came too fast, and was even like a gift of angels falling from the sky, quite a few among us became confused and even slipped up.

Prison, people say, is like its own world. An abnormal world – as I have already mentioned. But precisely because of its abnormality, life in prison can make the prisoner aware again of normality. The particular characteristics of a person come to be seen as multi-nuanced. So too the dimensions of concepts and words. All of them demand further scrutiny and re-evaluation. One's way of seeing black and white dichotomies, superficial and made in haste, comes to be questioned and challenged.

The extreme manifestation of this new awareness was found in many ways. Even before in the prison cell blocks, for instance, many political prisoners would make cynical sneers whenever they heard the call for 'solidarity' (*setia kawan*).

'Huh! You're still harping on about "solidarity". Give me a break! There's no such thing now. The only solidarity is your wife and kids and what you will give them when you finally go home …!'

They would sneer like this whenever they heard the opening lines of the poem by H.R. Bandaharo, 'no-one wants to return home/ even though death awaits them'. 'No-one wants to go home? Come on! You must be kidding. Everyone wants to go home instead of having a meaningless death lying in wait!'

There were other reactions, too, for instance towards the term '*diskusi*' (the Indonesian for 'discussion'). There was a group of prisoners, Kristian and his mates, who deliberately changed it to '*kusi-kusi*', a nonsense word, like the contents of the *diskusi* themselves. They also coined another phrase as a synonym, a play on words from the Javanese expression '*sahur-manuk*', meaning bird call. They coined '*manuk-manukan*' meaning 'to parrot'. It was a sarcastic jibe to refer to the way everyone would just parrot the words of the discussion leaders. And there was another term, *antuk-antukan,* from *antuk* meaning to nod, because what were called 'discussions' were in actual fact no more than sessions of nodding in agreement.

It was not only in the creation of new jargon that such new awareness could be seen. It also emerged in the themes and the main characters of the stories the prisoners told to their fellow prisoners. The storyteller did not have to search among class figures for his heroes. He found, or created, characters from ordinary people. He raised these characters not as models of superheroes, but as ordinary flesh and blood human figures, complete with all their human flaws.

The fact that storytellers no longer offered 'class figures' but replaced them with 'ordinary people' certainly had nothing to do with any fear of reprisal. It was chiefly because of a new awareness of their human dignity which was beginning to grow once more. Probably because of this too, many of the old leaders lost their mass following. A section of that earlier following no longer cared about organisations with all their membership problems, whilst another section – even though they still showed concern – no longer believed in all that was 'old' and 'of the past', because that meant 'the establishment', 'cowards', and 'smart-tongued'. They looked for new leaders from their own young cohorts – because young meant clean, brave and strong.

In addition to these two groups, there was another that was also looking for new leaders, but did not care if they were from the old group or the young one. What was important to them was the courage to think and speak up in a new way, even though what was 'new' was sometimes just political superstition and word acrobatics. It was from this group that 'info' flowed, 'info' which, deliberately or not, was contaminated with rumour, so much so that it was labelled, '*bom-boman*' or bombing.

Back to storytelling. The storytellers in the prison cells and blocks, or in the workplaces in the units at Buru, felt as though they were facing a much more open field of stories. They were no longer hesitant to tell stories that were 'purely' love stories to their audience who, *notabene*, were organisation cadres who carried with them a great deal of ideology. But they did not need to fear being branded 'bourgeois' even though they told tales of personal love between women and men, and not between supermen with their organisations and charged with ideological fervour.

And so, the old love stories like *Untung Surapati* and *Suzana*, *Damarwulan* and *Anjasmara*, *Sampek* and *Engtay*, became much-repeated repertoire. This meant that one aspect of the motto '*dua-tinggi*' (two-high), namely that art should be 'high in ideology', had to give way (or be broadened) from the ideology of the people to the ideology of humanity.

Untung Surapati, as we Indonesians know, was a Betawi slave who came from Bali. He had an illicit affair with a white woman, Suzana. Suzana's father was a Dutchman, a slave owner, and what's more, an officer of the Company! In short, there was layer upon layer of caste separating the two sweethearts. But there was not a single political prisoner, including those branded 'G30S/PKI', who protested and branded Untung Surapati as 'bourgeois' or accused him of being a traitor to his people or his class.

The second example is Damarwulan. He was a young man from the hills, and a favourite character in Javanese *ketoprak* and *langen-driyan* performances. He was a stable boy and grass cutter, who had the audacity to love Anjasmara, the daughter of the prime minister of the kingdom of Majapahit during the rule of Queen Kencana Wungu. When Anjasmara's twin older brothers Layang Seta and Layang Kumitir spy Anjasmara and Damarwulan together, they throw Damarwulan into a dungeon. Watching this story, the audience does not think Damarwulan got his just desserts but rather sheds tears when they hear Damarwulan sing in Javanese his verse of farewell to his love, Anjasmara:

> *Anjasmara ari mami*
> *Masmirah kulaka warta*
> *Dasihmu tumekeng layon …*
>
> Anjasmara my darling
> My jewel hear these words
> Your devoted servant is to die …

Now, we do not need here to go on about these legends. Actually, there are many stories that give messages like this; that is when making moral choices people do not approach it from a black and white dichotomy.

The second example is the issue of homosexuality among political prisoners, which I have written about in my essay 'Art and Entertainment in the New Order's Jails'.[1] The way I see it, homosexuality among political prisoners is nothing disgraceful that has to be covered up and handled with violence. Quite the contrary! It is a sincere statement and deserves to be defended. Nor should those concerned be branded as 'bourgeois'. Or, worse still, 'criminal'.

When there was a stabbing incident involving Sam and Adi, a couple at Unit XIV Bantalareja, I defended my homosexual friends. I wrote a poem titled 'On Love' that went like this:

---

1   See English translation by Keith Foulcher in *Indonesia* no. 59 (April 1995) pp 1–20.

On Love

love is like a cloud
that can absorb all
the sun and the moon
the drizzle and the storm

its setting the sky
infinitely wide
its power trembling
without end
it is the open flame
unextinguished

it becomes lament or worship
it becomes prayer or premise
mixed in the enchantment of sound

live!
my native land and country
live!
my people and nation
live!
my leader and ruler

only
live without humans
with humanity
live without love
that loves
merely
bubbles of froth

love is a word
whispered in silence
but turns desolate
disappears in the empty sky
and the cloud vanishes
sound is only echo
love is just a word
one
dry
word

Let's return to the *MV Tokala*. In short, it would not be an exaggeration to say that many of the prisoners were like 'horses freed from the stall'. They ran about everywhere, no less busy than the guards and officials who were accompanying us.

Among those prisoners busying themselves like this was someone who stood out to me. He was an engineer, still young, and the number on his shirt was 300 something. When he spoke he seemed to put on an air of authority. To get attention, he would pepper his talk with lots of gags and smutty jokes. I could never see what other attraction he had, but there were always lots of people flocking around him. And everyone who then flew off would carry with him some snippet to feed to his own group.

He was a sure 'storehouse of information', to use the term from Salemba. Yet to people who did not like this conspiracy-like sharing of information, figures like this Bigshot Engineer were just know-it-alls. They were like the snake-oil sellers at night markets, promoting some ointment that could cure all ills! To use the words of Njoto, the Deputy Head II of the Central Committee of the Communist Party, they 'know everything about something, and know something about everything.'

'Come on, brother. Let's have a bet!' one of Mr Engineer's satellites came over to challenge me.

'And precisely what do exiles like us have to bet with?' I replied.

'No, I mean let's bet with words. Do you know, brother?' And without even waiting for me to answer, to see if I was filled with anticipation, he immediately followed up his own words. 'This sea voyage is just to get far away from Jakarta. Once we reach the open sea, the *Tokala* is going to change direction. It's going to take us somewhere …'

'Like where?' I asked.

'Well, where do you think!'

He was ordering me to guess the answer to his riddle.

I knew. Of course, he meant the People's Republic of China, which at that time was seen as the first and last loyal bastion of the proletariat. But I truly did not know. Was this fellow joking, or did he mean it? His convinced tone and his serious face made me afraid to doubt him, let alone laugh at him.

It reminded me of the shadow-puppet story *'Bale Sigala-Gala'* about a shelter made from bamboo. At one time, the five Pandawa, their wife Dewi Drupadi and their mother Dewi Kunthi were shut in a bamboo shelter that caught fire – or, more correctly, was set on fire as a dastardly deed by the Kurawa. Suddenly a small, white, squirrel-like creature appeared and led them out of the flames. Carried by the mighty Bima, the Pandawa entered an underground space and continued underground until they reached the final layer under the earth. This was the seventh layer called Saptapratala where the dragon god Sanghyang Anantaboga or Nagaraja was meditating. This god, like the god Adas in the West, supports the earth. The difference is that Adas has a human form, whereas Anantaboga has the form of a giant dragon. It seemed that the Pandawa arrival was the will of the gods, for the dragon not only accepted them as refugees in need of assistance, but he gave his only daughter, Dewi Nagagini, to Bima as a wife. It was from this union of Bima and Nagagini that later was born Antasena, the Pandawa champion who could not be defeated by anyone until he was tricked by Visnu …

***

On the third day, the *MV Tokala* was still floating on the sea, following its appointed course. The *corvée* on duty to remove the filth from the overflowing toilets continued to work as on the previous two days. The *corvée* of young Tangerang prisoners 'on duty' to pilfer sugar, milk, salted fish, vitamin pills and anything that could be used to 'rehab' the invalids and the 'weak' continued to work every night when the guards and officers were asleep. And so all the prisoners, whether paralysed or not, whether weak or strong, whether convalescing or strong and healthy, all received a quota of the pilfered 'rehab' ration. Without exception.

Meanwhile, songs like '*Pohon Beringin*', '*Larilah Hai Kudaku*', '*Menanti di Bawah Pohon Kemboja*', '*Begawan Solo*' and others resounded on the boat. The hubbub made the temperature on deck feel even hotter.

But the white squirrel had still not arrived. Nor had the guards and crew been entered by the Holy Spirit so that they gladly turned the *MV Tokala* in the direction of Australia to the south or Macao to the North. And so, feeling his hopes of the magical white squirrel dashed, Mr Engineer's satellite came over to me again, to ease the situation. Needless to say, he was putting himself at ease, not me. This was on day four.

'Ah well! We'll be there in just a month or two at the most!' This was a retreat from his earlier conviction.

'And then?' I asked

'Then we will be taken back home to Java.'

'Who will take us?' I asked.

'Oh really! The point is we will be taken. Trust me!' said the uncompromising Mr Satellite.

Sure. There was no point in teasing him. I knew that politics is a process of contestation of power. And for the side that is under pressure or losing, but which is unwilling to acknowledge its position or defeat, it cajoles itself with dreams of glory.

But in order not to be branded as just a rumour-mongerer, which would mean the loss of his influence for distribution of information, Mr Satellite did not stop there. He swiftly followed up with a long sermon to back up his political predictions. Using heavy political language, he spoke about the global strategy of the three superpowers: the People's Republic of China, the United States, and the Soviet Union. He expounded on its impact on political life in Indonesia in general, and on the New Order policymakers in particular. As proof of his exposé, he reminded me of the 'info' that had circulated back in Salemba, namely about some political prisoners from Salemba and Tangerang, including Mohamad Munir,[2] who had been summoned to meet President Soeharto to discuss how to resolve the problem of the political prisoners and national harmony.

***

---

2   Mohamad Munir was appointed Head of the National Council of SOBSI in 1950. He was executed by the New Order regime on 15 May 1985, eighteen years after his arrest and thirteen years after being sentenced to death.

Song of the Voyage
– towards the 'Isle of Hope'

late afternoon floating on Jakarta Bay
splashed by foam of the past
slowly receding and vanishing
this is the moment
when distance is just a span of time

when the past is drowned
in the pits of victorious memories

this is the moment
when time is just empty space

when what is coming turns into fata morgana
far on the tip of the endless horizon

I see
the terns
flying in the shadows
I feel
the sunset's restlessness swoop
diving into the colour of the sky

yes, Jakarta
if this is the end of all dreams
then let your sky and sea
tempt in the far distance

yes, Jakarta
because from the far distance
the morning will come

the sun will come

     Jakarta Bay, 1971

The first day aboard ship a few people immediately lost their appetite. Many daydreamed, and many wept. Some were seasick and vomited. Inside the ship began to get hot and smelly. The stink of sweat, vomit, the oily smell of the rusting ship, and the ship's latrines which were soon blocked with the shit of 300 men.

The shit in the toilets piled up, and rocked by the waves spilt out of the toilets. Toilet-cleaning teams were formed – the WC *corvée*. My deck had to provide three men for the *corvée* every day. Except for those who were seriously ill or paralysed, we each had to take turns according to the number on our shirt, beginning with the lowest. In addition to the three men assigned to WC cleaning duty, we had to supply one more for kitchen duty. Their task, apart from cooking, was to hand out the prisoners' food and drink rations.

I calculated that my turn to join the toilet-cleaning team, if no-one before me suddenly got sick, would fall on day 14. Lucky me! This meant I would not get called up for this disgusting task, because according to the crew by then the *Tokala* would have already berthed at Namlea.

That first morning, when I went to take a poop, I wore my wooden sandals. I was so grateful for these sandals, which had come in my visiting parcel, and so impressed that my family could have such foresight. But when I stood in front of the door to the WC I could not stop vomiting and simply could not enter. The toilet had turned into a swirling lake of pee. There was no way I could poop. Even to pee, I had to stand on the barrier at the threshold of the door.

When I went back to my area, I sat staring at the sea. I made a decision: I would reduce all liquid intake, eat just once a day and restrict my movement. I did not want to join the visits to other holds or go up and down from one deck to another admiring the view of the open sea. My 'prayer' was this alone: please can I manage not to shit for eight days! And would this endanger my health?

Previously, in the 1950s, I had a 'younger brother'. He was a young poet from Solo and his name was Timbul Darmanto. He was the silent type, and extremely sensitive. Or the other way around: because he was so sensitive, he was a quiet type. His poems were like sea foam. Soft and beautiful, but just floating, without ever diving deep. He had a strong build and was chubby, rather round, always eating a lot three times a day. He also smoked too much. He had one problem: his bowel movements were never regular. Sometimes it would be once a week, sometimes once in nine or ten days! I too once suffered this problem when I lived in Semarang, although it was not as bad as Timbul.

'Don't worry', the doctor who examined me said. 'If after five days you still have not had a bowel movement, then come back to see me. Drink a lot. And exercise!'

'Aha! Exercise is the answer', I thought.

With that doctor's advice tucked away in my head, I wrestled with the anxiety and fear of falling ill. Such battles with myself had become second nature to me since becoming a political prisoner. When I was going to be interrogated, for instance. 'Lie, tell the truth; lie, tell the truth; lie … No! Lie! Two words of equal weight were fighting in my chest. When I heard the summons and was sure I would get some torture treatment, it would be: pain, no; pain, no; pain, no … No! No! No! Then I would close my eyes and sense the pain. The flower of pain is death, the Javanese say.

I do not know whether I really slept over those eight days and nights rocking on the sea. But as for bathing or washing my face, I know I did not. I just dipped two fingers into my drinking water and wiped them in the corner of my eyes. Once when I had been in isolation in prison, I had been told how to do the ritual ablution before Muslim prayer when there is no water available. You use dust or sand. And what if there is no dust or sand, like inside the cell? The religious teacher said, 'press the palm of your hands against the cell wall three times, then wipe them on your face, ears and arms up to the elbows, in the way you normally do when using water.'

And that is what I did each day. Not only for spiritual purposes, but also for normal physical needs. I paid no attention to the smell and faded whitewash of the cell wall, let alone the spots of dark red dried blood splattered on the walls. Yes, why not? If for prayer this sufficed, then of course it sufficed for washing one's face! So I got used to using dust or plaster from the wall every morning. I found it refreshing. Perhaps it was just the cool of the plaster wall that stuck to my palms, or maybe it was just auto-suggestion. Who knows?

In my group of fifty in the hold, was a former student of mine from when I taught at Taman Dewasa in Yogyakarta. His name was Bambang Irawan. He was the son of an older brother of Yogyakarta's Sultan Hamengku Buwono IX. Irawan became a political prisoner because he sinned against Soeharto's military regime, namely he was a member of the central leadership of the League of Indonesian Youth and Students (IPPI, Ikatan Pemuda Pelajar Indonesia).

'Do you regret it?' I whispered to him once during morning drill when we were together in I Block at Salemba.

'Why should I? I'm proud of it!' he answered, firmly.

'But isn't your uncle angry? And your parents?' I asked. Back then I did not know that he was already married with one child.

'Absolutely not. He once said to me. "If you want to be something, whatever that is, do it properly. Not half-heartedly."'

Irawan's delegated space was on the far corner because in this hold he was the lowest number: 401. But across from him was another young man whose number was 450. He was also a former member of IPPI but from the Jakarta branch. His name was Suwardi, but he was better known with the nickname Penjol. When he had been interrogated, in order to get a confession out of him, he was confronted with two IPPI members, a male and a female, who were accused of having been 'groomed' by him. In front of Sumardi's eyes, the two were stripped naked, tortured, then made to get on the interrogation table, one lying on top of the other. They were then bound with electric cable and forced to have sexual intercourse while the cable was switched on.

'Excuse me, Pak', Irawan said as he sat cross-legged in front of me. Suwardi Penjol was beside him. 'Penjol here would like to meet you.'

'And what have you told Bung Suwardi about me?' I asked, addressing Irawan with the Javanese term for brother, 'Mas'.

'Please don't call me 'Mas', Pak', he said

'Now why not? We are both adults, and both political prisoners. We are no longer in a teacher-student situation.'

'Why not call me 'Bung' like you the way you just addressed Penjol', he said.

'But I have only just been introduced to Bung Suwardi. Not like you. I have known you since you sat at the same desk as Bondan, the son of [the famous ketoprak actor] Kadariyah Kridomardi. Where is he now, by the way?'

'I don't know, Pak. I heard he was in Prambanan …'

I shook Suwardi's hand. His grasp was firm, as though he wanted to convey something: 'This is me. A comrade from the youth group. You can trust me!'

You should understand that after the incident at the end of September 1965, it was not easy to find a friend who could truly become a vessel of trust. But, actually from his over-enthusiastic handshake, I felt myself withdraw from him. In order to face a task, particularly some large task, people have to be aware of what in Taman Siswa we called 'neng-ning-nung-nang'. Do not flare-up. You need to be quiet (*meneng*) in order to become clear (*wening*) in your head, and from this would arise intuition (*nung*) as a condition for success (*wenang*).

Suwardi and Irawan took turns in talking about all kinds of things. These included the organisation of the unit: candidates for the barracks head and coordinator. How to be 'humanitarian' at the camp in Buru, what attitude to take towards informers, or 'cockroaches' as we called them, how to make contact with the local people and so on. Apart from that, they passed on information that seemed believable. The first item was that the *Tokala*, apart from carrying political prisoners, was also carrying enough food supplies for six months, along with medicines, tools, and various kinds of seeds. Secondly, that the group on the *Tokala* numbered 850 people, but when we arrived at Namlea at the transit camp, this group would be divided into two. The first group of 500 would be placed in Unit XIV, which was near Unit IV Savanajaya. This unit was apparently not far from the beach called Sanleko. The second group, made up of the remaining 350, would be placed in Unit XV, which was located further inland, near Units I and II.

There was one issue that required urgent attention; the 124 prisoners who were in 'weak condition' either because they were old or because of their health. Of this 124, 64 of them were in a serious condition and 14 of them were completely paralysed. The main problem while on board ship was how far some of them could be restored to health.

Secondly, once we berthed, how would we carry them in the march to the unit. We had to think ahead and prepare 'physically strong' teams to accompany, and if necessary support, those who were in 'weak condition'. We had to think about how we could make stretchers for those who were paralysed, what materials we could use, and who would be stretcher-bearers.

To help with the recuperation of the sick, 'ghost *corvée*' squads were formed whose job was to pilfer medicine, milk and sugar from the supplies hold. These squads were made up of the young ones who were nimble and experienced, most of them ex-Tangerang prisoners. The *Tokala* had two medical aides and one army doctor on board, but we could not trust them. Three prisoners among us with medical expertise, Dr Sumanto and medical aides Mulyono Munadi and Imam Sujono, were given the task of treating the sick and improving their health. Other prisoners with acupuncture expertise also helped whenever there was an opportunity.

On every deck, the loudspeaker ruled. There were 1950s keroncong songs, or even older hits like *'Menanti di Bawah Pohon Kamboja'* (Waiting Under the Frangipani Tree), *'Ombak Samudera'* (Ocean Waves), and *'Begawan Solo'*. The most interesting of all was the song *'Pohon Beringin'* (Banyan Tree). It is an old song that I learnt from my older siblings during the Japanese occupation. It was played over and over again, seemingly without stopping. Maybe the idea was to convey the mood of the recent elections (the banyan tree was the symbol of the government party, Golkar), or maybe to convey a message: 'Hey you political prisoners. Your life and death are in the hands of the banyan tree (the government)!'

One of the verses of the song goes like this:

> Banyan tree
> the oldest tree of all
> the most beautiful romance
> in the whole world

And the final lines of the song are like this:

> Banyan tree
> the place where priests pray
> worshipping while awaiting
> the gift of the gods.
>
> Gift of the gods!
> Gift of the gods who reign in the banyan tree.
> Without their beneficence,
> do not even hope that anything
> can happen to political prisoners.
> And what can the prisoners do?
> Work, worship and wait.

*　*　*

Bung Wardi left Irawan and me. He had to go and organise *corvée* duties – both the official duties of toilet cleaning and kitchen, as well as the unofficial 'pilfering' duty. Only the young, nimble and experienced were sent on this difficult task, and this meant the 'Tangerang boys' were dominant. The Salemba prisoners, who were considered the older ones, the intellectuals and prominent figures, were sort of 'extras'. What's more, there were fewer Salemba prisoners than those from Tangerang.

I felt as though there was a 'thought revolution' going on among the young group on the *Tokala*. Specifically, a 'revolution in thought' about cadres and leadership. It seemed as though two failed attempts by the older prisoners to build parties in Salemba (1968, Sri Wisnu Kuncahyo) and Tangerang (1970, Slamet Wijaya and Sabar Santoso Pangarso), had caused the older group to lose charisma in the eyes of the younger group, and trust. And their loss of trust was not only in the older group as a group, but more specifically their past importance, both politically as well as socially. And so there was the sense of a kind of 'cold war' going on between the 'cadre political prisoners' and the 'masses political prisoners', between the 'intellectual political prisoners' and the 'common political prisoners', between 'Salemba' and 'Tangerang'. One relied on brain, while the other relied on brawn; one was busy with discussions (*'kusi-kusi'*) while the other was busy pilfering (*'sat-set'*).

The ten candidates for head of barracks for my unit, Unit XIV, according to the news I received, were all young. Eight were from Tangerang and only two from Salemba. They included Irawan, my former student, and Aziz Belong (he was actually a 'to-and-fro' prisoner who had moved between Salemba and Tangerang) and who had been in the leadership of the Surabaya branch of CGMI (Consentrasi Gerakan Mahasiswa Indonesia, Indonesian Student Movement Concentration). The candidate for the coordinator of the ten barrack heads was Suwardi Penjol. Apart from being young and known as 'militant', he had been in the 'central cadre' camp at Salemba. He also had the support of someone I will call KM, as he did not want his full name used, a former head of the National Board of the All Indonesia Trade Union Federation, SOBSI, and the foremost figure of the older group. There were a few of the older ones who, because they did not want to feel left behind, took a stand like KM and secretly supported the young group. But the majority took the attitude of wait and see.

'The issues they are fanning are truly the ones that can attract the sympathy of the masses', Irawan said. He seemed to be fishing to see whether I was one of those 'them'.

'So I've heard', I said. 'They say that pilfering is no more than criminal stealing. And more stupid still, they say this is so because what they are stealing are our own rations.'

'And what do you think?' he asked me.

Once again this former student of mine was fishing with a question that had no need of an answer. Because ever since we had become detainees, especially political detainees with the appendage stamp 'G30S/PKI', we had lost all rights. The only remaining right was that right to pilfer. To steal at every opportunity to survive. Including the opportunity to escape.

'Our experience at Salemba and Tangerang was clear', I said. 'Even the parcels we received from our own families had been pilfered first, and we got what was left over, right? Even if it was just the bag and the label that at least gave us a sign that the family was still alive. Better than nothing!'

'*Kawruh begja*', right?' he said, laughing. It was a Javanese joke of finding 'good luck' (*begja*) in anything, and he knew that I used to hear that joke in the public discussions of Ki Ageng Suryamentaram called 'Jongkringan' held at his Kumendaman residence in Yogyakarta.

'Even though the contents of the parcels our families bring are the product of their own hard work. They're not state rations!'

'Huh. Rations!' Irawan grumbled. 'Without rights, without power, how can we talk about rations? Our very lives are no longer our ration …'

The loudspeakers were still blaring, this time with the song '*Di Bawah Sinar Bulan Purnama*' (Under the Full Moon). The sweet song composed by Arimah sounded like a taunt:

> Under the light of the full moon
> The sea flickers
> The waves rock and flow
> To the shore of joking and fun …

* * *

Every day the toilet-taming *corvée* for the day was hard at work. The quota of three people from my group was also going smoothly. No-one had suddenly fallen sick. Indeed it could be no other way. A must! Because to political prisoners, quotas were a duty carried out under the threat of violence, and under military guard the underlings knew: 'Yes sir!'

It was lucky for me, but unlucky for many of my friends. The last two numbers on my shorts were near the number 50, which meant I was among the last of the group and my turn for call up would come on the last days. I would be relieved of this duty as long as the others before me stayed healthy. Oh please let them all be healthy! That was my first and last prayer on board the *Tokala*.

The pilfering was actually something that started spontaneously among the young prisoners. It was a kind of rebellion against authority, showing their daring. And indeed there was no reason to step in and stop it. As I have said, it was a kind of declaration of the will to survive. The reason they gave, that pilfering was to 'rehab' the sick and weak prisoners, was in truth just a rationalisation. The fact was that even without this additional pilfered milk and sugar, which after all was only for about seven days, the nourishment on board was pretty good. Three times a day we had a dish full of white rice, with a piece of meat or a whole egg, as much sweet tea as we liked, and a between-meal snack of a mug of either milk or mung bean porridge every day.

Meanwhile, all the abuse and insults went quiet. The insulters and abuse hurlers were too busy. Even between prisoners this was so. They were too busy with their pilfering. Bashing and other torture were almost entirely absent except for when a prisoner was caught red-handed hiding an extra serving of food under his shirt. As for me – apart from being surprised at the elasticity of his stomach, I did not understand how he had managed to do it. Of course, he got a beating from the kitchen guards. The soldiers seemed pleased to have the opportunity to show off their profession as beat-up men. The prisoner concerned was a little older than me, so between the older and younger groups. But in the eyes of the young one, he was seen as both a 'prominent figure' and an intellectual. This was not good for him. He became the butt of the anger of two young prisoners, Tukimin (where are you now?) and Heru Santoso.

'What he did was criminal!' Irawan and his friends said, and this spread like wildfire. 'Even though he took the bosses' portion'.

The incident of beating up the 'criminal' almost became political. Two figures responsible for the illegal Communist Party at Tangerang were threatened. The person most angry and charged up was Ngari, formerly head of both the Sugar Union and the Kudus branch of Lekra. Luckily he did not leave any lasting marks except for a bump as big as a durian seed on the chin of his former leader.

At sea

Sea
Speak sea
So the fishermen's children
Will sing a song of exile

Tern
Cry tern
So the lightning
Will not go dark soundless

When the long night has dreams
What is there to paint

when portholes
Are fenced by army guns

When the long day has words
What is there to hear

When between day and night
There is only a border of colour

Yes ocean
Yes lightning

Breathe the breath of the storm
Into my chest

And you, soldiers
present your fence of guns

surround the dreaming terns
and capture the shadows of their wings

you own the day
but the night

will follow it
because the sea

the land of exile
will not go dry

because the lightning
the sky of exile

will not go dark

    Java Sea, 1971

Chapter 6

TANGERANG VERSUS SALEMBA

The '*Tokala* shipment' was the third group of political prisoners sent to Buru. The group comprised 850 men who were later divided into two units. Five hundred were settled in Unit XIV Bantalareja, and the remaining 350 – plus another 150 who were about to follow from Jakarta – were to be housed in Unit XV. Unit XIV was later known as the 'Pure Jakarta Unit' because all the inmates had been sent from Jakarta, namely from the Salemba and Tangerang jails. Apart from being called the 'Pure Jakarta Unit', Unit XIV was also known as the 'Masses Unit' and the 'Youth Unit'.

And indeed that name was right, because there were probably at the most only 25 older men, meaning those aged between 50 and 70 years. Many were around my age, between 30 and 45 years, but the majority were under 30 years old. For instance, there was a prisoner whose nickname was Bogel – I never knew what his real name was – who was only 14 when he was 'picked up' in 1966. Another prisoner called Purwadji who had been an IPPI activist (Ikatan Pemuda Pelajar Indonesia, League of Indonesian Youth and Students) was only in third grade of junior high school when he was captured, also in 1966. According to him, this spoiled only child still liked to suck his thumb secretly at recess times at school, or go to the cinema.

Among the 500 people in my unit, there were only seven who had had any tertiary education. There were many who had a high-school education, but the majority had only a junior high school or primary school education, and there were quite a few who could barely even write. Seen from the organisational viewpoint of the Indonesian Communist Party, the great majority were just ordinary members of mass organisations.

Back to the *Tokala*. I have already mentioned that in the crisis of trust in the old leadership and older figures, it was the young group who were part of this mass membership who dominated. They still had ambitions to rise up and lead. But seeing the uncertainty of the situation, they kept these ambitions close to their chest, until the right opportunity arose and the time would be ripe. They, and the middle-aged prisoners of my own age, became the targets of attention of a few of the mid-ranking figures and intellectuals who were reluctant to become part of the mass under the leadership of the young generation.

And so very quickly there were three power groups jostling one another. The first, the largest group and the one currently on top, we can call simply 'the young group'. The second, which was a small group but no less active than the first, was the 'intellectual group'. The third was an incomplete grouping of the older prisoners. This group was divided into two. A small number of them secretly supported the young group, and the rest were like cats. They appeared to be just sitting minding their own business in a corner, hiding their claws of ambition. But all the while their sharp eyes were flitting all over the place.

Amidst all these groupings, I myself was a newcomer. I was a cadre from the cultural movement – and prior to that had been in the student group – and I had been promoted too quickly. After not even a year in charge of developing and promoting the Yogyakarta branch of Lekra

(Lembaga Kebudayaan Rakyat, Institute of People's Culture), I had been promoted to lead Lekra for Central Java. I had not even been a year in that position, organising the cultural movement and activities at a regional level without any process of 'caderization' at national level, before I was 'thrown upstairs'. I was moved to Colombo, the capital of Ceylon (now Sri Lanka) to the Asia-Africa Writers Bureau. My position was as representative of all the Nasakom (Nationalist, Religious and Communist) cultural organisations on the Indonesian National Committee for the Asia-Africa Writers Conference.

I returned to Jakarta on August 24, 1965, not for a bit of rest and recreation, or an international conference or such. No, I had been forced to leave Colombo because the Asia-Africa Writers Bureau had been closed by the new powers in Sri Lanka who were anti the Asia-Africa movement. All the Asia-Africa workers, the representatives of thirteen Asian and African countries, were made persona-non-grata and given 48 hours to leave the country. I arrived in Jakarta utterly exhausted, back to the home of my family who were totally unprepared for my arrival. I felt foreign in the capital city and that city saw me as foreign too. Probably this was one factor why when all the sweeping was going on after the 30 September 1965, I was able to spend four more years playing cat and mouse night and day in Jakarta. My face was unknown to Intelligence and my name was not on the lists of people to be picked up. It was not only Intelligence – even my friends and comrades in Jakarta did not really know me, nor me them.

And it was like that too on the *Tokala*. There were only one or two who knew me, namely those who had lived and been active in Yogyakarta or other towns in Central Java. I could count them on my fingers. There was Irawan, my former student; Ngari, Mudakir, Kho Dji Tjhai, and Soleh Amat, the Lekra leaders for Kudus, Pati,

Magelang and Semarang; Suhardi, a teaching colleague at Taman Siswa, Yogyakarta; Martin Lapangnuli, a student from the Music School in Yogyakarta; Basuki Effendy, a very well-known figure from the national film world whom I had met a few times at the Lekra national secretariat in Jakarta. Yes, that was about it for my 'old comrades'.

On board the *Tokala* floating on the open seas, in the midst of the cadres and masses from the capital, I truly felt alone. I felt like some object in the sky all by itself somewhere, free from all the clusters of stars. They were all orbiting according to their designated orbits. Or, in performance terms, it was as though I was looking at a performance on stage, but I was the one and only person sitting in the audience. There at the front of the stage all the actors were moving in a drama following the same scenario. But behind that stage were other, different stages. Each had its own actors, all of whom moved in a narrative framework according to the scenario of each of their directors.

One thing that unites people, clever people say, is similarity of fate. People pay no heed to differences in race, skin colour, religion, language or anything else when they unite to confront the same calamity. Yes, calamity is a better word than fate. For good fate or destiny often gives rise to competition, which in turn causes splintering.

There is a Malay saying that illustrates this: *biduk lalu kiambang bertaut* (after the barge passes the duckweed re-entangles). Once the calamity, like a barge, has passed, the duckweed clumps together again. But people are not duckweed. The duckweed has no problem to face in joining up again once the barge has passed. Not like people. They each individually have the right to their opinion, to declare that opinion before others, whether with words, deeds, or words and deeds together. There is just one condition: daring.

And so people with daring come to the fore, those who in the eyes of the majority have leadership quality. And there are never many people like this. Not like those who are wishy-washy or cowards, their number is always greater. And like suns, the few daring figures suddenly appear along with their admirers around them, moving to create a field of orbit around their sun. And suppose we take another analogy for this, drama, and the line of orbit is the storyline, then the sun is the one who determines the story, or the dalang who wants to direct the way the story unfolds.

On the surface, there was only one performance going on. It was the play titled Bapreru (Badan Pelaksana Resettlement dan Rehabilitasi Buru, Body for the Administration of Buru Resettlement and Rehabilitation). It had a single dalang sitting on a high, high throne way over there in the capital city, Soeharto. But beneath him were lots of other dalangs, who were performing their own plays, each one competing for the attention of the masses. I felt as though I was part of the mass being fought over by two competing orbiting stars. On the one side, it was clear, namely the young group of whom the most prominent were Suwardi, Irawan and Heru Santoso. On the other side was the intellectual and middle-class group, also represented by three figures from Jakarta, but I did not know any of them.

But what we see as 'worth' or 'value' is not fixed, operating forever and in all corners of the earth and sky. What is of value in the world outside can have no worth at all in the prison world. What is polite today is not necessarily polite tomorrow, and might not have been so polite yesterday. Take the example of when I came out of isolation. We were still at the operational detention centre at the Paskoarma II headquarters in Cilandak, Jakarta. There were three of us in one cell. My two companions were from Klaten, which was a base for the

Central Java branch of the Indonesian Communist Party. One was Suprapto, and the other was Pak Hadi. Suprapto had been a member of the Pemuda Rakyat (People's Youth) who was only in the second class of junior high school when he was captured, and Pak Hadi said that he was 'nothing at all', but his wife had been a member of the Indonesian Women's Movement (Gerwani).

The three of us were eating lunch. Suddenly, Prapto farted, which he deliberately let off loudly. Maybe it was to express his annoyance because the food ration was so small.

'Hey, Prap!', Bu Hadi called from the cell next door. 'When mixing with high-class people (*priyayi*) you should know some manners!'

'Priyayi? Come on!' Prapto replied, grumbling.

Now the word *'priyayi'* was clearly directed at me. I was surprised at the explosion from Prapto's muffler. But not because my 'high-class sensitivities' were offended, but because gas emitted from the backside is not nice when eating or chatting. Values in emergency situations cannot be expressed the same way as before, but they do not have to be dismissed completely but rather accommodated to the new situation. As for me, whenever I felt a fart coming, I would take my backside over to the bars in the cell door, and let the gas out slowly. Yes, if you think about it jokingly, Soeharto's crimes were truly too many. It wasn't just that we had to keep our mouths closed, but people could not even fart freely.

Part II

Buru Stories

Chapter 7

FROM SANLEKO TO BANTALAREJA

One by one, we were made to jump off the landing boat into the sea, and we did not know how deep it was. Our rucksacks, mats and anything else we were carrying were on our backs, held above our shoulders or on our heads so they did not get wet and therefore were even heavier to carry.

I was amazed. Quite a few of the prisoners were carrying mattresses. Maybe they were attached to them because they had made them themselves when in prison at Tangerang. Among the former Tangerang inmates, especially the older ones, many were carrying mattresses. They looked like the Javanese villagers during Dutch times sent off to 'colonise' Lampung in Sumatra. Maybe because the soldiers saw how much the feeble old bodies were weighed down, they 'freed' them of their burden. Without worrying whether there were sharp weapons or other banned items hidden inside.

There was one of these older ones with me. We usually called him Pak Haji Rauf. He was a tried and true communist from the 1926 era. Apart from his mattress and pillow, he was also carrying two rucksacks. One was pretty heavy, the other less so, although even this lighter one was heavier than my own rucksack. This old man is still building his nest, I thought. Like a bird, collecting all kinds of twigs and dried grass for his home. When I asked him what all the stuff he had was, he didn't know. 'All kinds of things', he would say. At the transit unit, I already decided that I would help him by carrying something for him.

Here I was ready to jump, like the prisoners ahead of me. I could see the undertow from the shore crashing against the waves rolling in. I felt dizzy, scared and acrophobic and regretted never having learnt how to swim! The boat seemed to be holding us back, as though it did not want its prisoners to leave. The sea around the boat churned even more as the load on the boat lightened.

Number after number we jumped down one by one. I could see the sea was up to their armpits! They floated forward a few steps, pushed by the weight of their bodies and the stuff they were carrying, and were thrown by the surging of the sea.

My turn had come. My number had been called. There was nothing to do but do exactly what the others had done before me. I replied to the order by calling out the identification number on my photograph as loud as I could and … jumped! My vertigo disappeared and seemed like it had been a dream. How had I managed to jump? Hadn't I just been staggering? Didn't the soles of my feet tread on coral …? When I got to the shore, Pak Haji Rauf came over to me. His rucksack, which I had held on my head, was only a little wet from the splashing. But my own rucksack, which I had on my back, was as soaked as my body.

'*Alhamdulillah*', I said to him, counting my blessings for survival.

He answered with a smile of exhaustion.

We then quickly formed lines for our march. The sand on Sanleko beach was scorching hot in the midday August sun, making shimmering waves before our eyes. Waves of fata morganic shadows. When one's past life is history that will not return. When one's future life is an indescribable riddle.

Probably it was around two in the afternoon by the time everyone had landed and then lined up according to the numbers on our shirts. Pak Haji Rauf was in Barracks VI, the number on his shirt was 300 and something, and I was in line for Barracks IX because the number on my shirt was 438. I carried my wet knapsack on my chest and Pak Haji's heavier rucksack on my back. My state-issued rolled-up mat and pillow I carried in my hands. When the lines were given orders to march, my legs felt too heavy to move. Apart from the weight of the wet rucksack, it was also because of exhaustion from lining up and standing under the hot midday sun, anxiety, and on top of all that, a hungry stomach. Since leaving the transit Unit Jiku Kecil, we had not had anything at all to eat. And not a single drop of water!

Fishing boat skeletons lay sprawled around Sanleko beach. Here and there were mangroves ending in shrubs. Behind a bit there was a rise with yellow cogon grass and eucalyptus trees. At the beginning of the road, we were greeted by a crude gateway made from rough whitewashed planks. The gateway was far too small standing as it did in front of the wide-open sea and Sanleko's long beach, but it was also too fancy for the four-metre wide unpaved road. '26th Anniversary of Indonesia's Proclamation of Independence' the sign on top of the gateway read. The style of the gateway and the lettering betrayed a city hand. The decoration was that of the last decade, but without the muscled arm and clenched fist, the style of A. Rachmad from People's Artists (Pelukis Rakyat). But it was clear: this was the handiwork of an artist political prisoner who had adapted to the challenge of a 'New Life'.

Behind the gateway, beside the road left and right, were two buildings with tin roofs and coconut wooden walls, which were different to the houses of the local population made out of coconut palm fronds with thatched roofs of dried leaves. One of the buildings was the army's guard post, and the one across from it was a warehouse for the agricultural tools and food for the lower units. It was a kind of 'transit warehouse' between the warehouse at Namlea and the lower units. 'Lower units' meant the four units in the Wai Bini valley: Unit IV Savanajaya, Unit XIV Bantalareja, Unit XV Indrapura, and Unit XVI Indrakarya. The 'upper units' were all the others, situated behind the hill and across the Wai Apo River.

In Buru island terms, the village of Sanleko was considered large. It consisted of about twenty or so houses. They all faced the road. Behind the houses was a thicket, and every house was surrounded by plants, including pineapple and banana trees and some even had coffee and clove trees. In the yard of the first house, after passing the army guard post, there were two big signposts. The first said Sanliku Village; (even though it was normally pronounced 'Sanleko') and the other one had the Golkar symbol: the banyan tree. There were no symbols of the other two 'competing' parties, the Ka'abah (PPP) or the Buffalo head (PDI). But the vacancy left by the Ka'abah was filled by a mosque which was far too big for this village of straw huts. The village head at Sanleko, whose name was Mangke – supposed to be an abbreviation from 'Uncle from the island of Lei', was said to be Muslim. He lived as a trader and plantation owner. He owned the big coconut plantation at the village of Marloso, about seven kilometres behind Sanleko. People said he had already been on the Haj twice and had close relations with the current big shots in Jakarta.

Pak Mangke's own house was quite close to the road where the cogon grass was thicker and the colour of the soil blacker. There were also sturdier trees: *kedondong*, jackfruit, eucalyptus and clumps of bamboo. In the yard of his house stood a sign saying 'Village Head of Sanleko', not 'Sanliku' like the sign at the edge of the beach. A few goats were roaming around his house, which was also a display of his wealth compared to all the other people around. The villagers hunted as a group for deer or wild pig, then divided the spoils among those who had joined in, including the dogs – except, that is, for the village head, who received a portion even if he did not go along. Pak Mangke's house looked too fancy. It was made of stone with glass windows, the window frames painted green.

Almost at the end of this village road, there was a branch to the right that went to the villages of Marloso and Jamilo (sometimes spelt Jamilu). At the corner of the turn-off, there was a house with coconut palm walls and a dried sago-leaf roof, like the houses of the other inhabitants, but this one was neat and clean. Its owner was a young woman who lived alone, whose clothes and way of talking was that of an urban Javanese. She had pale skin and a face that was too pretty for the swamps and savanna. She was known as Ibu Fatimah, and the gossip was that she had been a figure in the Parmusi party (*Partai Muslimin Indonesia*, Indonesian Muslims' Party), and that she knew Tien Soeharto (the president's wife) well. My Unit IV Savanajaya fellows were warned not to be too eager to chat with the smiling, talkative Ibu Fatimah. All the stories and warnings about Ibu Fatimah reminded me of the time of fighting for independence, of the stories about the beautiful women, most of them mestizo Indo-Dutch, who looked for sexual partners but were actually spies for the Dutch colonial army. The republicans called them 'golden chains'. If Ibu Fatimah was a kind of New Order 'golden chain', then how stupid their Intelligence agency was, I thought, and on the other hand, how powerful the network of political prisoners was!

The Sanleko village road was barely one kilometre long, but oh how long it felt to go along it. After passing the banana trees and bamboo groves, before us lay yellow-green ricefields. Yet another gate greeted us. It was no different to the one on the shore, apart from the greeting written above. This was the gate to Unit IV Savanajaya and had written on it the words 'Happy 26th Anniversary of the Republic of Indonesia's Proclamation of Independence.' Now was this a hesitant welcome? Slapdash? Or was it the opposite, a cynical, critical greeting? The wording was not praise for the country or the people of Indonesia, but just a kind of 'happy birthday' for August 17, 1971. The long days prior to and following on from that date were a series of days of suffering for the era's current slaves.

Behind the gate, where the road turned right, there was a board measuring about 1.5 x 2 metres. The words on this board were not praise, but magical mantra words written in large capital letters: SPREAD AND SECURE PANCASILA. Beneath it were the rows of the five state principles or *sila*, one after another, according to the wording of the 1945 Jakarta Charter, complete with their respective symbols: the yellow star, the linked circular chain, the banyan tree, the head of the buffalo, and the bunch of flowering cotton and rice. Beside the sign with its mantras was another sign in the shape of an arrow, pointing in the direction of the road: TOWARDS A NEW LIFE. And so, there it was. All complete. The praises, the slogans of prayer and magical mantras. All that awaited was to take a step: Towards a New Life! No matter whether it would be better or worse than the old life, the new was still new, an embryo of a life of suspense to the curious.

For years my eyes had been bound by the walls of a 1.5 x 2 metre prison cell, now as the stretch of ricefields of Unit IV Savanajaya opened out before me, it truly felt like seeing 'as far as the eye could see'. In the distance was a range of hills and trees, dark in colour. Just like my imaginings as a child when at school the teacher told me to draw whatever I liked. Blue hills in the distance, a long straight road, telephone poles and trees beside the road getting smaller and smaller into the distance, ricefields with their borders becoming narrower in the distance, and a few birds flying in the empty sky.

Empty! A new Life that was empty and quiet?

In front of this view before me were the roofs of shining tin buildings, among them the 'giant' mosque dome built in the style of Istiqlal Mosque in Jakarta. In the quiet, people do indeed like to wander, following the trails of 'the origin and destination' of creatures, a search for what the Javanese call *'sangkan paraning dumadi'*. And God's House was waiting with its room for this. Well, so I hoped. Not haunted by the 'religion police' like at the Salemba prison.

The road was named Gajah Mada, clearly to remind people of Indonesia's great Majapahit warrior and conqueror, the prime minister of that name. It was normal that the commander of the Military Police wanted to promote the name Gajah Mada, who was a legendary leader and hero to the Military Police corps. The width and length of the road seemed to have been made following the example of the Jakarta bypass boulevard. Five metres wide on the left and right lanes divided by a two-metre wide separation planted with red and white *turi* trees in a row. The road was spotless, as though it had been swept, without sand or dust. The packed dry clay, white with no humus, seemed to convey a message. A bone dry New Life was awaiting us!

There were no houses along the Gajah Mada road. You could see only a few shacks in the ricefields here and there. Everything was totally empty. There was not a single person to be seen working in the ricefields. Much later we found out that on the day of our arrival, our fellow prisoners at Unit IV Savanajaya had been ordered not to work that day and had been confined to their barracks. But for all the 1001 prohibitions and no matter how many security police were around, there would always be 1001 'criminals' clever at slipping through the nets and creeping around.

All along the 'boulevard', at distances of 20-30 metres or so, kettles or even drums of tea had been placed beside the road. Complete with a dipper and aluminium cups. Also baskets or plastic buckets filled with boiled cassava or mashed cassava cake, cucumber and *sinole* (fried sago starch). All this had been prepared voluntarily, of course, by our fellow prisoners at Unit IV Savanajaya. They knew from their own experience a year previously that when arriving at our unit we would be exhausted, thirsty and hungry. This was solidarity in suffering, something that had already faded in many prisons in Java, but here in this arid land of exile had suddenly blossomed once again.

'*Alhamdulillah!*' Pak Haji Rauf exclaimed spontaneously as he gulped down a mug of tea. This expression of gratitude was deep and sincere. It is this sense of solidarity that arises from sincerity, I said to myself, and becomes the capital of conviction and resolve. Return to furthering the struggle: grasp life with one's head held high!

* * *

Almost every 100 metres we stopped, looking for what was left of the cassava and the tea. While sitting for a moment beside the road, we would bathe our hot feet. When we got close to the fancy shining Savanajaya mosque, the road branched: straight ahead went to the Savanajaya Unit, and left went to what was to be our unit. Bantalareja.

The road to the left was short. At its end, it petered out into a path that people called the 'pig road'. It wound into the thick vetiver grass and the cogon grass that was taller than a man.

As we neared this left turn we saw an open buffalo cart coming towards us. But it was not pulled by buffalo, cows or horses. It was being pushed by some men, all bare-chested. As it was still at a distance, we thought they were locals, but when the cart got close it turned out they were all prisoners. Prisoners from Unit IV Savanajaya. Among those pushing and pulling the cart were faces vaguely familiar to me.

'Pak Haji, you go on ahead!' I said, deliberately loud so that the guard behind could hear. 'I need to pee!'

I stopped. Stopped and faced the ricefields. The sergeant guard kept walking, without rebuking me, following Pak Haji. The cart was now close to where I was standing. These prisoners, I thought, had, with the excuse of doing their appointed work, come to see what was going on. To look and see if there was anyone they recognised. I turned and deliberately looked at them. I too wanted to know who they were, those faces, vaguely familiar. Sure enough, the horse pulling the cart was called Hutajulu. He was one of the former leaders of the Yogyakarta branch of CGMI (Consentrasi Gerakan Mahasiswa Indonesia, Indonesian Student Movement Concentration) in 1950-something. Of course, we had known each other well back then. He was one of four who had been detained for a few days by the Yogyakarta state security police for leading a demonstration against the initiation 'games' for students at Gadjah Mada University.

One of those at the back of the cart on the left suddenly ran to the right and approached where I was standing.

'Mas'... he greeted, quietly.

'Ssst!' his companions warned, even more quietly.

But suddenly he stopped his pushing behind the cart and clasped his two fists together in front of his chest like Chinese people do when they are honouring their gods. Then he raised four fingers on his right hand, as high as his chest. He was giving me a sign that he was in Barracks IV.

'Push!' shouted the horse-Hutajulu giving the command. His voice was a little hoarse. Maybe his voice was like that before when I knew him.

'Come on, push!' the others all shouted together.

And the empty cart ran off, throwing its clattering noise into the curtain of dusk on the walls of the Savanajaya-Bantalareja forest.

The one who had called out 'Mas' to me, was Sudarno As. He was a former student of mine at the Teachers Training section of Taman Siswa in Yogyakarta, who went on to become a teacher at the Cilacap branch of Taman Siswa for adults. He had created a few 'new creation' (*kreasi baru*) dances, as they were called at the time, including 'Butterfly Dance' and 'Fishing Net Dance', and he was also clever at painting the intricate designs on leather puppets (*wayang kulit*). He had led the Cilacap branch of Lekra until he was captured in 1966 when Lekra was banned by the New Order regime.

I ran to catch up with Pak Haji Rauf. The sergeant guard was still walking a few steps behind him. Probably he was deliberately walking slowly, waiting until I came back to accompany this old man who seemed fragile.

'It's not the same, is it?' Pak Haji whispered, grumbling.

'What's not the same?'

'The reality compared to the news. Just look!' he said while pointing at the ricefields. 'Infested and yellow rice shoots like that? There's no sign at all of them being fertile!'

'It's what you call propaganda, Pak Haji.'

'No! Propaganda is what they do! But the news came from our own comrades!'

'Yes, but where was the source of the news, Pak Haji? Isn't it still them?'

'So it was just 'bombing' then. Not real news …'

Once at Salemba prison, a friend who was also a political prisoner and had formerly been a journalist for a Jakarta newspaper, spread a snippet of news. With whispers of course. Who knows where the news was from and how exactly he had managed to get it, he never said. The spreading of rumour (we called it *'sasus'*) was indeed sometimes mixed up with a deliberate 'little bird' telling campaign. The New Order rulers called this 'political guerilla tactics', and the prisoners called it *bom-boman*, or dropping bombs. And all the rumours and gossip and 'little-bird-told-me's' were wrapped up as though operating in the press in the free world: 'From a reliable source!'

The news was big news for life in prison, which was closed and locked tight. 'A Letter from Pak Prapto in Buru island'. This would probably have been the headline had it been in the press. 'Pak Prapto' was Prof. Dr. Suprapto SH, who had defended in court those involved in the July 3, 1946 incident and the Madiun Incident of 1948. He was also the one who had drawn up the Tedjasukmana Labour Laws, which had been opposed by members of SOBSI. Tedjasukmana was the Minister of Labour in the Burhanudin Harahap cabinet of 1955.

Pak Prapto was one of the first group of political prisoners sent out to Buru in 1969 and settled in Unit III Wanayasa, which we knew as 'Big Shots Unit' (Unit Gembong) because it housed people like the writers Pramoedya Ananta Toer and Rivai Apin; a member of the Central Committee of the Communist Party, Anwar Sanusi; editor of *Bintang Merah*, the magazine on Marxist-Leninist politics and theory, F Runturambi; the national Lekra figure Oey Hay Djoen and many others.

The Pak Prapto letter, so the news went, was smuggled out to his family in Jakarta. In the letter, Pak Prapto asked to be sent twenty-five rupiah which he needed as capital to invest in a chicken farm on Buru. This snippet of news of course ballooned. There is a Javanese saying '*sadawa-dawane lurung isih dawa gurung*', which is literally 'no matter how long the road, the windpipe is longer still'. News spreads far and wide and is made bigger in the spreading. If a big shot prisoner like Dr Suprapto SH had been given freedom, just imagine then what the 'little fry' prisoners who were just from the mass organisations would get!

So the story was embellished more and more. For instance, Buru prisoners would be able to have their own business. Prisoners could roam around freely. Prisoners there could find their own new lives. Prisoners from now on would no longer be imprisoned, but just exiled …

But those pathetic infested rice plants were the reality. Not a single prisoner as far as the eye could see; that was the reality. Prohibited to speak to any of the local population or any prisoner from another unit; that was the reality. The flash of Hutajulu's glance; that was the reality. Human beings replacing buffaloes pulling carts; that was the reality.

The sun was tilting more to the west, going behind the range of hills. I grew up in a village and had learnt as a child how to read the time just by looking at the shadows of bodies and the smell of the blowing wind. It was near dusk. There were no more kettles or drums of water and buckets and baskets of boiled cassava. Pak Haji Rauf and

I entered the 'pig track'. We stopped. I bathed my feet in the ricefield ditch. There were not many others behind us. Only the sick, and those who were even older than Pak Haji Rauf.

'Hurry up now!' our sergeant guard whose name was Andi Sose, said. He spoke patiently and without a snarling tone. He stopped for a moment, deliberately giving us time to catch up. 'It will be dark soon. We still have about a third of the way to go …'

'Still another third?'

'Yes, after we go through this bit ahead, we turn again to the right. You can see your unit from there.'

I glanced at Pak Haji's face. It looked as though he was trying to hold back tears. I did not say a word. Nor did he say a word. His eyes, though, said too much.

'Where are you from, Mas?' asked the Sergeant, using the friendly Javanese term of address for 'brother'. I thought the question was directed at me.

'Java, Pak'

'Java. Java again. Communists are always Javanese.'

We kept quiet.

'Now if you Javanese want to live, let me warn you. Don't ever get the guards angry. Don't wake sleeping tigers!'

His warning and threat came through loud and clear, even though it was said in polite language.

'Obey all the commandant's commands. Obey us. Because every single thing that the New Order government gives to you comes via our bosses. For all of you.'

We let Sergeant Andi Sose continue.

'The New Order government's aim is good. It wants to restore you to being true Pancasila-ists. Remember that!'

He suddenly stopped and turned to those of us who were a few steps behind him.

'And so don't you ever try anything!' he stressed. 'The law is in our hands. We can kill you whenever we want!'

Andi Sose's friendly tone had vanished. It was replaced with the accessory of power of a harsh army sergeant. While talking, he had changed the way he addressed us. The friendly 'Mas' had changed to '*kalian*' (you all), then to '*kamu*', the top-down term in the style of the Dutch colonial soldiers addressing the natives, and now '*tuan*', a term of respect he was using in mockery. He was drawing a sharp line of division between those up there and us down here.

After going through the path surrounded by clumps of young sago, we turned to the right. On and on, it was just jungle cogon grass. Our hands were busy parting the sharp cutting grass, the scratches itched our skin, and we lifted our feet carefully. The shoots pierced the soles of our feet and were as sharp as thorns when we trod on them. The jungle cogon grass was so thick and so high that we could not see the earth clearly.

'There it is!' Sergeant Andi yelled. 'You can see your unit now.'

Yes. Far behind the stretch of jungle grass, you could see the tin roofs of buildings shining.

'That's where you will eat, drink, sleep, work, and … don't forget … pray. Forever. Until you die.'

Pak Haji Rauf stopped walking. He pretended to be rolling up the cuffs of his long trousers. He waved to me with his eyes to wait for him. I understood. Even though he was a dyed-in-the-wool communist who had been imprisoned and exiled I don't know how many times, he was very aware that he was old now, and those last words the sergeant uttered had deeply shaken him.

'It's okay', Pak Haji, I whispered. 'History always writes its own story.'

'Meaning?'

'It depends neither on statesmen of world-class calibre nor a thousand generals compact as one …'

'Insya Allah!'

'Hey, what did you say?' Sergeant Sose turned and asked.

'I was just offering thanks to God, Pak. We have got to the end …'

'Have you ever been to Arab countries?'

'Yes, I have, Pak. When I went on the Haj.'

'You too?' he asked looking at me.

'Not yet, Pak. I only got to study some basic Arabic alphabet when I was at Salemba.'

Sergeant Andi continued walking without turning round. We dragged our feet along behind him. The unit was closer now. The barbed wire around it was also clear. The Red and White flag was flying near one of the buildings with the tin roof. That had to be where the office of the unit was located, or where the Camp Commander stayed.

A few prisoners behind us caught up and wanted to pass us, but the sergeant guard walking in front of us stopped them.

'Hey, you Chink!' Sergeant Andi said, turning.

'I am not Chinese, Pak' Syamsuddin Gobel replied. He did have pale skin, slightly slanting eyes and rather protruding cheekbones. Like a Mongolian woman.

'I am from Gorontalo, Pak'.

'Gorontalo?' Sergeant Andi repeated. This had to be because he felt that he too came from a similar place.

'Gorontalo in Sulawesi?'

'Yes, Pak.'

'Liar! How could someone from Sulawesi become communist?'

Gobel did not reply.

'What schooling did you have?'

'Primary school, Pak.'

'Liar. I know that those Javanese are all smart … but how could you go to primary school? And you, Old Man, what school did you go to?'

'Islamic boarding school, Pak.'

'And how could a Muslim like you turn communist?'

Pak Haji Rauf did not answer. None of us said anything. There was no point, it would only bring trouble.

We had arrived at the unit complex.

The sunset greeted us. Its rays no longer had heat in them, as they beamed from the forest and the swamp, entering the wire fence from the west. To the left of the entrance gate there was a barracks building, like our own barracks, but with a tin roof and wooden plank walls. This was the guards' barracks. They called it a 'mess', not 'barracks'. On the right of the entrance gate, outside of the barbed wire, was the building we had seen from a distance flying the Red and White flag. This was not a barracks, but a normal house. This was the office of the unit and the residence of the commander. They called it the Commander's villa or *'wisma'*.

This was the reality of the hierarchy of the society of political prisoners on the island of Buru in matters of accommodation: A villa or *wisma* for the Commander, a mess for the platoon of guards, and barracks for prisoners. Each had their own values. Each had its rights and duties. But for the one called barracks, there were no rights. Just duties.

All three had a single law and etiquette that had its source and flowed from the Commander's wisma!

Chapter 8

STARTING AT NAMLEA

Namlea. The capital of the island of Buru. The Isle of Hope. Suppose Indonesia had never made history by crushing the Indonesian Communist Party and overturning President Sukarno, with the pretext of crushing the movement they called G30S/PKI in the early hours of 1 October 1965, then probably the words Buru and Namlea – the town situated on the north coast of the island – would have remained hidden from maps and the news.

Now those two words can be found easily on the Winkler Prins map of the world (Elsevier MCMLXXXVII) or the Wolters-Nordoff map of forests (1993). Even the prestigious Encyclopædia Britannica has an entry for the island of Buru, which says:

'Situated 42 miles (68 km) to the west of the island of Seram, across the Manippa Strait, with an area of around 3670 square miles (9505 square kilometres). Hilly and with dense forest, the coast is narrow, having a port and airport in Namlea, the most important town, on the north-east coast. The highest point is 7967 feet (2428 metres) above sea level. The island was taken by the Dutch (1652-1658). It produces forest products and sago. The population (1971) is 37,624.'

As we approached the shore aboard the *Tokala*, the view that first struck me was the tin mosque dome shining in the sun. After stepping ashore and having left the port, our marching file was ordered to stop on the four-metre wide highway and squat in front of the Military Police office beside the local government office. In the opposite direction, in front of the shining tin-domed mosque, there was a stall with a name painted in green: Rice Stall (*Warung Nasi*). On either side of this earthen highway were four or five doors of Chinese shops. They were all general stores.

We were left squatting there for hours in front of the offices of the two highest authorities at the time. Waiting and waiting. But we had no idea what we were waiting for. There was no announcement.

The sun burnt hot and the sky seemed as though it had never been dampened by the rain. Every now and then men wearing headcloths would pass, walking on the far side as though afraid to be anywhere near the lines of newcomers who had just got off the boat, Javanese wearing identical clothing in khaki green shirts with numbers on their chests. The men passing by were carrying staffs and bore on their shoulders something strange that I was seeing for the first time. It was the shape of a capsule about the size of a betel nut branch and wrapped in a kind of young coconut frond, sometimes green and sometimes dry and brown. Later on, I found out that this capsule is a measure of sago starch, called a *tumangan* and weighing about 10 kilograms. The wrapping is made from sago leaves that resemble coconut leaves, but sago leaves are a little wider and have soft thorns.

The *tumangan* is at once a way of storing sago starch and a measure. It looks like a long tube and is about one span of the hand plus three fingers long. The circumference of the *tumangan* cylinder measures the same as the circumference of the head of the person who made it. To make the frame of the leaf structure, thin strips of the fronds are used, or coconut fronds, or sometimes strips of the bark of a plant called *bamban*. This is a swamp plant that has long sections between the nodes, and long pointed leaves like the medicinal plant we know in Java called *temu ireng*. *Bamban* leaves are also usually used to wrap *midong*, which is the larva of the sago beetle before it is baked.

After the capsule is filled with wet sago, it is stopped with something called *ela*, which is the sour-smelling fibre residue of pounded sago that has been left to ferment. This is made into a convex-shaped stopper and enclosed with the edges of the leaves. The whole capsule is then tied with frond strips or *bamban* bark strips, from top to bottom.

Because the *tumangan* are made in a standard size, the contents will also be more or less standard in weight, namely two-and-a-half kilograms. This is the way that sago is traded in the region, as far as Ambon. When it gets to the city, the sago that is already dry is pounded again and moulded into small bricks. Those bricks of sago are what is sold in the markets in Java and neighbourhood shops in Jakarta, and were also an alternative to bulgur cracked wheat in the food parcels for political prisoners from poorer families.

In Buru itself, and probably also on the islands of Seram and others around, sago was an article and measure of trade. Goods were measured in sago. People would ask the price of a knife or a piece of cloth, for instance, by asking 'how many *tumang*?' The sago *tumang* was the unifying basic measure for exchange. This did not apply, though, for bride price, which was calculated differently and called *harta*. For instance, one spear or knife was one *harta*, seven pieces of white cloth were worth one *harta*, and so on.

* * *

Behind the rows of houses lining the roadside, for about 50 metres there were two or three more rows of roofs. The houses on the right side of the road when you came out of the port led directly to the shore of

Kayeli Bay, and those on the left led into the panorama of barren hills, although not as barren as the limestone hills in Karangmojo, Gunung Kidul, Yogyakarta. The most striking sights of Namlea were the jungle grass (*alang-alang*), the eucalyptus trees, fan palms, the *gempol* fruit tree, and a thin tree with lots of branches, which I later learned was called the *laban* tree. Its branches were hard and with smooth bark, which we later found made them good for making handles for tools, like hoes. There were one or two clumps of banana trees behind the houses here and there, their leaves battered by the ceaseless heavy winds.

I was feeling the blistering heat of the sun. But I would soon realise just how strong the wind could be on this barren island. In Java, strong winds usually bring outbreaks of influenza and children's illnesses like measles. But in villages, among the farmers, strong winds are signs that there might soon be plagues of locusts and grasshoppers. My initial impression of the nature on arrival already signalled to me that we were in for a difficult life ahead.

That day we were forced to fast, after being spoilt for seven days and nights at sea with nonstop delicious food and drink. On this day none of us received any ration. Not even a drop of drinking water. There were one or two local people who took pity and secretly left out a kettle of water and some pieces of boiled cassava.

'Pak Hersi', Heru said to me, 'Have you still got any money in your pocket?'

Dammit! I thought. He had sharp eyes. The pocket of my trousers was too thin!

'What are you taking it to the unit for?' he asked, before I even had time to reply.

'We're not going to live only until today', I replied, rather annoyed.

'Ah, so you're keeping it as a reserve for the unit, then?'

'Yes,' I said. 'We're going to feel even hungrier after we have been walking for however long we have to. Who wants to feed 500 people? Who is going to serve us all? We're not guests, Heru!'

'No, you're right, we're not guests', he said. 'But, what if there's no place selling stuff there? What if it's just dry jungle grass like over there?' He nodded his head in the direction of the barren panorama.

Secretly, I agreed with him, but I kept quiet. I pretended not to pay attention.

'Have you already forgotten what we experienced at Salemba, Pak? You might have your rucksack in your hands or your visitor's parcel on your lap and you get a summons. We could never think about what might happen later on or tomorrow, right? Where is there a prisoner like that? Careful, you might be getting old and forgetful!'

'That's enough!' I gave in. I pretended to be mad. 'This is all about you dying for a cigarette, right? You're drooling over that black tobacco that your friends bought, right?'

With a grin he took the note I handed him, a red one. It was the one and only hundred rupiah note in my pocket, which my younger brother had sent me on my last day at Tangerang.

'Over there. Tobacco for you, and palm sugar for me.'

He slipped between two houses that bordered the shore. There were a couple of traders from Buton there earning profit from Coca Cola, Sprite, cigarettes, tobacco and palm sugar. In the hope of 'profit', they had not been scared off by the propaganda the authorities circulated in the days before our arrival: 'Watch out! The army of murderers from Crocodile Hole in Java is about to arrive.'

A few moments later, Heru came back. He was carrying a roll of Bugis tobacco about as long as a finger and five centimetres thick. It was black and packed firm. It had cost 60 rupiah. With the remaining

40 rupiah he had bought four pieces of palm sugar, each about the same size as the roll of tobacco. We divided two of the pieces of sugar into four, for Heru, Irawan, Penjol and me. Then the four of us inhaled the smoke from the Bugis tobacco, which was so pungent it seemed to hit you in the nose!

In prison life, nicotine smoke and sweet palm sugar were like 'weapons of last resort', the ultimate remedy. Nicotine smoke calmed anxiety, and palm sugar was believed to keep fever away or reduce it.

There is a story about Bung Djono, who was a fellow prisoner in my Barracks IX at Unit XV Indrapura. In the free world, before the New Order army captured him, he had been a member of the Kendal branch of Lekra in Central Java and worked as a primary school teacher in that small town. After he was captured, before being locked up at Nusa Kambangan prison, he was detained at Pekalongan prison, which was known for its cruelty. At one time, he was suffering from beri-beri and his condition was serious. He could do nothing except lie sprawled on the floor of his cell waiting for his end to come. Back then, between 1966 and 1968, in Salemba jail too, every day there were prisoners dying in cells in prison blocks here and there. Some days there might be up to ten, other days less, but there were rarely fewer than five bodies.

So it was. Because death had become a routine event in the prison, the authorities in the Pekalongan prison made a special duty, the corpse *corvée*, made up of six people. They were fully equipped with their work tools, spades and hoes, along with an open cart to carry the bodies, minus the horse to pull the cart. One of the six in the team had to become the horse pulling the cart, three others had to push it, and the other two pushed from left and right.

The duty of the corpse *corvée* took place every morning after roll call, under the supervision of a prison guard who carried the keys. They checked cell after cell, taking out the bodies they found and carrying them one by one into the cart. Then, supervised by one or two army guards, they went to Pekalongan beach to bury the bodies.

When they got to the beach, the bodies were taken down from the cart and lined up on the sand without any covering at all. Meanwhile, the hot sun of the Java coast got higher in the sky, reaching its zenith. The sand on the beach was so hot that it stung.

The corpse squad looked for places that they thought would not be reached by high tide, where they would dig the number of graves necessary. Each hole was about one metre deep, and sometimes not even that. One by one, they would put the bodies into the holes they had dug, then close the hole with sand. With no ceremony or prayer other than a 'farewell' from those six on the squad.

On this day there were seven bodies to be buried. One among the seven was the 'body' of Bung Djono. The seven holes were ready. Two men stood in the holes, ready to receive the body about to be lowered, while the other four in the team carried the bodies one by one over to the holes. Two soldiers were sitting in the shade under a tree.

'Hey, one isn't dead yet!' someone suddenly yelled.

'You're right. He's not dead!' shouted the other three, bending over and scrutinising the 'body'.

'Who is it?' shouted one of them from inside the hole, while jumping up. He was the head of the squad.

'It's Djono!'

Bung Djono was moving his lips. Weakly. Maybe he was trying to show signs of life, from the shock of the hot sand. But he had no energy.

'Yes. He's alive', someone said, feeling for the pulse in his neck.

'Bring him over to the shade!' the head of the squad said, as an order. 'Rub his lips. Have we got any water?'

'What for?' someone retorted.

'We're taking him back. I will report to the Commander.'

'What's the point? He'll just die anyway. Might as well just bury him now …'

'How could you? I don't agree', the head of the squad said emphatically. 'If he dies later that is a matter for later. But now is now and he is still alive. We're taking him back to the cell block. His fellow prisoners will care for him'.

And so it was that the 'body' of Bung Djono was put back on the cart, covered with the clothing of his friends, and taken back to prison to the cell he had been taken from. He was patiently and lovingly nursed by his cellmates. They took turns to rub his lips with liquid palm sugar. And those lips, from only being able to tremble, slowly managed to take some of the liquid, drop by drop. And his eyes, from being tightly closed, could slowly open and see the faces of his friends. Eventually, Bung Djono returned to health.

The story of how he had once been a 'body' and had come back to life was one that Djono himself told us one day when we were having a midday break in the fertiliser shed.

* * *

It was already well past midday when we heard the signal to get ready. The columns of prisoners had scattered somewhat, but now immediately went back into formation. Ten groups, each with fifty men, lined up according to the numbers on their shorts. After all the organising was done, the columns received the order, 'about turn riiiight … march!' We all faced right, towards the end of the road that went who knows where. But we were herded towards a place called Jiku Kecil where there was a transit camp, where we would be in transit before continuing our march to our new abode, Unit XIV Bantalareja.

Jiku Kecil was on the edge of Kayeli Bay, about four kilometres from Namlea. The four-metre wide road leading to the transit camp was built by the political prisoners who arrived before us, namely those from Unit IV Savanajaya, which is closest to Namlea. The road was made from coral, earth and sand.

We all had to walk quickly, interspersed with jogging. If there were some among us who were thought too slow, then the platoon guard would prod them in the back with the barrel of his rifle. If the column got too messy, then gunshots fired in the air gave the sign to get the columns back into neat formation. Of course, this was accompanied by abuse and barks of anger.

After about one and a half kilometres, we came to a hilly rise of white stones like limestone. On the right of the road was a big graveyard surrounded by shady trees, and with trees in the centre too. The guards shouted an order that moved down the line: 'Cease march …!' The order to stop, right in front of a large graveyard, seemed to come out of the blue and made the hairs on my neck stand on end. A cold shiver of fear went down my spine. I thought I was not the only one who was feeling like this. But before I even had time to try to calm my soaring blood pressure, there came follow-up orders. Again, it went down the line from the front to the back. Order one, we had to all squat down with our linked hands behind our necks; and the second order, we had to all face the graveyard.

'Pak', Heru whispered to me. 'We're not going to be killed right here, are we?'

We were all quiet. You could sense the fear gripping us all.

'What's this?' Slamet Kondor grumbled, with a deliberately loud voice, as though he wanted to get those of us near him fired up. In the 'time before the incident', he had been a security guard at the office of the Central Committee of the Communist Party in Jalan Kramat Raya.

'Do we just want to sit here waiting until the bullets kill us all?'

'Don't be a fool, Bung!', Alibasah said. 'This isn't a graveyard of our fellow prisoners. Do you think they would ever be given headstones?'

'Don't worry', Alibasah went on, in a low tone. 'How could they kill 500 people at once in full daylight? And anyway, do you see any graves dug? None, right?'

I had known Alibasah well when we were both in G Block at Salemba prison. If it got to his personal political stance, then he was no less fervent and vocal than Slamet Karyadi alias Slamet Kondor. But his experience as a former leader of the Air Force Workers Union (Serbaud, Serikat Buruh Angkatan Udara) had made him smarter at using his brain than Slamet Kondor who was used to using his brawn.

Slamet Kondor went quiet. We were all quiet. But our fear began to subside.

It turned out that Alibasah was right. The soldiers 'only' wanted to give us a fright and to crush our spirit. We were ordered to crouch because they wanted to count us, not with a roll call, but by hitting us on the head with a stick, one by one. And every single recipient of that blow on the head from these young, low-ranking soldiers, whether old or young, university graduate or illiterate, had to yell out the number following on from the number just called. Right down the line.

The 'graveyard roll call' as Heru called it, took about half an hour. We were given the order to be 'at the ready' and then, 'quick maaarch!'

And the column of 500 political prisoners, in ten groups, continued their march towards Jiku Kecil. With a feeling of exhaustion and oppression, but also relief because it turned out there had been no serious torture during the 'graveyard roll call'.

Chapter 9

FIRST SUNSET AT BANTALAREJA

I walked through the entrance gate to the unit with a steeled heart. The gate was wide open. A huge padlock hung mute. Straight across on the other side was the exit gate. Shut. You could see the padlock and chains. There was jungle grass higher than me growing in front of the lines of barracks. Five on the left and five on the right. All of them had roofs of plaited leaves and walls of split bamboo. Beyond the exit gate was thick scrub. It was the same behind the barracks. Only in front, beside the wisma and the mess, there was a stretch of jungle grass and cogon grass with eucalyptus trees and other local trees.

The area directly in front of the guards' mess had been cleared for a security post. When we went in, there were two guards sitting behind a table. A few carbines were hanging on the wall behind them. In front of them, on a pole at the entry door, was a bell made from an old bomb casing about a metre long. It was hung from the verandah rafters. Later we got to know that apart from being a marker of time, that bell would order our every breath day and night.

'Go and report at the guard post!' ordered Sergeant Andi Sose as he went into the mess.

We reported. It was all military style. Take off your straw hat, then bow, just as we had to do during the Japanese occupation.

'Reporting!' said with an attitude of being totally alert. Standing up straight, ankles together, eyes looking directly ahead, two arms by

First Sunset at Bantalareja

your side with fists clenched. Then state your name, followed by your full identity, meaning the number on your shirt and the number of your photo. It was Pak Haji's turn after me. The same thing. One of the guards heard our report while checking it against a big book in front of him, while the other one looked at us with eyes of vengeance.

'You know your barracks?' he asked.

'Mine is nine. This man's is six', I said, answering for Pak Haji.

I also had a chance to glance at their names: Jance and Sumual. One red stripe on the arm. Soldier, second rank. Later on, we got to know that these two were the most arrogant, swaggering soldiers, and as wild as wolves. They liked to casually terrify by firing their guns in the air. As though the price of a bullet was worth less than our daily ration of a plate of cracked wheat.

We went through a barbed-wire fence, then walked along a path bordering the mess. The barracks furthest away was Barracks VI which was where Pak Haji Rauf was going to 'stay forever until he died', as Sergeant Andi Sose said. I went to my own barracks, which was the second to last on the right. Barracks IX.

The earth under the awning of the barracks was muddy. There were muddy pools of water here and there. This was not like the earth in villages in Central Java. Here, after rain, the clay earth outside our unit turned to mud. It was slippery and stuck to the soles of your feet.

When I entered my barracks, it was already dark inside. It was not yet past sunset, but the sunlight was already trapped behind the hill covered with thick scrub to the west. This is also why the soil was muddy and damp. The heat of the sun could never fully penetrate the surface of the earth.

'You've just got here, Pak', Irawan greeted me at the door.

Our head-of-barracks-to-be was a pure blue blood with the Javanese aristocratic title of Raden Mas, and he was a cousin of Sultan Hamengku Buwono IX. He had formerly led the governing body for the League of Indonesian Youth and Students (IPPI, Ikatan Pemuda Pelajar Indonesia) together with Robby Sumolang who was another inmate of our unit.

'Yes, I was keeping Pak Haji Rauf company.'

'Ha ha! The one who carries so much stuff?'

'Yes, I was surprised too. But remember that he is old.'

'True. Even in Tangerang we knew he was already squirrelling stuff away.'

I looked around me. My fellow inmates were dangling their legs in their tiny allotments, sitting on the edge of the split bamboo ledge that ran the length of the barracks on both sides. There was nothing else they could do. They couldn't stretch their muddy legs. If they got down, then the entire floor of the barracks would be like a muddy open drain.

'Where do the low numbers start?' I asked.

'Over there on the left. You are on the right, around the middle, beside Heru.'

'How come?' I said. Because according to the number on my shirt, I should be between Syamsudin Gobel and Mohamad Soleh Amat. Gobel was a former member of People's Youth (Pemuda Rakyat) and had been one of the security guards of Njoto, the third-ranking member of the Central Committee of the Communist Party. Soleh Amat had been in the central leadership of the Motor Vehicle Workers Union (SBKB, Serikat Buruh Kendaraan Bermotor), in Salemba he had been my teacher for Qur'anic reading, and before that he had been the first secretary of the Semarang branch of Lekra.

'It's all sorted, Pak!' Heru called, hearing the tone of my confusion.

Heru was sitting relaxed like the others. Around his neck, he had a small white hand towel, just as he did when I first met him at Salemba. He was leaning on the leg of his sleeping platform, against a barracks pillar. The barracks pillars were made from branches of mangrove, eucalyptus or the meranti tree. The branches had just been stripped of smaller branches and leaves, and not treated, shaved or shaped in any way. In fact, some of them were showing signs of regrowth.

'I asked if I could change places with Pak Soleh', he said, half whispering.

'Why bother changing when it's just to sleep?'

'Sleeping time is the only chance we'll get to talk.'

Before I had the opportunity to answer Heru, Slamet Kondor entered the barracks, held by a friend from another barracks. His face was squinting with pain. His two hands were clutching his groin, and he was dragging his feet. Heru jumped down, and together with Irawan they supported him and lay him down on his bunk. It was number 440. It was just one away from me, to the left of Heru. A pillow and some rucksacks were piled up to raise his legs higher than his body.

Actually, his real name was Slamet Karyadi. He had formerly been a member of the security guard for the Jakarta Branch of the Communist Party. He had been captured when the army attacked the Central Committee offices of the Communist Party at Jalan Kramat Raya, as a shield for the mass actions by the student groups KAMI and KAPPI (KAMI Kekatuan Aksi Mahasiswa Indonesia, KAPPI Kesatuan Aksi Pemuda dan Pelajar Indonesia). I had been a witness in the crowd, standing watching on the roadside. Slamet Karyadi and some other security guards tried to hold out by throwing stones from inside. Meanwhile, outside the 'KAMI-KAPPI' group pushed forward, under the cover of rifle shots. Not even an hour later, trucks went in and then came out carrying files and prisoners.

Like his fellow guards, Slamet Karyadi was well trained in martial arts. He underwent severe torture in the first bout of interrogation at Central Intelligence. From then on, he suffered a serious hernia in his scrotum, which is why he was known with the Javanese word for scrotal hernia, *kondor* – he became Slamet Kondor.

'Where is Mas Setiawan?', using my more 'official' name.

I heard a loud voice behind me. When I turned, there was a young man with a thin moustache, bright eyes and dark skin, jumping in through the window.

Irawan was about to say something but I cut him off with a sign.

'Tedja Bayu!' I shouted. I ran to meet the young man, embraced and kissed him.

'Mas Setiawan is dead!' I said, deliberately rather loud. 'This is me, Hersri. Setiawan's younger brother. Do you remember?'

Now it was Tedja Bayu's turn to hug me. I could see his eyes filled with tears. Of course, all the memories came flooding back. From when we were still in Yogyakarta. From when he was in the second grade of junior high school and lived in a brick house in Jalan Pakuningratan. Then when he became a student at Gadjah Mada University and was active in the students' organisation CGMI, and lived in a bamboo house on the banks of Gajah Wong River, together with his mother and younger brothers and sisters.

'How are your mother and brothers and sisters?'

'I heard the news from Ambarawa camp that Mas Setiawan was dead.'

'Good news, isn't it? In the midst of this chaos, when we get the news that someone is dead, that is good.'

'It's good if it isn't true. But if it's true?'

'True or not, just accept it ... Don't question it, don't bother searching. If it is true that someone is dead, then there's nothing to be done, is there?'

We were quiet then for a moment or two. Each was digesting his own words. We were both remembering the peaceful times so many years ago.

'How are your mother and brothers and sisters?' I asked the question again that he still had not answered.

Then I told him about my last meeting with his mother, Mia Bustam. It had been about a month before the 'Incident', on the verandah of a building next door to the Communist Party headquarters building. His mother had not said much, but just looked at me hard and long. It was as though there was just too much to say, so that she did not know where to start. But the situation also was not right.

We were taking a break at the time, having just eaten lunch. Some people were sitting on chairs on the verandah, some were chatting while they stood and smoked, some were busily reading the newspaper. I was chatting to Sugiarti Siswadi while leafing through a collection of Betawi and regional folk songs. The songs had been given musical arrangement by Mohamad Sutiyoso, and given new words by someone, I thought probably S.W. Kuntjahjo, Subronto K. Atmodjo and Sudharnoto. We were going to make stencil copies of the text to give to regional delegates who were coming to the gathering to commemorate the first anniversary of the Conference of Revolutionary Art and Literature (KSSR, Konferensi Seni dan Sastra Revolusioner), and to the Dwikora volunteers who were undergoing training at Halim. Sugiarti Siswadi, who was standing beside my chair, was a prominent female Leftist writer, along with S. Rukiah

Kertapati who was head of the committee for the KSSR anniversary celebrations, and I was secretary of that committee. Standing on the other side of me was Mia Bustam who was whispering to Rumini, the wife of the late Basuki Resobowo. I had no idea what they were talking about. Maybe about the sessions planned for the celebrations, or maybe about the general situation, which did indeed feel like it was getting hotter by the minute.

Suddenly Aidit's car passed in front of us, leaving the Party building and heading towards another office building. Government offices. At that time Aidit, as head of the Communist Party, had been made 'Minister Coordinator/ Deputy Head of MPRS [The Temporary People's Consultative Assembly]' – that was his official title. Immediately everyone sitting rose from their chairs, except for me, and they all stood as Bung Aidit passed and left the building precinct.

'Why didn't you stand?' one of them asked, in a nasty tone.

'Do I have to stand?' I asked, innocently. Not because I wanted to challenge. But I, who had returned from Colombo not even a month before, did not know this new habit among the 'Party family'.

'Of course! Bung Aidit is a minister!' she said.

'He's a minister if he's over there. But here with us, he is our head, isn't he?'

'Shhh. You'd better not say that again …!'

The atmosphere calmed. I tried to remember what I had glanced when the car had gone past. What I saw rather than glanced was that his face had changed. He was smiling as usual. Was it an empty smile? Or was it a smile of surprise to see a cadre who did not know the new routine since he had become a minister? Of course, only he knew.

'Yes, when mother got home, she told us about that incident', Tedja Bayu said.

'Where is your mother now?'

'In Plantungan jail.'

'Plantungan?' I replied, shocked.

I went silent. Mia Bustam captured too, and even sent to the women's camp in Plantungan! This made no sense at all. Such a well-mannered woman, patient, one who could never discuss politics in a strident tone. I could imagine her being arrested, because she was the former wife of the well-known Leftist artist, S. Sudjojono, or because she was a member of the leadership of the Yogyakarta branch of Lekra. Because she was the mother of Tedja Bayu who was a CGMI activist. But it truly made absolutely no sense at all that she could be imprisoned at the Plantungan camp along with people like the MPRS member Salawati Daud, the Regional House of Representatives (DPRD) member Ny. D Susanto, or Dr Sumiarsi who had been labelled the 'Crocodile Hole doctor', and other female political figures. This was totally crazy.

'And your brothers and sisters?' I asked.

'I don't know what's happening with them now. Nasti had to take on the role of mother to the others. Sometimes Pak Salam and Pak Yudho help her.'

* * *

Suddenly there was the sound of the bell ringing. Everyone's eyes and I am sure mine too, were suddenly wide open, startled. This was the first time in my life, in our life, that there was the sound of a bell to give signals, which as yet we did not understand. I was familiar with the striking of the wooden block in my village. That was a sign there were bad spirits roaming around, or an enemy air raid. The warning for spirits was for the spirits that accompanied the Queen of the South

Seas as she passed towards the Progo River heading for Kyahi Dhiwut Merapi on the Merapi volcano.

'That's the bell for roll call!' Tedjo called, telling us. He had already been an inmate in Unit IV Savanajaya for a year. He was used to hearing the toll of the bell at any time whatever.

'Savanajaya has roll call at six in the evening. After that, there will still be another. The night roll call, before sleep. Around nine o'clock.'

'Well, why are you still here then? You'll be late …'

'I am still on *corvée* duty', he said. 'I helped build this unit. From measuring out the land, clearing it, felling the trees for building, through to fastening the last thatched-leaf roof panel.'

'But the sergeant said that military construction engineers made it?'

'All they did was hold the plans, give orders, and hit people …' He headed for the window.

'I am in barracks number one', he said, turning back as he jumped out the window. And he was gone, disappeared into the scrub. Like a wild deer.

As I waited for the guard taking the roll to arrive at our barracks, Barracks IX, my thoughts wandered back to the Sudjojono family in Yogyakarta after their husband and father had left for Jakarta. The stories from when he became a member of parliament from the Communist Party faction, then divorced his wife and married the singer Rose Pandanwangi. About the newspaper Harian Rakjat which had announced his expulsion from membership of the party because of his second marriage. About Tedja Bayu and his six younger brothers and sisters, all of whom were still small. I knew all this through letters his mother sent me when I was in Colombo, over the five years leading up to 1965. After her divorce from her husband, she had given up using his name, (as 'mBak Djon'), taken the name Mia Bustam, and intensified her own study of painting. In 1964 I got the news that Mia Bustam – along with other artists like S. Ruliyati, Kartika Affandi and Edhi Sunarso's wife (I forget her name) – had exhibited her works. One of Mia Bustam's paintings that she particularly liked, showed her family facing a difficult future, but with courage radiating from their faces. Mia Bustam is the central figure, while to her left and right are Tedja Bayu and his six younger brothers and sisters. The bottom left corner of the painting feels empty. Who knows what imaginary face was to be added there.

Chapter 10

FIRST NIGHT ROLL CALL

It was the evening of the first day we spent at our camp, Unit XIV Bantalareja. I personally thought that this was where I would live forevermore. It could only be through some miraculous power if at some time in the future we could leave this place, what's more return home safely! And I did not mean those whose health would not stand it, and who would be buried here. But, for those who would end up being buried here, I consoled myself with the words of Rabindranath Tagore: they are like falling autumn leaves, and their decay will fertilise the soil. Or I calmed my feelings with the lyrics of a song we had to learn during the Japanese occupation, '*Oemi Yukaba*', which went like this:

> Battle at sea, buried in water
> Battle on land, buried in earth
> Sacrifice yourself for ookimi
> Sincerely and without regret

It turned out that once we had cleared the jungle and scrub around our unit and after the road to Sanleko beach had been built, the distance between Sanleko and Bantalareja was actually not so far. It was about five kilometres, maybe a little more. So a sixty-year-old man could walk that distance in about an hour, an hour and a half at the most. But on that first day when we arrived, August 17, 1971, how far it felt! And it was far, as the time it took us shows. Only two

First Night Roll Call

to three kilometres of it was wide road, namely the section built by the prisoners from Unit IV Savanajaya who had arrived about a year earlier. The rest of the way was just a path, or, as we later called it, a 'pig track' that wound through the scrub and the jungle grass that was taller than us, and occasionally crossed swamps and ditches. All barefoot of course, because since we had left the prison, shoes had become forbidden items. And for years, all our bare feet had walked on was concrete floors or the prison yard.

Another reason our journey took so long was that among us were 62 lame prisoners, semi-paralysed as a result of months of isolation at Tangerang prison, and we had to take turns at carrying them. On top of that, there were many old people who were not only frail physically, but also mentally, and so needed companions on the march. I accompanied Pak Haji Rauf and carried his knapsack. But I must say that I was secretly amazed that someone old like him, who had relatives in Sumatra, would carry so much heavy stuff! What on earth could he be carrying? Oh well, I thought, old people do hoard. Building nests, as the Javanese say. They collect anything, just like a bird collecting all kinds of things to build a nest. Maybe Pak Haji was at that stage.

The five hundred prisoners all had to jump off the landing craft on Sanleko beach, at around three in the afternoon. After roll call on the beach, we began our march to the unit. I arrived at the unit just at sunset. That meant that it took me about three hours to walk from Sanleko to Bantalreja. But there were lots of others who arrived later than me. Some of them did not get there until after the bell rang at 9 pm.

It was dark and muddy everywhere. The barracks, which measured 6 x 30 metres inside, was lit by only two 15-watt light bulbs. The walls were made of split bamboo, and the roof of plaited sago leaves, which would shift in a strong wind and did not allow in any outside natural light. Our unit, apart from the area in front outside the barbed-wire fence, where the Commander's residence and the guards' mess were, was still entirely surrounded by forest, scrub and cogon grass. Even the empty places between the barracks and in the centre of the unit which overall was about one hectare, was still thick, high jungle grass. Needless to say, this was a haven for all kinds of creepy-crawly bugs: *wereng*, the pest that ate our rice and crops (apart, that is, from the 'green worms' in army uniforms, namely the guards!), gnats and mosquitoes who would buzz and attack our bodies until dawn light.

I felt unbelievably exhausted, tired and hungry. But of course, my fellow prisoners must have been feeling the same. We sat at the edge of our allotted spaces, under the mosquito nets to avoid the biting gnats and mosquitoes. We sat cross-legged, trying to find some warmth from our legs. The barracks floor was muddy and had puddles of cold water everywhere, like a mudhole. This was because no sun could get through the surrounding jungle, and there were still no drains built. Now who do you think wants to build them? That was our task beginning the very next morning: land clearing and digging drains to the far swampy corner of the unit. The soil on Buru island was still young, and so it still had only a thin layer of humus. When it was soaked in water, and not even a lot of water, the soil would immediately turn to sticky mud. Like the earth in the kampungs in Jakarta.

That was why, that evening, none of us wanted to get out of our allotted spaces after arriving at the barracks. We just put up mosquito nets and sat under them. We had no idea when our rations would arrive from the kitchen. Ten kettles of hot water for one whole barracks, and dinner of bulgur cracked wheat or rice. But apart from that there was still one all-important ritual before sleep, the nightly roll call.

First Night Roll Call

There was no escaping it. There had to be a roll call in each barracks. We had not even made an area outside for it yet, and even if we had, it was already dark. There was no way the guards would take risks of holding the roll call in some open space.

There were three people to take roll call: the platoon security Commander, together with two platoon guards. They went from one barracks to the next, over the whole ten barracks. Our barracks was number IX. Our barracks head gave us a sign as the Platoon Commander stood at the front entrance into the barracks, with his pistol at his hip. The two platoon guards then walked around us, one holding his carbine with a bayonet, the other holding a lamp that looked like a marine lamp, or miner's lamp.

When the barracks head had given the sign for 'count', the two guards walked slowly, examining us one by one, beginning with the inhabitant with the lowest number on his shirt (401, who was Sugiri, the deputy barracks head), through to the highest number (450, which was Bambang Irawan, the barracks head). The guard carrying the lamp held the lamp right in front of our faces as each of us yelled out (it had to be a loud yell, as befitting the etiquette of the soldiers of our republic!) and the carbine-toting guard scrutinised our faces.

Sure, we had learnt the correct soldier method of roll call back in prison. But this military-style roll call carried out in this particular situation was truly something new for us. Even when we had been in the transit unit in Jiku Kecil in Namlea from August 12-17, 1971, (this transit unit later became the punishment unit, before it moved to 'Ancol' in 1974), the nightly roll call had not been like this first night at Bantalreja. It was really terrifying!

So when we heard that the roll call guards had already got to barracks number seven, we were already nervous and thought we must get ready. What else could we do? Stand up there in the cold muddy muck. All mosquito nets had to be tied up high, so the sleeping platform could be clearly seen to be free of anything hidden; we each had to stand by our platforms wearing our 'numbered' shirts, in the correct order with no-one changing places. When the roll was called, you were not allowed to utter a single word except for answering the roll, and were not allowed to make any movement unless you were given a sign to do so. You must ignore the heat and all gnats and mosquitoes biting away.

Two of our fellow prisoners, we already knew from our time at the transit camp, were particularly susceptible to behaviour that could attract punishment for the whole group, even though group punishment might be relatively slight, like making prisoners box each other, doing push-ups, rolling, walking duck fashion and so forth. Those two were Supardjo P.A. and Kromoredjo.

Supardjo P.A. was a former teacher at Cawang II primary school in South Jakarta who had been accused of taking part in military training at Crocodile Hole (Lubang Buaya). According to him, his initials P.A. stood for *Purworedjo Asli* – or True Purworedjan. And indeed, he came from Purworedjo in Central Java – but he also said that the P.A. stood for *Pikiran Abnormal* or abnormal mind. Whether or not his mind truly was abnormal, or whether he just acted like that, only he knew. What was clear was that he would just blurt out whatever went through his mind. When he was in that state, his communication with the world outside seemed to be suddenly cut off. He could not hear anything other than what was in his own head and heart. Usually, he would sing. As a former primary school teacher, he had certainly memorised a lot of songs, like *'Yen ing tawang ana lintang'*, *'Bintang Kecil'* (prison version), *'Rek, ayo rek'*, *'Walang Kekek'* and so on. He had also memorised his own particular version of the text of the five principles, Pancasila, and many other things besides.

Kromoredjo was another kettle of fish entirely. He was short and stout. The right kind of person to have been the leader of the railway workers union. He had been the head of its Cilacap branch before the event of 30 September 1965. You could also imagine how strong and energetic he had been when working as a young machinist during the Japanese occupation. So it was not surprising that he was signed up for the *romusha* – which opponents deliberately twisted to '*remukrusak*' (crushed and broken) – the forced labour unit used to build the Burma railway, nor that he then became a machinist on the railway in Burma (now Myanmar). He returned to Indonesia in 1947, leaving behind a wife and two-year-old daughter in Burma.

While the danger from Supardjo P.A. was from his 'abnormality', there were two problems with Kromoredjo. The first was that he was nervous speaking, and the second was that his Indonesian was barely comprehensible. He had a strong Bagelen accent, which often made people laugh, but he was also still extremely narrow-minded – even though he had been the leader of a workers union at the kabupaten level. Kromoredjo was the exact opposite of Supardjo P.A. whose Indonesian was excellent, and who also was clever at thinking and speaking.

At last the roll call reached barracks number IX. We were all standing alert and ready (as still as statues, arms straight at our sides with our hands as fists, and looking directly ahead). The tension was increased by the buzzing of mosquitoes around our ears and by the heat and gnats that could bite right through our khaki.

We had passed test number one. When Supardjo P.A.'s face was illuminated by the lamp and the guard stood before him, he was able to shout out his number, 'eight' loud and clear, even though mumbling was P.A's speciality! Then, in front of Kromoredjo, the roll call train suddenly stopped short. The consonant 'd' (for the word *dua*, two) seemed to be stuck in his throat.

The entire barracks was silent. At almost the same moment that the Commander roared and the platoon guard's hand was ready to strike Kromoredjo's cheek, he managed to yell, '*d…d…d…dua likur!*' Using the Javanese way of counting, meaning twenty-two, which in Indonesian is *dua puluh dua*.

And at the same moment, we heard Supardjo P.A. explode in laughter. Even though he tried desperately to stifle his mouth with his two hands, but nothing could stop it.

'Who was that?' roared the Platoon Commander.

He began to walk over to Supardjo.

'Pak. No. He can't help it. He's like that.'

'Like this?' the Commander said, doing the 'mad person' signal as he put his index finger askew on his forehead.

'Pikiran Abnormal, Pak' chimed in Supardjo himself.

'What?' the Platoon Commander roared even louder.

'He's mad, Pak', Irawan answered, just as loud.

The barracks was silent. So too the barracks on either side, numbers eight and ten. They could hear what was going on and were waiting to hear what would happen next. The prisoners waited for punishment, and the Platoon Commander was finding the way to declare his power.

'On the ground, all of you!' he ordered.

And we all immediately lay prone in the stinking muck.

'Push-ups!'

And we all did push-ups.

First Night Roll Call

The guards with the lamp and the carbine did their rounds. They checked the movements of fifty prisoners doing push-ups. If there was anyone not doing them properly, they would give him a kick or tread on his back pushing him into the muck. But the push-up punishment finally ended. That was when Aki Aminto Kemo, the oldest prisoner who came from Indramayu, and Mang Sadli, a prisoner with TB who came from Subang, fell on their backs unable to move any more.

Chapter 11

FIRSTS AT UNIT XIV BANTALAREJA

The tolls of the bell on the first evening were over. We had got through the first roll call in our barracks. Not to mention the first group punishment when our unfortunate fellow inmate, Kromoredjo, had yelled out his number in Javanese instead of Indonesian.

We had all stifled our laughter. Including me. The way we did that was by straightening our necks, and pulling in our chins. All of us at Buru had to learn certain techniques of stifling a laugh, a cough, or a fart. As the famous Javanese poem, *Wulangreh*, says, we had to train our spiritual and physical skills (*ngelmu* and *laku*). The poem's author says that you can only gain spiritual control once you have mastered the physical.

Political prisoners became masters at both, thanks to being forged in situations of emergency and under the constant threat of punishment. Living among many other people could produce unpredictable things. And those unpredictable things could make those who saw, heard or felt them react spontaneously. Meanwhile, the 'other side', namely the soldiers and unit authorities, were of course always on the lookout for reasons to indulge their anger. For instance, in the early hours of the morning after roll call, we had to all go quickly to our appointed workplaces. As we walked past the guard post at the front, it might happen that a prisoner coughed or sneezed. He could be called up by the guard on duty and accused of insulting or deliberately startling the guard. After the sinner had been given the required beating, all those who had been walking behind him were given group punishment; push-ups, made to box one another, or do 'duck-walking'.

Sometimes it was even sillier. It would still be morning, before the heat set in. The group of prisoners would be walking to their workplaces, having almost navigated the guard post, when they thought someone ahead in the line had begun running. Actually it often happened that the guards on duty at the guard post – for whatever reason – would order the prisoners to run as they went past the guard post. Thinking that was the case, the prisoners behind would begin to run too. Chaos! The guards became startled and angry and stopped the movement by firing their carbines into the air. The prisoners were ordered to line up, stand at attention in front of the guard post, and await their punishment.

To the guards, political prisoners were more interesting than buffalo and cattle are to farmers, for apart from being work equipment, they were also playthings. Buffalo and cattle, however, are the farmers' faithful work companions, are fed well, and when they are out working in the fields are lulled with songs and poetry as the farmers lead them with the plough.

But back now to the disaster of the first night's roll call. After Supardjo P.A was unable to stifle his laughter and we were all punished with push-ups, finally it came to an end.

'Get up' the roll-caller ordered. And we all stood.

As we dripped with the filthy, stinking cold water, we all stood to attention and listened to our first briefing from the Platoon Commander. The briefing consisted of a list of prohibitions and rules; do this, do that, don't do this, don't do that.

'Attention', he yelled. 'We are telling you "gentlemen". Don't you even think of waking a sleeping tiger. Guns can talk. Understand?'

'Understand!' we all yelled in reply.

Yelling replies in this way was the etiquette of underlings towards their bosses in the soldier world. You copied the word exactly as it had been uttered, and yelled back in the loudest voice you had.

'That is rule number one!' he went on. 'Rule number two. You are forbidden from talking in languages. Understand?'

'Understand!' we yelled back in chorus, even though actually we had no idea what he meant by 'languages' (*bahasa-bahasa*). Only later did we get to know that it meant regional Indonesian languages. We were not allowed to speak any regional language, but only the national language, Indonesian.

'Rule number three!' he continued. 'After roll call, the head of the barracks must meet the Unit Commander. Briefing! Any of you who report to the Unit Commander about your things, like shoes, clothes, sandals, rings, watches or other stuff that you handed over to the guards at Namlea will know the consequences. Get it?'

'Get it …!' replied the choir, but the lyrics had changed. 'Understand' had become 'Get it'.

Exhausted and tense as I was, I remembered. In the late afternoon of August 17, 1971, in the transit barracks at Jiku Kecil, many guards had come in and out of our barracks. They lay around and offered us cigarettes of 'black tobacco' that the prisoners found so tempting, then chatted about this and that, full of smiles. None of us knew that all this was actually like the old proverb 'crabs lie under rocks'. After about 30-40 minutes of chatting, the crabs suddenly leapt out from behind the rock. To honour the day of Indonesia's proclamation of independence, they said, they wanted to look their best for the ceremony tomorrow.

Patriotic, right? Therefore, they said, they would like to borrow this or that from us. After the ceremony was over, they would give the things back. Makes sense, right? After all, those who borrow always return things when they say so.

The roll call guards had left our barracks. We were free of disaster for the moment. The prisoners on kitchen duty arrived with five kettles of hot tea. The aluminium mugs, gifts of the state which had been distributed at Tanjung Priok harbour, now came out of our packs. Under the flickering light of two weak bulbs that were like the light from a lighthouse seen from afar, we enjoyed our first hot tea on Buru island. It tasted mouldy but at least it was hot, and this helped lessen our exhaustion and anxiety.

'Food…!' yelled Pardimin.

Pardimin was a young prisoner from Tangerang who didn't care that his feet were filthy and wet, but just lay down in his place near the back door to the barracks. Earlier in the evening, I had seen how fit he was. He was like a monkey when he heard a friend shout 'Snake! Snake!' While taking off his belt, he climbed to the top of a pole and dangled from the rafters. A python about as thick as one's big toe was crawling down the roof, and he whipped it with his belt. When the snake fell, Pardimin jumped down. He grabbed the snake just under the head with one hand, and with the other, he gave the body of the snake a sudden jerk. Immediately the snake coiled on Pardimin's arm and then collapsed, dead.

When the roll call was over and the three roll-calling guards had left the barracks, we sat on our platforms, dangling our feet. Worn out.

'Won't be long now', shouted Tarzan, the head of kitchen duty, answering Pardimin's yell.

'Better not!' came the voice of Mustihar Umar, in his strong Betawi-Malay accent.

Meanwhile, Irawan and Heru were busy talking together by the front door to the barracks. It must be about the briefing at the Commander's quarters, I thought. I heard that one of the matters at hand was naming our barracks.

But there were still three more agenda items before we could sleep. First: eat; second, final roll call; and third, and most important, listen to the news about the briefing of the heads of all ten barracks with the Unit Commander.

'*Kawan-kawan!*'

This was the first time I had heard this term of address, meaning 'comrade' or 'friend' used publicly for a long time. At Salemba prison it was replaced with the less political terms '*bapak*' or '*saudara*'.

'While waiting for our evening food ration, let's get to work and clean up our barracks.'

'You're joking! We're starving! Exhausted!' came the replies from here and there.

'For the sake of the health of us all', Irawan defended his order.

'The old ones can pull out the grass and weeds under the tables and sleeping platforms, and the young ones can get rid of the water …'

'Get rid of the water? Water that is still flowing?' Rohiman protested. 'And just how are we supposed to use to do that, Mr Engineer?'

'Don't you have any common sense?' Irawan replied. 'Use your mugs and bowls, of course.'

Apart from Irawan himself, Suwardi Penjol who was the candidate for unit coordinator, and the barrack's head assistant Heru Santoso, none of us wanted to follow this order.

'Heru! You organise the barracks. Penjol and I have to go to the Commander's', Irawan ordered.

'Come on, *kawan-kawan*. What are you waiting for?' Heru took up the call, seeing that we were all staying in our places.

'No point in being afraid of the mud. Tomorrow we'll work in the ricefields. It's all mud there. Heru, you take over now!' Irawan said as he left the barracks with Penjol.

'Come on now, comrades!' Heru pleaded.

He looked in my direction. Maybe he was secretly hoping that I would enthusiastically support this idea of barracks cleaning duty on that first night, and so provide an 'example' to the old and young from Tangerang.

Beneath the calm exterior, in actual fact there was a clash between the ex-Tangerang prisoners and the ex-Salemba prisoners. Of the two groups, the ex-Tangerang prisoners were mainly from the lower classes – the masses – whereas the ex-Salemba prisoners were mainly upper-middle cadres and educated city types.

'*Ayo Bung*!' Heru said, using the rousing phrase used back in the days fighting for Indonesia's independence. 'Come on, brother! We're wet and filthy, like it or not. We're in Buru now, like it or not. What are you waiting for? This is our reality now. Come on …!'

He spoke like that while setting an example. He used his bowl to scoop up water and throw it out of the barracks. And all of us reluctantly got down too and followed his example even though we had no stomach for it, and we used our mugs and bowls to scoop water. But as fast as we scooped, the water kept on flowing. The barracks floor was like a water spring. It would not stop!

Without waiting for Heru's approval, I went and joined the old men, pulling the weeds and grass out from under the tables. I did not want to use my mug and bowl for the filthy water. In the camps in Jakarta and Tangerang it used to make me furious if a cellmate took my plate to the toilet to use for washing himself. And often without even asking! It turned out that the old men were just squatting under the sleeping platform, not doing anything. I could not bring myself to pretend to be a 'good revolutionary' and do what the barracks head had ordered. If I did, it would look like I was trying to show the old ones up. But if I did nothing at all and just squatted quietly, that was also not fair to the one or two prisoners actually working. And so I moved, from one place to another, until under the dining table there were a couple of old prisoners idly pulling out some jungle grass. What I call the 'dining table' was three planks of wood on legs about a metre high, placed in the centre between the sleeping platforms on both sides. And it was not only weeds and grass growing underneath. The table legs and even the benches had sprouted shoots!

'Don't you have a bowl, Pak Hersi?' Heru asked me. To my ears, that was clearly Javanese-style criticism levelled 'politely' at someone older than oneself. Because of course he knew I had a bowl! What he meant was, 'What are you doing here with the old men?'

'Didn't you just say yourself that this is our reality now …' I replied.

'Meaning?'

'Meaning, don't just look at the reality of the muddy barracks, but take a look at the reality of the fact that we are all exhausted. Exhausted and anxious. Aren't you exhausted yourself?'

'Heru!' interrupted Rohiman, in his thick Betawi accent. 'Whose idea is this, anyway? Scrubbing this muck?'

'Putting on revolutionary airs, yeah?' Mustihar chimed in with his even stronger Betawi accent.

'Careful, Mus! Combining "putting on" with "revolutionary"!'

'Well? It's "overdose", that's what it is, Roh. Do you understand what the word "overdose" means?'

'Well, what is it? Think you're an intellectual, Mus?'

'Once a kampung boy, always a kampung boy, Roh. "Overdose" is when you should take two pills but you take six at once. And then – you can drop dead. Like us here right now.'

'Yes, Heru. Mustihar's right. This is too much. Apart from being wrecked from the push-ups, there's the walking … we're hungry. It's enough, Heru!'

Seeing that Heru was cornered, toothless Pak Aminto Kemo began to speak.

'Mas Heru', he said softly.

'What, Ki?' Heru answered him in Sundanese, using the term of address 'Ki' for grandfather. Many of the prisoners used that term for Pak Kemo, who had been a village water official in Kuningan, Cirebon, and leader of a branch of the Indonesian Peasants Front (BTI Barisan Tani Indonesia) there. Needless to say, he knew a thing or two about water and working in the fields.

'This water is not coming from inside the barracks. This is a swamp. The jungle around the barracks has not been cleared. No drains have been dug. So I think it is pointless to keep cleaning …'

Having weathered the attack from the Betawi brigade, and now with the advice from the experienced farmer Grandfather Aminto Kemo, Heru stood and took a deep breath. He went slowly to the middle of the barracks.

'My fellows' he said (using '*saudara-saudara*' now, and not the revolutionary '*kawan-kawan*'). 'Our work *corvée* for cleaning the barracks is ceased for tonight. We will continue tomorrow. I will take full responsibility to inform the barracks head that this work of drying out the barracks must be included in the work duties of the whole unit.'

'That's more like it!' a chorus of voices responded.

'That's the way!' Rohiman said. 'Why should we do it all for nothing?'

'Yes, Roh! What was it you said before, 'putting on revolutionary airs …'

Bang-bang-bang! Heru hit his fist on the table.

'That'll do! That's enough, *saudara-saudara*. The guard post will hear you, and we'll get even more punishment. Let's rest now while we wait for our food. Those who want to go to the river to bathe, carry a lamp and report to the guard. Thank you!'

'Bathe? He must be joking! Rohiman said. We'll have the next roll call in a moment!'

'More push-ups,' came the hoarse voice of Pardjo P.A., which the rest answered with laughter.

The last roll call on that first night went smoothly. Pak Kromoredjo spent the three hours before it memorising 'twenty-two' in Indonesian. *'Dua puluh dua,* he practised so he would not say *'dua likur'*. And he learnt how to shout out the number so that he would not get suddenly nervous again. We hoped that the guard doing the roll call would do it in the same order as in the evening, namely from the far left corner with Sugiri and then progressing in order, and that he would not do it in reverse, or start from behind. We were longing for the bell for sleep.

Meanwhile, the barracks heads had been authorised by the Unit and Platoon Commanders to tell us what had gone on in the briefing. 'Briefing' meant no more than being told the work schedule for the following day, so in actual fact it was the same as the briefing from the guard at the end of roll call. The guard would give a thousand rules and prohibitions. 'Don't do this'. 'Don't do that'. The Unit Commander

Firsts at Unit XIV Bantalareja

would give a thousand commands. 'Do this'. 'You must do that'. Their rules and commands could not be questioned in any way. For instance: when the morning bell was struck five times all prisoners had to get up, have breakfast and be ready for roll call. All prisoners, except those on general kitchen duty, or on kitchen duty in the wisma and the guards' mess, had to be at their workplace at 6 am. During work hours, the barracks had to be empty. All mosquito nets had to be folded. No sick prisoners could remain in the barracks. Not going to work because of sickness had to have the approval of the Unit Commander and the health official. During the break from 12:00-13:00, prisoners had to remain at their workplaces until the signal for 'finish work' was given … and on, and on, and on …!

Not long after receiving this gift of briefing notes from the wisma, we heard the bell ordering us to sleep. That meant that from that moment on there was to be no more talking, and no-one was permitted to leave the barracks without carrying a lamp and reporting to the guards.

On that first night not a single one of us went to bathe. It was too late. And anyway, the barracks and the unit complex were still jungle, bushes and swamp, making it paradise for mosquitoes and gnats. Probably snakes, scorpions and centipedes as well. Within the barbed-wire enclosure of the unit there was no well or bathing place. Our bathing place was the open air, a little creek behind the unit. This shallow creek, called Wai Tui, did not even come up halfway to our knees, and it barely flowed because the water was stopped by the swamp and by the slight slope of the land.

After we changed into dry clothes that we had in our rucksacks, and put up our mosquito nets, we all threw ourselves down. Crept in behind the mosquito net and the oppression of power. On that first night, how keenly we felt that the beautiful and costly value of freedom was far, far out of reach. All that remained were images of difficulty and impossibility, leaping in unrestrained sounds as we slept. Sighs and moans could be heard from that side and this: 'owww ...' *'Astagfirullah*! ...' My entire body felt pain. All my joints and muscles went into spasms.

The unit was totally quiet.

Through the cracks in the thatched-leaf roof I could see stars twinkling. Like the winking eyes of a lonely land. I could not sleep. The snores and grunts from here and there seemed to be in competition, snatching whatever freedom and peace they could. A fragment of opportunity entered in the dreams of night. Night dreams in the middle of a world full of prohibitions.

Chapter 12

TALES OF UNIT XIV BANTALAREJA CLUSTERS

Words are like money. Apart from having intrinsic value, money has market value. The intrinsic value is the value intended by those who make or distribute money, as is written in ciphers and letters on the money itself. The market value, however, is the value given the money by the 'market', beyond the intention of the makers, as the product of negotiation between supply and demand. It is not written on the money. And so it is with words, which always have two meanings. There is the literal meaning of words, which can be compared to the intrinsic value of money; and there is the social value of words, which can be compared to the market value of money.

According to its literal meaning, the Indonesian word *'gundukan'* means a 'pile' or 'stack' or other synonyms for 'clump', 'accumulation', or 'group'. It is from that last synonym that the word in Buru prisoner parlance took on its social meaning, and more sharply still, its social meaning with political overtones. It came to mean the same as 'cell', meaning the smallest part of an organism, and in this sense 'organism' included 'organisations'.

Back in Jakarta in the 'cat-and-mouse' time after the bloody events of 30 September 1965, I was not familiar with the term *gundukan*. Back then we used the terms 'group' (*grup*) or 'network' (*jaringan*). The word 'cell' (*sel*) was not common. This was probably a deliberate avoidance, because the conspiratorial connotations were extremely sensitive, and could also be associated with images of 'cells' in prison.

So the terms 'group' and 'network' arose, 'one-three-one-three-one ...' and so on, as a link of chains. Because of the effective New Order strategy of 'use a thief to catch a thief', coupled with increasingly savage acts of repression, this strategy of one-three-one proved to be the most secure form of organising underground opposition. The kind of 'if one dies, everyone dies' spirit we knew of Diponegoro's soldiers, and which were familiar from performances of traditional theatre, took on ironic forms like 'if one gets caught, all get caught' or 'if one gets caught, all disband'.

The network system 1-3-1 was discarded around the time of the South Blitar movement in 1966. The underground resistance movement found a new form, 'one-one-one' for its linking chains. We called this system 'frogs' eggs' and it was devised to limit the number of victims. If one person was captured, tortured, and then 'squealed', he or she could not name two others of the group, but only one other person.

But in response to this new network system, the New Order increased its repression, and at the same time intensified its strategy of 'using a thief to catch a thief'. It brings to mind the strategy of the Dutch Captain Tack when he faced the staunch opposition of Diponegoro's soldiers by strengthening his 'fortress system' while spreading the net as wide as possible to bring in 'thieves' at the top – including netting Kiai Mojo, Basah Sentot and Gus Tasripin who ended up as a big landowner in East Semarang.

And the number of G30S 'thieves' that the New Order Intelligence netted kept getting bigger. Bigger in terms of number, but also bigger in position as 'big shot' thieves, from Suyono Pradigdo from the Party

Central Committee, right down to the small-fry who ... *astaghfirullah al-azim* ... were countless in number, from party circles and from its mass organisations! I would say that every prisoner who was caught alive in, say, the first month after the 'incident', had in their memory lists of names of 'thieves'. I am not exaggerating when I say that a very large number of the victims of the G30S incident – including victims who died as well as those imprisoned and exiled – actually were victims of the behaviour of their fellow 'thieves' or comrades.

The irony of 'one gets caught, all get caught' then took on a more real form: we called it 'train carriages' (*sepur-sepuran*). We called it that because like a series of train carriages, the one in front pulls along all the others linked behind it, one after another. So punishment imposed upon them was 'train-carriage punishment', or 'chain punishment'. If one got it, everyone did.

Indonesia's political stage turned into the stage of a *wayang* play. The story performed was a new play from the episode '*Pendhawa Tundhung*'. One person gambles and loses, namely Yudhistira, and his four brothers and their mother are equally punished. They are all exiled (*tundhung*) from the kingdom of Indraprasta for thirteen years, with the heavy imposition that they had to discard all signs of their identities.

It was only after failure upon failure, every time paid for dearly, that we arrived at the organisational structure for a way of working that was called 'organisation without structure' (*organisasi tak berbentuk*). It was a way of organising and working that was extremely easy to say, but extremely difficult to put into practice, because even the phrase itself is a contradiction in terms.

The word 'organisation' has at its root the word 'organ', or body. The body is a vessel. Its spirit has no form. But how can that be in the physical body? Maybe this was the context of meaning that people used to understand or interpret a phrase from one of the countless sayings of Bung Karno; 'to commemorate something is to understand and light a fire of that something'. He went on, 'therefore don't just pick up its ashes now and then, even if you want to put those ashes in a golden vase.'

An organisation without structure should be interpreted as no longer about restoring or reviving form, but rather perpetuating the spirit or fire anywhere and at any time. Because it is the 'spirit' that is important, not the body. Because the spirit never dies, whereas the body knows only death. *Ars longa vita brevis*, the saying goes. In the words of Ki Hadjar Dewantara:

> 'All full, correct understandings about an endeavour can be recognised with four measures, namely; its nature and its form, its contents and its rhythm or way of carrying it out. Of those, the only one that cannot change is its 'nature', because this is the basis of its point of departure, its foundation, its essence; whereas its 'form', not to mention its 'contents' and 'rhythm' must always be adjusted according to the times and in normal conditions they are continuously changing.' (*Taman Siswa 30 Tahun 1922-1952*, 1956:53)

* * *

The 850 of us from Salemba and Tangerang prisons, arrived at Namlea on August 12, 1971. From the 850 men, 500 were taken to Unit XIV Bantalareja, and the remaining 350 to Unit XV Indrapura. A few months later another group of prisoners arrived, which was also divided into two upon their arrival at Namlea. Some of them were sent to Unit XV which only had 350 prisoners, and the remainder were sent to a new unit, Unit XVI Indrakarya.

Because of the way the prisoners were distributed, the barracks I was in, Unit XIV Bantalareja, was dubbed the 'pure Jakarta' unit. The day-to-day language among prisoners in my unit was Betawi Malay. In Unit IV Savanajaya, where the prisoners had come from camps in central Java, the day-to-day language among prisoners was everyday common (*ngoko*) Javanese. The Unit XV Indrapura was different again. The prisoners there came from West Java and Banten, and so the usual language was Sundanese. The Unit III Wanayasa was different. The majority of prisoners there came from camps in East Java, so the prisoners usually spoke East Javanese Surabaya dialect among themselves. But these patterns of daily language lived only within the barbed-wire compounds, and not beyond, for instance in the Commander's quarters (the *wisma*) or the guards' mess.

The wisma housed the high officials, namely the Commander and the Deputy Commander, the head of health, the head of agriculture, and the head of stores. The first three were all Javanese, and the other two, Ambonese. Combined with the Platoon Commander and deputy Platoon Commander, who were also Ambonese, there were only four non-Javanese officials. The officials spoke Indonesian with each other. This was very different from the scenario among prisoners. For example, one day when I eavesdropped on a conversation between the prisoner Alexander Syamon (deceased) from Manado who lived in Jakarta for years, and Christian Tambayong, a mixed-blood Belgian-Manado prisoner who before his capture had lived for years in Malang and Surabaya, it turned out they were speaking in an East Java dialect of Javanese.

So it seemed that the language used 'over there' at the front of the camp followed the line of power – because among them, the Unit Commander was the one with the most power. This meant that the language patterns moving on down to the lower levels followed the top. But 'over there' behind the barbed wire, there was not a system of top and bottom or high and low ranks, so the language patterns tended to follow the habits of social intercourse, where the group feeling itself in the minority adapted to the group seen as bigger or the biggest. On that basis, if indeed this is what was going on, then the 'strong theory' in culture (which can of course be applied to matters of language) that says that 'the culture of a people or society in any one period is the culture of the class that rules over that people or society at that time', actually turns out to be too narrow as a measure. For in each of those two groups, the inter-prisoner group within the barbed wire and the inter-ruler group outside of it, the matter of class did not come into it at all. There was only the matter of structure. Within the prisoner group, the structural division was the majority group and the minority group, and in the governing group, it was high ranking and low ranking.

So perhaps the principle above can be given a wider and more 'fluid' variant, namely that 'culture is subservient to structure'. But the structural groups were not made up of class, and therefore not charged with ideology and politics, so they did not get called '*gundukan*' according to the understanding outlined above. There was never any mention of the 'Betawi *gundukan*', the 'Sunda *gundukan*', the 'Jawa *gundukan*' or the Manado *gundukan*'.

There was an occasion in our unit when the 'seven earth *gundukan*' caused disaster for its inhabitants, specifically for one called Sawal. This disaster was hurled by the 'group over there', outside the barbed wire, at the 'group here', behind the barbed wire. The punishment was imposed by the group structurally powerful but without culture, upon those culturally powerful; but not structurally powerful, by the 'group that won' upon the 'group that lost' including various political *'gundukan'* within.

Sawal was a young prisoner from Tangerang prison, a member of barracks number five in our unit. He was small in stature with a child-like face, and he was always quiet. Once he started working, you could not stop him. Perhaps he also had some mental disability, although not as pronounced as Supardjo P.A.

When I later moved to Unit XV Indrapura in 1974, there was another prisoner who was mentally disturbed. Tardjo was his name. The head of his barracks put him on kitchen duty. He was a quiet young man, and diligent. He had a strange habit. When he saw a cassava leaf that was turning yellow or had gone dry but was still attached to the plant, he would pick it and put it beneath the plant, with his mouth twisting and turning all the while. Perhaps he was saying a prayer to the plant, because he knew that fifty inmates depended on this very plant.

Sawal had a different habit. He didn't sing as Supardjo did, and he paid no attention to leaves turning yellow falling back to earth. What you would hear him muttering was the Lord's Prayer. For Sawal was a Protestant.

One day, the Platoon Commander ordered him to make a 'flower garden' in front of the mess. He had to do this from the afternoon until evening, after his work cooking in the kitchen was over. After a few days of working hard by himself, the flower garden was completed. There were a few mounds of earth planted with flowers that he had got from around the unit, and there were wild orchids hanging from the fence poles. He had built the fence from some pieces of bamboo to prevent the chickens from getting in and ruining the garden.

Suddenly, one evening, after the bell to signal the end of work, there was another bell signal – the repeated toll, which meant danger! This signalled an order for all prisoners to gather at once in the yard, and line up in groups according to their respective barracks. When we got there, all the top brass of the unit were already there facing us. Sawal was standing in front of them. Bare-chested, his head bowed, with black eyes and his face swollen and bruised. He looked utterly exhausted. It was clear he had just been beaten black and blue. And it was clear, too, that this was why we had all been summoned.

While we were secretly questioning what all this could be about, the Platoon Commander's voice yelled in anger. With two guards at his side he marched barracks by barracks to the area in front of the guards' mess, and ordered us to look carefully at the flower garden that Sawal had made.

'And what do you see here?' he yelled once we were all assembled.

We were all quiet.

'Are you deaf? Raise your hand. Who knows …?!'

Even more quiet. Probably my fellow prisoners, like me, were working out where this questioning was going.

'Hey you, Coordinator!' he yelled at Basuki Effendy. 'Speak up. Now!'

Basuki Effendy, who also did not understand the point of the question, said what he saw. There were mounds of earth planted with all kinds of flowers, and a neat bamboo fence …

'Shut up! Liar! Communist scum!'

'How many mounds are there?' piped in the head of agriculture, who never went anywhere without his carbine on his shoulder.

Basuki Effendy did not reply. We were all quiet too. Not a single one of us counted the mounds. What was the point of counting them?

'Sawal. Answer! How many mounds did you make?' Now it was the health officer's turn. He was a young man from Semarang who did not want to miss the opportunity to show his power.

This health officer, who claimed to be a student in the medical faculty of Diponegoro University, had skills at about the level of the medicine sellers in the town square in Yogyakarta, who I used to see every day back when I walked to junior high school. He had one kind of medicine that he claimed to be a cure-all. The difference was that the medicine seller in the square had a few black pills, whereas Mr Health Officer had his fist.

'What's wrong with you?' He would ask the prisoner who had come to the clinic asking for medicine.

'It's my stomach, sir', the prisoner would answer politely.

'Stand up!' Mr Health Officer would order.

The prisoner would stand, and receive a series of punches on his stomach from Mr Health Officer.

'Please stop! It hurts!', the prisoner would howl.

'Oh still hurts, does it?' the officer would say, and continue his treatment. The prisoner, aware now that the word 'hurt' was inviting trouble, would change his approach.

'Stop, sir! It's not hurting any more!'

'Off to work with you. Right now. Even buffaloes work if they want to eat. Understand?' And the prisoner would run off to his workplace.

It was the same when prisoners came complaining of headaches. He would hit their head until the prisoner was forced to say:

'It's gone! No headache any more!' And now nursing an even worse headache the prisoner would run to his workplace.

Health officers expert in curing all illnesses without using medicine apart from his fists and commands were found in other units too. Or at least I know it was the case in Unit III Wanayasa. I know this from something that happened to a close friend of mine, Drs Dilar Darmawan, an alumini from Gadjah Mada University who had been in the leadership of the Solo branch of the Association of Indonesian Graduates (HIS, Himpunan Sarjana Indonesia). He was a lecturer at Saraswati University which was taken over by the New Order and renamed Universitas Sebelas Maret (University of 11 March).

He suffered from malarial fever and also had tuberculosis. When he went to the polyclinic suffering from chills and fever, the health officer prescribed for him the medicine of running laps around the prison yard, which was more than a hectare in area. He was not allowed to stop until his chills stopped. But Dilar was so weak that he had not even got halfway around his first lap before he collapsed. He was taken to hospital and did not leave his bed until the time when the second influx of prisoners from Java arrived in Buru.

The Three Heavies dragged Sawal before the flower garden he had made himself. The Platoon Commander with his fancy command stick, the agriculture officer who always carried his carbine, and the health officer who used his fists as a cure-all. They ordered Sawal to count the number of mounds.

'Seven, Sir!'

'Why are there seven?'

He did not answer. It was of course because the stretch of earth there only allowed for seven mounds. But he could not explain, especially because he did not understand the point of the question. And it was not that Sawal was not quite the full pound, even we had no idea why the number seven had set off the fuse of this evening's summons. What we then saw was Sawal being made the sacrificial feast for the three top-ranking unit officials. The commando's staff beat down upon him at the same time as he was showered with fists on his bare chest and prodded with the rifle. Sawal collapsed.

'There are seven mounds of earth!' shrieked the health officer after the three of them stood in front of us again.

'And what is the number seven?'

Silence. We were silently asking ourselves that question. We did not understand what the number meant. Not like the number 'three', which we had known for a long time was taboo. This word was supposed to signify the 'Three Flames of the Party' (Tripanji Partai), a Communist Party work program that made the New Order tremble.

'Liars, all of you! Liars!' The health officer yelled even louder. 'That is the number of generals, our heroes, who you lot murdered at Crocodile Hole'.

We went even more silent. Now we were beginning to understand what all this accusation of being liars was about. Especially that medical student from Diponegoro University, who we had hoped would enlighten us. It turned out that it was actually him who had dreamed up this interpretation of the 'symbolic meaning' of Sawal's flower garden.

'Watch it! Don't you lot even think of trying us!' the Platoon Commander went on. 'Just try it, and you're dead, the whole lot of you!'

We were dismissed.

That evening the coordinator was ordered to demolish Sawal's flower garden in front of the guards' mess, which he had completed just that day. Sawal was taken off to the hospital. Apart from the bruising all over his body, one of his ribs was shattered.

**

I had met Musayid one day back in the cat-and-mouse days in Jakarta, after the bloody events of 30 September 1965. Before that, when I had been head of the Central Java branch of Lekra, Musayid had been the 'second man' in the Party leadership for the province. When the 'first man' graduated and was moved up to the centre in Jakarta, Musayid took over his position. Our meeting took place on the banks of the Ciliwung River, at the edge of the Kebon Baru kampung beside Jalan Gatot Subroto heading towards Cawang.

Among the things we talked about was his sense of shame because after all this time he had not been taken in. He was well aware of his own prestige, and this made him uncomfortable. While his 'underlings' had been scooped up everywhere, he who had been the provincial head was still free. He didn't say 'not captured', he said 'not yet captured'.

'How do I appear to you now?' He asked me. 'How is it that I am living free? Do I no longer look red?'

I laughed. 'Isn't that a good thing?' I said. 'They say there are wise words from the Chinese experience. At times like this, we should be like the watermelon. Outside green, but still red on the inside.'

'That's right. But I still want to know. What do people think of me now? Do they think I still look red or not? What do you think?'

'How can I think anything? We've only met twice. And anyway, what does it matter what people think?'

I finished talking with a laugh. But maybe it was precisely that laugh that made him think I was hiding something about what I thought of him. He wanted to know what I knew about what people were saying about him. That he was trading in batik cloth together with Rantiyem, that he had a young wife and about their child who was born in hiding … but all of this I only heard much, much later from Doctor Djayus who had been together with him in Nusakambangan prison, and who told me when I visited him at his house in Ambarawa.

So the essence of what Musayid was talking about was his sense of shame. Because he thought that in the eyes of the Intelligence he did not look red. And more ashamed because he thought this was the case in the eyes of his fellow comrades. But to me, the question was, why did this sense of shame arise in him? Did it arise in the form of his awareness of his responsibility as head of an organisation? Or did it arise as the effect of awareness of the morals and behaviour, good and bad, of the members of the organisation – including taking responsibility versus washing one's hands, a sense of discipline versus just letting things be, a sense of service versus personal ambition, and so on?

Organisations linked to political parties, like those linked to the Indonesian Communist Party, are not organisations like sports clubs or neighbourhood gatherings, where people can enter and exit as they please. Nor are they like other political organisations, which are established only to grab power. The organisations linked to the Indonesian Communist Party were established upon a basis of ideology, like religious or faith-based organisations. This kind of organisation, or at least as I think they should be, must prioritise the business of, as the Bible says, 'building heaven on earth and the kingdom in heaven.'

But I could also see that on the other side, because of their conviction, political party organisations with such ideological foundations could become closed. As a condition of entry you have to take vows, make an oath of allegiance, or be baptised. Probably it is this closed nature of the organisation that makes people feel ashamed towards other members once they leave the organisation, or even look different from the others. When Mao Zedong took to wearing a closed blue jacket, hundreds of millions of people in the People's Republic of China did the same. When the 'progressives' in Jakarta censured long hair, then all the young men in the large community of 'progressives' neatly shaved and cut their hair!

I used to have neighbours who lived across from me in my kampung in Yogyakarta. It was a husband and wife (when will that common phrase ever be reversed to 'wife and husband'?), Kariyo Tukiyur and Kariyo Ijah. When times were good for them, as good Catholics they regularly attended mass. When times turned bad for them, which began during the Japanese occupation, they no longer set foot inside a church.

'Why don't you go to church any more, Aunty? I asked Ijah one day as we sat under the rose apple tree in our yard.

'Ah, I am ashamed. Could I visit the Lord naked like this?' she said, while feeding the young child sitting on her knee.

Ijah's usual clothes were her bodice and an old wrap-around cloth. 'Wash and wear', the kampung people would joke, meaning you washed your clothes and put them back on as soon as they were dry. Her husband, Tukiyur, did the same. He wore knee-length baggy black trousers. They were good for climbing up on his neighbours' roofs to solder their gutters when they leaked. They were good to wear when digging graves for neighbours who died. They were good to wear when he cradled his children to sleep with lullabies.

'What do you mean, ashamed?' I said. 'The Lord Jesus does not look at your clothes.'

'I'm not talking about the Lord Jesus!' she replied. 'It's the congregation. Who would want to sit next to me? They would all scatter. I would scatter. The priest would probably scatter too …'

I thought she was right.

Probably it was because of this same kind of shame that, in the early months of being in Unit XIV at Bantarareja, without giving it deeper thought, I quickly became involved in 'activities' of two political groups. Our unit, as I have already said, was known as the 'pure Jakarta unit'. The majority of the inmates were still young, under 35 years of age. The criteria of 'old and young' referred to the standards used by the management of Buru 'Resettlement Plan', who recruited political prisoners for labour on the sago swamps and the eucalyptus and meranti tree savanna.

The majority of these young prisoners were from Tangerang prison, and as a result of their experience there and since, they had lost faith in organisations and in the leadership figures. Their cynicism was shown in the way they changed the words of H.R. Bandaharo's poem 'and no-one wanted to return home' to 'and everyone wanted to return home'. When 'solidarity' was mentioned, for instance about sharing food sent by families, they would respond yelling 'solidarity is over!' They labelled the prisoners from Salemba 'intellectuals' or 'upper class' or 'leaders', showing how fed up they were with anything to do with organisations and with the ways that organisation leaders worked in the past.

Over the eight-day sea journey from Jakarta to Namlea, the young prisoners appeared busy indeed. Wandering from here to there, passing information on this and that, making 'lines' about what would have to be done later on, taking control of the kitchen, serving the food and drink rations and so on. Some others were busy 'pilfering' whatever they could from the storerooms for the 'rehabilitation' of the old and sick. Meanwhile, the older prisoners, most of whom came from Salemba prison, mostly kept quiet and bided their time, and many of them just sat cross-legged in their assigned places lamenting their fate.

But compared to the problems faced over a few days at sea, those faced in the unit were not only much more numerous, they were also much more complex. They could not be overcome by just the energy of youth, dexterity and daring. The work of organisation was not just the task of seeing who had the most strength and daring. The young

Tangerang inmates got to realise that 'brain' and 'brawn' had to work together. And so collaboration developed between the younger ones, regardless of which prison they had come from. I saw that there was a tendency for the 'upper class' Salemba prisoners to become dominant, even though the 'old ones' were still marginalised. This, of course, was because, as I have already said, most of the Tangerang prisoners were from the masses, who were indeed more skilled in practical work. The organisation of the 'illegal' party within the Tangerang prison, which relied on the strength of the young group, seemed to have been incapable of, or had neglected to develop their organisational skills as cadres. I think this was why, when we arrived at the unit, these young Tangerang prisoners went back to doing their own thing at the bottom, as workers with agility and skill but not many were capable of leading. The young prisoners from Salemba, however, were more experienced.

Take my own barracks, Barracks IX. The barracks head and deputy head were Bambang Irawan and Soleh Amat. Irawan was a young prisoner from Salemba. Soleh Amat, who was around my age, was also from Salemba. Irawan had been in the central leadership of the Motor Vehicle Workers Union (SBKB, Serikat Buruh Kendaraan Bermotor). The unit coordinator, Suwardi Penjol, also from my unit, was a young prisoner from Salemba. The deputy coordinator Aziz Belong, from barracks X was one of the young men from Tangerang; the prisoner in charge of unit affairs, Purnomo (Pung) from Barracks VIII, was also a young man from Tangerang. Penjol had been in the leadership of IPPI central Jakarta, Aziz had been in the leadership of CGMI for East Java, and Pung had been a member of the leadership of the Yogyakarta branch of CGMI.

The 'old' group, meanwhile, who were marginalised from discussions, just took the attitude of wait and see. They kept a low profile.

Or at least this became their defence against attacks of being 'hungry to lead', and was also a tactic to restore the confidence of the young ones. But of course, they were not just like cats waiting to catch mice, sitting quietly in the corner of the room while they sharpened their gaze and pulled in their claws. Secretly, the prominent old cadres were employing the 'classic method' of personal approach first, a method called 'breaking in'. They were not uncomfortable with this term, which compared the potential cadre still to be broken in, with virgin soil that had to be ploughed or a virgin to be seduced. It is another example of how a word with social meaning can take on socio-political meaning.

'Bung!' Kadis Margono said to me one day. He was in the same barracks as me. I had known him for a long time, since we had both been involved in Central Java branches of mass organisations in Semarang. I was leading Lekra, and he was leading SOBSI. Later, I moved to Colombo to the Asia-Africa Writers Bureau and he moved to Jakarta as one of the leaders of the central national board of SOBSI.

'Those young ones will come back to us older ones soon enough. Who else will they have to turn to when the time comes?' he whispered conspiratorially.

'Like what?'

'Penjol has started talking to me a lot. That is why I feel I need you now.'

What was this game he was playing, I wondered. 'Well, if I can help. What, do you need precisely?' I asked.

'Penjol has left it to me to organise. But Irawan would be better. Irawan was your former student at Taman Siswa, wasn't he? As for his deputy, even though he used to be in Lekra Semarang, that can be me. Both of us are from labour union backgrounds.'

I kept quiet.

'What we have to organise here is the agricultural work', I finally said. 'Our Tangerang comrades are experienced in this. As for me, I have no experience at all. So am I needed at all?'

'Of course you are!'

'For what?'

'Well, for work morale. So we work together as one. Should we give it our all to make the program succeed, or work in a limited way, meaning we just do the required work quota, or should we do all-out sabotage? And we haven't yet discussed the matter of 'self-criticism' sessions.'

'Whoa there! Leave all that self-criticism stuff to the ones not in prison. I don't think this is the time or place. It will only give rise to conflict between us, and the danger is too great if the authorities hear us.'

'Alright then. We'll forget about self-criticism. But what about our stand? You must have heard already what is going on at Unit II. Nurjaslan has composed a march called *'Bapreru* March' (Buru Resettlement March) to fire up enthusiasm to make the work project a success. You must know him. He's a Lekra man. And as you yourself are from Lekra, you know better than I do about the power of songs …'

I was surprised when the word 'Lekra' was uttered that way as a challenge to me. I felt insulted. I looked Kadis Margono in the eye.

'What do you mean, linking the *'Bapreru* March', Nurjaslan and Lekra and then talking to me about it? Are you expecting me to share the blame for his sins? Surely you have heard about our last day at Tangerang? Bung Ripto, who is also from Lekra, and I composed a song 'Rucksack March'. Do you remember? So don't go lumping us all together for 'punishment'. That's the first thing. The second thing is this. You can drop all those old judgements that Lekra is a nest of liberal cadres ...'

'But this is something that involves us all, isn't it?'

'That's right. But the way I see it, the issue of responsibility for the stand to be taken is every individual's affair. We can insist on responsibility later on, at the right time. When we are all outside, if there is a chance, and more importantly, if there's any point in talking about it ...'

'Very well. But actually what I meant was talking about how we approach the work project.'

'And what are your thoughts on that?'

'Well, if we're just talking about the basics, then of course I reject the two extreme positions, namely complete sabotage and complete participation. So I think we just do the minimum. But it's not enough to just stop at that.'

'Yes!'

'So, that's our problem. How to make this middle way the way we all accept together, rejecting either of the extreme positions, without creating any open contradictions. I am asking you to help me think about this. And then there is something related, something concrete, that I need to ask your help with.'

'And what's that?'

'As someone formerly from Central Java, I think that among our unit inmates you are the only one who has many friends and acquaintances in the neighbouring unit, Unit IV Savanajaya. Bung Sugeng is also there, who used to be with me in the regional leadership of SOBSI.'

'So you want me to contact Bung Sugeng about this'

'Yes. But not only for this. We need to know what is going on. We are just like the proverbial frogs under the coconut shell, knowing nothing of the world outside. Savanajaya has been established longer.

Maybe they have contact with the local population who listen to the news on the radio ... so I would like you to find information. So that we know what the political situation is outside ...'

He used the jargon word '*sitpol*' for 'political situation', and I inwardly laughed to hear it. How could he still believe in any news of the '*sitpol*' that was circulating in our place of exile? When we were back in Salemba prison, we had replaced that word with another, '*bom-boman*' – dropping bombs, because what was called 'information' about the '*sitpol*' was no more than a battle of gossip. One of the inmates, from his frustration and disgust at this, fashioned his own bombs and sprinkled them with sophisticated logic and analysis. Then he dropped those 'bombs' to a friend in a highly conspiratorial whisper, and sure enough the bomb about that '*sitpol*' did the prison rounds until it came back to his own ears, much elaborated. He laughed to show how his made-up '*sitpol*' was gobbled up by his fellow prisoners.

'Here it can't be like when we were in Salemba, can it?' I spontaneously replied. 'We can't go asking spirits?'

'Don't be like that ...' Kadis said, getting my mocking tone, but pretending to laugh.

'Very well. I will meet Bung Sugeng. But where and when?'

'He likes to work in the vegetable garden. The shed for that garden is near the path to the Walgan Lama kampung. It is across from our unit's plot G.'

'Oh no ... near Walgan Lama?'

'What's the matter?' He asked. He seemed to have realised my anxiety.

'That's where the guards like to walk around. I sometimes go by there on my way to the mangroves, looking for snails. Amat Jawa lives in that kampung.'

'Who is Amat Jawa?'

'According to our Unit IV friends, he's a spy. He's often hanging out with the guards.'

'But why would Sugeng point out that place to meet, if he thought it was not safe?'

I did not reply. Because that was clearly not a question to be answered. It was a 'line'. And I was a cadre being groomed. What was the point of making problems? Better to go along with it, because despite everything, I found myself interested to know more about what this 'group' of Kadis-Sugeng was up to. So to face this danger, all I could do was build up my confidence. Compared to the kampungs and the sago forests at Rawa Tui that I had already entered, the Walgan Lama kampung and path was nothing much. The thing that really had to be taken account of was the informer, Amat Jawa, who himself carried a gun. He said that early in the Pacific war he had been drafted as a soldier for the Japanese in Ambon.

'When?'

'He said on Wednesday, at midday break time'.

'Tell Penjol to arrange for the barracks head to give me work placement in plot D or E next Wednesday, and be free with the time. Give me half a day off work duties, because if the situation is unsafe it will take at least half an hour to get to the shed ...'

And this is was what happened.

From that Wednesday, and every Wednesday thereafter, I was in the 'SOBSI, Kadis-Sugeng, Bantala-Savana' group. In actual fact, it was still the same old Jakarta-Central Java group, the same one that had promoted the 'Three Flames of the Party' or 'Tripanji Partai'. It was focused on building a front whilst maintaining the order of priorities of the three principles.

After a few Wednesday meetings, I felt that I had gained nothing at all of importance. It turned out that the Savanajaya prisoners were going along in a pragmatic way as far as taking a stand towards projects and steering between the two extreme positions were concerned, without drawing conclusions. Perhaps this was the best way, because it meant no more tension between the prisoners and the probability of repression from the authorities. What I took from those Wednesday meetings was, as I had previously guessed, no more than scraps of information on the '*sitpol*', which were just intended to soothe one's dreams. News about the gathering force of the rebellion against the New Order and of the increasing power of the international communist movement.

Maybe three or four months after joining the Wednesday meetings, one evening as I walked home through the scrub a fellow Savanajaya inmate, Wahyono, stopped me. He signed to me that he wanted to meet the following Friday in the vegetable shed, but this time at Barracks IV, almost directly across from plot B of Unit XIV. Wahyono had been a participant at the Central Java branch of the Party School at provincial level (SPDB, Sekolah Partai Daerah Besar), where I was once a teacher. All those years ago I had been his teacher of theory. But now, all these years later, he was my mentor in matters of revolution in practice!

The Friday meeting went on to become a regular event. It was a group of a different nature. I called this group the 'Central Java North Coast' group. It too was promoting the same Three Party Principles, or Tripanji Partai, with the same order or priority. But for them, the principle that was mentioned most was the Armed Struggle Program (*program perjuta, program perjuangan bersenjata*). Modern revisionism, subjectivism, left and right opportunism were all attacked mercilessly, while Lenin-Stalin-Mao Zedong were praised to the hilt. Given this was their frame, apart from Nurjaslan, who was attacked as being reactionary, Sugeng and Kadis Margono were seen as modern revisionists.

'Why do you keep meeting Sugeng?' Wahyono asked me one day after we had met on Friday a few times.

'Why, does it bother you?'

'What's the point of that modern revisionist SOBSI group?'

'Well, what about your group? Can you convince me what the point of it is?'

He was silent. I was silent. I knew that both of us were irritated, and both of us were fed up. But we restrained ourselves. Nonetheless, we could not talk without shouting because suddenly it started teeming with rain. The plaited leaf roof could not keep out the rain that seemed to be poured from the sky.

After a while, when the rain still did not stop, I said I had to go. I was afraid there might be a roll call. Once the rain began to fall as heavy as this, often it did not stop for several days. But actually, aside from the fact that I thought the rain was not going to stop, nor did not want to spend a moment longer in that shed, just the two of us.

I had a feeling of unease as I left that shed. Uneasy because conflict had appeared between us, but also because I was afraid I would miss a roll call. In the middle of the incessant heavy rain, I instinctively picked two or three cassava plants. I trimmed the leafy branches and carried the sticks and the cassava on my shoulder. I did not take the 'pigs track' between the bushes, as I usually did, but walked on the main road between Savanajaya Unit and Bantalareja. This was so I could get back quickly, but also because the rain was so hard now I thought it would be safer. But, sure enough, just as I got through the Savanajaya cassava plot, a guard stepped in front of me.

'What's your unit?'

'Fourteen, Pak', I answered, shivering with cold.

'Where have you been?'

'Looking for cassava, Pak. I was hungry.'

He looked at me, half believing, half not. But because of the heavy rain, he surely understood the word 'hungry'. He was probably hungry himself, having walked about five kilometres from the Sanleko beach in the middle of the cold and rain too.

'What's your shirt number?'

I unfurled my soaking wet shirt, which I had rolled up and put on my shoulder to cushion the weight of the sticks and cassava. He took a good look at the number. He fumbled with the button on his shirt, probably wanting to take out his notebook. But his hand did not make it. Perhaps because he didn't have a notebook, or perhaps because he did not want to get soaked in the rain. He looked at my shirt number. His mouth was working.

'Let's see if you can memorise it!' I was saying secretly to myself.

We parted, continuing our journeys. The heavy rain had protected me from torture. He went on to his unit by the road. I left the road and took the 'pig track' back to the barracks. I was certain the guard would not be able to remember my number. Even so, my heart beat fast as I thought about the punishment I would get later that evening or tomorrow morning. And at the same time, I gave thanks for my instinct earlier. What would have happened if I had not been carrying the cassava? That cassava was my shield if I was called up later that evening, or tomorrow …

When I got to the barracks, I gave the three cassava plants, which weighed around 15 kilograms, to the head of the barracks. But I asked him not to cook them straight away, but to wait until it was clear whether I was going to be called up or not. That night, at around eight o'clock, after the heads of the barracks, the coordinators and the unit staff had finished their work-placement briefing and returned to their units, I met the unit coordinator, Basuki Effendy.

'Ah, so it was you the guard caught stealing cassava earlier?' he said. 'The guard reported it to the Commander.'

I laughed.

'Cut that out. You be more careful next time!'

I laughed again.

'I'm always careful. It was just bad luck. But what did the Commander say?'

'He said it was up to me to deal with the thief.'

'And then?'

'I said 'How can I do that, Pak, if I don't know which barracks he is from, and don't know the number on his shirt? Or even if he is from our unit. What if he was from another unit but just happened to be going home from his work placement? What is the point of having a roll call for five hundred prisoners over that, Pak? In this heavy rain?'

'And then?'

'Kirno said, "Okay, leave it."'

The person he was referring to was Sukirno, First Lieutenant of the Military Police, the Unit Commander.

'So, the case is closed?'

'Yes'.

I embraced him, spontaneously. And I wandered back to my barracks.

'You're a damn nuisance!' he said.

'Come on! How can someone who is just hungry be a damn nuisance' I said from the doorway.

Needless to say, I never mentioned anything about the Kadis group and the Wahyono group. If Basuki should find out at some stage, let him hear it from elsewhere. Not from me.

From that day I stopped my participation in those two groups competing for truth in a vacuum. I told Kadis Margono it was because I was intercepted by the guard and was afraid of further trouble. As for Wahyono, my colleague from Jepara branch of the Party's executive committee in Jepara, I never told him anything at all.

Actually, I could have said no to both of them, from the start. Why did I go along with them? One reason among many, if I want to be honest with myself, was that I still harboured a sense of shame. Shame as a former Lekra leader who felt his honour had been challenged. Shame as a person who felt humiliated because he was considered a coward. Shame as someone who had dared to choose a path of struggle but who was judged as having avoided responsibility.

Some years ago I presented a paper in Amsterdam and Utrech about the culture of shame as one aspect of feudal Javanese culture. A sense of shame in a negative sense. Now I see that it would be better to call this awareness of shame a sense of 'self-esteem'. The positive aspect that I think is there in every human being.

Chapter 13

TAP WATER COMES TO UNIT XV INDRAPURA

I had just recovered from illness. The usual, fever. Fever was so common that quite a few of the lazy prisoners, sometimes lazy because of their 'principles' of opposing the regime, would often use it as an excuse.

It was easy to play that game, because at the unit polyclinic there was no government doctor or health officer, and perhaps the acting agriculture officer was not up to the task of also being a doctor. Otherwise, there were only other prisoners who had been assigned nursing duties, though in earlier 'normal times' there might have been a real nurse or even a health officer in place.

Early in the morning, when the bell for roll call rang and everyone hastened to the yard, the prisoners 'putting on the fever' would stay behind. They would not roll up their mosquito nets. But other prisoners got to know the ones who sought asylum behind their mosquito nets with the word 'fever'. They referred to this with the Javanese word '*ngula*', meaning acting like a snake – clever at slipping away.

Probably because of these 'sick shows', a particular jargon arose among the prisoners on Buru. I have no idea who created the jargon. Most likely, as we would say in Lekra, it was more the product of 'communal wisdom' than the product of individual creativity. Who knows who the creator was! But in my unit, and particularly in my barracks, namely Barracks IX Unit XV Indrapura, I first heard it from Christian Tembayong, the mixed-blood Belgian-Indonesian from Malang who was previously in unit XVIII Argapura. If he – and soon all of us – saw that someone's mosquito net had not been rolled up, he would say of that person – let's call him A – 'Hey, A's shit is white'. The first sign a chicken is sick is that its shit is runny and white. If it is a rooster, then its cockscomb will go blue. So the next shout would be, 'Better check. Is his cockscomb blue?' The sick chicken, if seriously ill, will have mucus discharge from its nose and then will choke repeatedly. These are the symptoms of bird plague and it is extremely contagious, just like the human plague spread by fleas on rats – there had been an epidemic in Yogyakarta in 1947. People used to say that 'if you fell ill in the morning you would be dead by nightfall, and if you fell ill at nightfall you would be dead by morning.'

Apart from the 'white shit' phrase for those who were sick – whether pretending or not – there was another, which I also heard for the first time from the same source – the Belgian-Indonesian. The sick person was said to be 'at work' extracting sugar palm juice – the Javanese word for this work is *nderes*. This was because the barracks head would always give some palm sugar to the prisoners who were 'behind their mosquito nets' without checking whether they were really sick or just doing the snake act. For his generosity, the barracks head would later get criticised, to his face or behind his back. 'Why bother giving rehabilitation to the ones pretending to be sick. Our barracks would be none the worse if they died!'

This tradition of giving palm sugar to the sick had actually begun in prison before we came to Buru. Consciously or not, this was an example of good practice of solidarity between comrades. Or, if not between comrades, between human beings. Because we had absolutely no medicines at all, the head of the block would ask all prisoners who had a supply of palm sugar to share it with the sick. We called it rehabilitation, for we saw that it was extra food that could increase one's power to survive.

As a barracks member who had just recovered from illness, I was assigned 'light duties'. Usually, light duties for people recovering from relatively light illness meant a couple of day's work inside, not out in the field. The term that prisoners used for this was *inreyen*. It was Buru slang from the Dutch word *inrijden*, meaning to 'break in' a new car by driving it slowly.

In actual fact, the barracks benefitted from this unwritten convention of giving 'light duties' to those who were still recuperating, because with *inreyen*, the non-field workers, who were mainly the elderly and weak, and assigned to administrative tasks, received extra support. The younger and stronger prisoners took on extra regular duties in the field. Once their routine daily tasks were completed they were assigned duties of barracks maintenance such as working in the garden, making new leaf thatching to repair the roof, looking for rattan to make things to sell, helping in the sago swamp, and various other things.

The work given to the recuperating patients was varied. After the rice harvest, they would spread the rice out to dry; after the vegetable harvest they would set out the corn, soya beans and peanuts to dry in the sun; between planting and harvest seasons they would husk the corn, peel peanuts, and grind or mill the corn or unhusked rice. Later on, when the Command Headquarters owned a huller and polisher for the rice, all units had to go there to do their hulling. Needless to say, we had to pay the head command for this privilege. (Readers can find more on this payment system in Pramoedya Ananta Toer's book *The Mute's Soliloquy*).

After my allotted three days of recuperative light duties, the barracks head, Bung Subari Marta Atmaja, for some reason did not think I should return to working in the field. Apart from the heavy workload, the hot burning Buru sun took its toll and you could not take a rest whenever you liked. Working in a team meant you had to keep up with the rhythm of the group. It was better to work actively and swiftly than fall out with the rest of the group, and there was always the daily work target to achieve and the possibility of a visit from the authorities checking up on things at any time. The feeling of inner anxiety was another burden that was just as heavy.

On this occasion, the barracks head assigned me to work in the barracks kitchen. For me, the most arduous task was fetching water to fill the three drums in the kitchen. The barracks in our unit were situated on a small hill about 15 metres high. Clear water flowed at the foot of the hill. To fill the drums, we had to walk up and down the hill. Balancing across our shoulders two 18-20-litre containers. It would take about 20 loads in the morning and 24 in the evening to fill the drums. Apart from providing water for the kitchen, it was also used for cleaning teeth morning and night, and for ablutions before prayer for those who did the ritual Muslim prayers.

One day, the head of Barracks VII, Bung Mudakir, heard that I had recently been ill, and he dropped into the kitchen to check how I was doing.

'I heard you have just been ill', Mudakir asked that day. 'Are you strong enough to carry water?'

'Right now I can do it. But in five years' time I don't think I can', I said while taking deep breaths. Sweat was pouring down my chest and back.

'And who will do it then?' I went on. 'There are only about a hundred younger than me, and very young ones like Bogel. We are going to need them to work in the fields ... and because of our condition, we older ones will probably die earlier. Have you thought about all this?'

'Yes, you're right. We have not thought about it, but all the barracks heads should.'

The two of us then talked about all kinds of things, but the essence was how to delay death. It was not just a case of living with as much strength as possible, but also as long as possible. Indeed, this was the core of our last fight, the political prisoners' fight for victory in exile. Because the real purpose of the Buru 'humanitarian project', no matter what name and rationale given to it, was no more nor less than a bloodless murder of prisoners. It was as though they had been handed over to the whims of the law of nature. In practice, their lives rested on the bodies of ageing prisoners, on forced labour duties that never lessened, accompanied by mental and physical torture at every moment. So the victory that political prisoners had to find was not through individual escape, nor through some communal act of seizing weapons and cutting telephone lines.

We also talked about the possibility of proposing that our unit move to flat land, and the pros and cons of having our unit situated on a hill. I was suddenly drawn into the memory of my experience in a vegetable garden in the high hills of Dieng all those years ago.

* * *

It was a time when I had just recuperated from three or four months of typhoid in the Ambarawa hospital. I was then Secretary of the Central Java organising committee for the Regional branch of the National

Front, where I represented Lekra artists, together with others: Mas Tedjo who was Editor-in-Chief of the Semarang daily *Tempo* and representing journalists (Democratic Youth, Pemuda Demokrat); and Pak Pringgo who was head of the Central Java branch of the Murba political party.

I did not work for the National Front for long, at the most maybe a year. However, even though the time was short, I learnt a lot about life and the conditions of the people in the lower rungs of society in Central Java. I was involved from the early days of the National Front. Together with two or three others we went around the districts forming small local organisational branches. One of my many experiences was in Dieng in a mountainous region of Central Java I had heard about as a child.

As a child, though, all I knew of Dieng were stories about its high plateau with extinct or almost extinct volcanoes and many old temple ruins named after figures of the Mahabharata, like Bima, Arjuna and Aswatama.

As Secretary of the National Front I was no longer a child, needless to say. So what I found interesting about Dieng was not only the ancient, eerie ruins and views of babbling mud at the base of craters belching sulphurous gas. I was attracted to the way the local farmers grew vegetables in this colder climate, like carrots, radishes and white cabbage. Running between the vegetable plots were bamboo pipes branching off to the left and right, tied with string made from sugar palm fibre.

'This system is rather recent', the local district head explained to us. 'Before this the people had to go back and forth with watering cans, like the onion farmers do at Brebes.'

'How does this system work?' Suparlan asked.

Suparlan was a member of the National Front committee from BTI, the Indonesian Peasants Front. There were three National Front members who most frequently visited districts like this; Suparlan, myself, and Mas Mario who was from the nationalists (PNI, Indonesian National Party). Sometimes there were four of us when Dr Sutopo joined us. He represented the 1945 generation, and was from the Communist Party.

'The people did this themselves, communally, from gathering the bamboo, to preparing it and the installation …'

'What is the sugar palm fibre string for …?'

'Ah, that is a good question. Come and look …' The district head squatted down beside a pipe that had what looked like a string 'bandage'. We squatted beside him. He explained that the fibre string is found at every section of bamboo. Inside bamboo there are sections, and the bamboo must be cut at these points so the water can go through. The bamboo is then rejoined by wrapping the leaves back around it and tying with sugar palm fibre string. This string does not perish in the sun or in water.

'It rains a lot in Dieng, you see'.

'Are there enough sugar palm trees in Dieng?'

'Fortunately, yes.'

'This must be a legacy of the Hindu era', Mario said.

'Why are you going right back to the Hindu era?' Suparlan asked.

'Well, of course! Look at Bali today. Palm sugar is not only tapped to make alcohol. They also make string from the fibre and use it for their temple roofs, their ceremonial houses …'

'Is what Mario says true?' Suparlan asked me.

'Absolutely!' I joked. 'A Marhaenist is never wrong!'

We laughed. Dieng's district head, who was also from PNI and so a Marhaenist, laughed too. In those days, this kind of banter between friends who were from different political parties was common. I am not sure about today. Probably it invites fights?

'Why don't they use a different kind of bamboo, the thicker kind called *apus*?'

'*Apus* bamboo is thicker, but its sections are shorter compared to this bamboo, *wulung*. There is an even thicker kind of bamboo called *aur*, but its sections are shorter still.'

It is common knowledge, at least as far as I know in Java, that if you want to use bamboo for building, you have to soak it in water first. The longer the better. This makes the bamboo stronger and also more resistant to the little insects that bore into it. Pieces of bamboo of the *wulung* variety with longish sections are selected and split in half or into thin strips and then soaked in water, taken out and dried. Only then are they used; the strips are used to make woven bamboo panels, and the larger pieces to make roofs, frames for the panels, or mats for drying rice, corn and so on.

* * *

After Mudakir and I talked together that day, he brought up the subject of water at the next meeting of the barracks heads, and they immediately responded. They not only agreed to the idea of working on a piping system, but also agreed to carry out the idea. This was helped along by the fact that some of the prisoners were engineers. There was Kamal Uddin, for instance, who had once been a senior in B.J. Habibie's class when he studied in Germany, and there was also Sukarno and Bambang Sasmoyo. Not to mention Anay Rahma who was an alumnus of ITB and had experience in planning.

Behind out unit it was virtually jungle. Down below in the jungle and swamp, near the boundary between Unit IV Savanajaya and Unit XIV Bantalareja, were many sugar palm trees. All around the unit were groves of bamboo of the *petung* variety and about 1500 metres above and behind our unit was a valley with the little stream that was the source of our water.

The most difficult problem to solve, or should I say that was made to be difficult, was the 'political stand' or 'ideological consideration' towards the idea of piping water to the unit. Those in agreement, needless to say, saw the common sense in the idea and also thought of the future, namely the need to maintain the health and energy of everyone, as much as possible. Those who did not agree upheld the consideration of 'holding resolutely to class opinion', namely they demanded a stance of being anti-regime. The water-piping project would only mean that directly or indirectly the political prisoners were voluntarily extending the time of their own oppression.

A middle path was found, through an 'internal meeting'. The unit water-piping project would be carried out in a limited fashion. The bamboo pipes would service only the kitchens of the ten barracks. They would not service the Commander's wisma and the guards' mess, which were at the foot of the hill, or even the polyclinic, which was situated below the barracks. And anyway, those three places already had their own water pumps. We also agreed to keep the project secret from the authorities. The situation of the unit and the terrain made this possible.

As I have said, the ten barracks were situated on a rise, whereas the wisma and the mess were by the front gate down below. Along the road running towards Unit XIV Bantalareja, for a distance of five or six kilometres, in flat alluvial soil from the Wai Bini stream, we had planted crops and wet rice. Behind the hill where the barracks were situated were more hills and the source of our water. Below, running parallel with the unit fields was thick forest and groves of bamboo. This was where we had made our vegetable gardens, out of sight of the unit. Funnily enough, the unit guards and even the commander never came to this 'dark area', maybe because they were afraid.

This is how our water pipe project was able to proceed and remain a secret from day one until the water had already been running for a few days, filling the containers at the barracks. A secret project cannot be whispered about to every one of the five hundred prisoners in the barracks. The secret would then be a secret no more. And there were always one or two who, for the 'wow' factor, would want to tell others, to show they are in the know. When living in isolation, knowing 'secrets' has a value, especially when the people who want to know the secret are people you think are important. So the one who tells the secret will gain kudos in the telling.

It was time for evening prayers that day, and there were visitors attending, the official in charge of 'mental development' was visiting the unit from Jakarta, and he was attended by the assistant in mental development from Command Headquarters and staff. The proceedings were opened with a sermon and a talk from Pak Sarwono – a political prisoner said to be a retired army brigadier general, a devoted attendee at the mosque who was also deputy unit religious affairs officer. He was the one who told the secret that was actually no longer secret. Wanting to show off his skills with the Muslim prisoners and also the prestige of his unit, he told the visitors about the water pipe project. So from after evening prayers that night and for a few days afterwards, Sarwono was the target of verbal abuse from everyone in the unit. A few came to his defence, but they were greatly outnumbered. He was attacked from the point of view of 'political stand' and 'ideological considerations', and this criticism was sharp indeed. Even though I thought that these reasons were overly dramatised. Because whether our bamboo pipe system was there or not, the camp authorities themselves never had to pump or fetch water. When the water began to flow freely through those bamboo pipes and reached the wisma, mess and polyclinic, it was not the commander, staff and guards who were the first to enjoy it, but the prisoners who were now relieved of one of their arduous tasks.

* * *

Over time, the accusations died down. They flowed away like the water in the bamboo pipes that flowed constantly. But before that happened, while all the whispering and accusing was still going on, I had an attack of my stomach ulcer. Mudakir probably suffered from the same anxiety. Even though the pipes were our idea, when it was taken on as a group idea and carried out as a group, then the idea and its realisation became the group's responsibility.

But the problem remained of where to find that communal yardstick, and where it should be placed.

Chapter 14

COMMAND HEADQUARTERS BAND

Watching the news of war all over the world is a dilemma. If you don't watch, then you don't keep up with the aggression of the neo-colonial imperialists of the early 21st century; but if you do watch, your eyes and heart cannot bear to see the victims' suffering. Children and babies that are born to live, and the women who give birth to these seeds of new life must suddenly die. And as a sacrifice for what, and who has to be sacrificed so dearly? And those pictures are not some series in a 'historical film' but are scenes of real 'historical events'!

But it is not the news broadcasts of war that jolts my memory to write these notes. What jolts me are the 'commercials'. This is the polite journalistic term in The Netherlands for the advertisements that continually interrupt every program. The exception, of course, is a speech from the Queen or a high-ranking government official. Suddenly there on the television screen are wild horses, freed of their bridles, galloping away. I am imagining a scene from a novel by Soewarsih Djojopoespito (*Buiten het Gareel*, 1939). My eyes are drawn by the camera to follow one of the horses, from close up to medium shot to long shot. The stallion rises on its two hind legs in the middle of a desert. Then comes a commercial message from 'Johnnie Walker', the famous brand of whisky known from the 1800s!

My memory wanders then to my fellow prisoner in Unit XIV Bantalareja, Lie Bok Hoo, to his high forehead, his stocky body and short neck. But when he sang, even though he had a short neck, he could draw a very long breath. He was just as good as the famous singer from Malaya (there was no Malaysia yet) S. Effendy. When he sang *'Bahtera Laju'* and got to the words *'bersama angin utara'* his voice was as sweet as the singer Paulina Robot in her prime when she sang her most well-known song *'Si Gembala Sapai'*.

But it seemed that Lie did not like either the song *'Bahtera Laju'* or *'Si Gembala Sapai'*. In Buru, at Unit XIV Bantalareja, he was known for, and later known as *'Hai, Kudaku Lari'* (Run, my horse, Run!). While the singer Effendy could draw out the final 'a' in the final word 'utara' of *'Bahtera Laju'*, Lie could hold the sound 'ai' in the word *'hai'*. He would always draw a huge round of applause whenever he appeared on our 'arts stage' at Bantalareja. The song would not have ended, he would still be singing the 'ai' and it would reverberate around the walls of the surrounding jungle.

But that is not what happened on this particular night at Namlea. Quite the opposite! 'Run, my horse, Run!' was always greeted with whistles, cheers and applause in our unit, including from the top brass in the wisma and the mess, for the soldiers in Namlea seemed to be like a difficult homework problem. After his performance, Lie Bok Hoo was called in, 'interrogated' and beaten up! Others who got the same treatment were Cak Buang from Unit III Wanayasa, a former performer from Ludruk Marhaen, because on stage he had repeated a verse by Cak Durasim *'gupon omah dara, melok Nippon tambah sara'* (doves live in a dovecot, under the Japanese life gets more miserable); and Basuki Effendy.

And what were their offences? Old, thin Cak Buang was accused of insulting the guards by using 'Japanese' as an allusion. For Basuki Effendy and Lie it was because on that stage at Namlea, they also sang the song 'Come Back to Sorrento', which was a favourite in our unit and had become a favourite too of our band, Bantala Nada, led by Martin Lapanguli. Lie was accused of giving a secret sign to prisoners to escape, because of the words 'Run, my horse, Run', which he sang very clearly, drawing out the notes. Basuki Effendy was accused of encouraging his Communist Party cohorts who were still in hiding and at work underground to quickly stage a 'comeback' and continue the fight!

I have no idea what happened to Cak Buang after he returned to his unit that night, but at Unit XIV Bantalareja, Lie Bok Hoo's and Basuki Effendy's punishment continued. They were not allowed to return to their barracks, but had to squat under the tables of the two guards on the porch of the guardhouse the whole night long.

The next morning there was a special roll call. The roll was called not by the Platoon Commander or his deputy, but by the Unit Commander, First Lieutenant (Military Police Corps) Sukirno himself. Lie and Basuki were brought out and made to stand in front of us all. After all the usual kinds of procedures, like stand, on your guard, turn right, turn left, straighten your lines and at ease, all of which were led by the Platoon Commander. It was now the turn of the Unit Commander to give his address. The content of this address, from the first words until the end, was just you this and you that, abuse and threats of shooting us dead.

Lie Bok Hoo was warned yet again never to repeat his call for 'running away'. All of us were warned that we had to report to the authorities anyone who at any time encouraged escape. Basuki Effendy was warned not to give signs to his comrades to stage a 'comeback'. All of us were warned to get rid of any dreams we might have about 'comebacks'. Anyone at all who dared to challenge authority would be dealt with: 'shot dead!' And with that final word he took out his pistol and 'bang'! shattered the dawn. The bats and birds were all startled and flew off screeching ...

This was when the announcement was made that the Unit Commander was firing Basuki Effendy from his position as work coordinator of Unit XIV Bantalareja. From that moment too, the treasure chest of New Order prohibitions was enriched further with two more songs. Since late 1965 all 'Lekra songs', 'p-k-i songs' and the song *Genjer Genjer* had been banned. To this list was now added '*Larilah, Hai, Kudaku*! – Run, my horse, Run!' and 'Come Back to Sorrento', a Western song that had been popular in Indonesia in the 1950s long before the 30th September event ever happened. There was no connection between Sorrento, a town in Italy, and the Indonesian Communist Party, just as there was no connection between the 'obstinate horse' that the handsome singer S. Effendy sang about, with the political prisoners from the 30th September event called G30S/PKI!

The incident I am relating happened in late 1972 or early 1973, and coincided with the change of senior military personnel at Buru, which happened in the last three months or first three months every year. The previous Commander of the 'Rehabilitation Centre' of Buru, Lieutenant Colonel A.S. Rangkuti was replaced by Lieutenant Colonel Samsi M.S.

Cak Buang was invited to participate in the festivities to farewell the former Buru Commander and welcome the new one, because in the register of Unit III Wanayasa it was noted that Buang was formerly a performer in a *ludruk* theatre group. What's more, he came from the group called Ludruk Marhaen in Surabaya, which had been directed by Cak Syamsudin and in the early 1960s was the most famous group in all Indonesia. Ludruk Marhaen had not only performed at the National Palace (Istana Negara) in Jakarta, but had also entertained the troops on the front line during the campaign to liberate West Irian. The film director Tan Sing Hwat had filmed one performance of their repertoire ('*Mawar Merah Lembah Merapi*').

This was probably also true of Basuki Effendy. Apart from being known as our work duties coordinator, Basuki was also known as a singer and famous figure in national film. The Buru Camp Commander who was ending his tour of duty, A.S. Rangkuti, was said to have also been a film actor back when he was in Medan. He had made a show of his friendliness from the moment we 500 political prisoners disembarked from the *MV Tokala* and set foot in Namlea on August 12, 1971. He sought out Basuki Effendy from among the lines of coolie hats and uniform khaki and shook his hand. It was an attempt to transfer his old acting skills on the silver screen into a real-life history drama, maybe titled 'Humanitarian Greeting' set in Buru scorched by the hot midday sun.

But what about Lie Bok Hoo? Outside his unit, Lie Bok Hoo was nothing. He had been asked to take part in the event at Namlea not because he was 'the horse who ran fast', but because he was a singer in the Bantala Nada band. This band, from Unit XIV, was the one and only band in all of the units at that time. So it was not Lie himself, but the band that had been asked to take part. Or the more correct term would be 'given string duties' for the musicians, and 'windpipe duties' for the singers, Lie, Basuki Effendy and some others.

Our unit, Bantalareja was not at all like its name, *reja*, meaning prosperous. The absolute opposite was true. The prisoners in our neighbouring units Savanajaya and Indrapura, called our unit the 'beggars unit' or the 'thieves unit'. This was because for almost two years, the inmates of Bantalareja, either clandestinely on a one-to-one basis, or more 'officially' as a unit, asked for corn and cassava from the two neighbouring units. It was also called the 'Jakarta' unit because almost all the inmates came from the two prisons in Jakarta, Salemba and Tangerang. The ones from Tangerang were comparatively young, and already had agricultural work experience in the farming project run by the Military Command V. Because of this, they were clever at pilfering things.

Because we were stamped as beggars and thieves, Unit Bantalareja was also given another bad name – the 'liberal unit'. 'Liberal' meant tending towards being lax. Lax, that is, in terms of following the old norms of the organisation and ideology. This attitude originated among the young prisoners at Tangerang who brought it with them to Buru where it spread to all units. It is no exaggeration if I say that this was the main cause of the destruction of a collective spirit and the spread of an individualistic spirit on Buru. But nor can this be separated from events that happened in Tangerang prison previously.

Signs of a fracturing of the spirit of solidarity had also been evident at Salemba. Prisoners mockingly replaced the word 'solidarity' with the word *'sodakoh'*, meaning alms. The old Javanese proverb *'mangan ora mangan waton kumpul'* ('whether we eat or not, the important thing is to be together'), was turned on its head to become *'kumpul ora kumpul waton mangan'* ('whether we get together or not, the important thing is to eat'). The food-sharing groups fell apart and were replaced with 'every man for himself'.

Needless to say, this fading of the collective spirit brought with it a fading sense of comradeship – to an extent that even the term of address 'comrade' (*kawan*), suddenly became taboo and was replaced by all kinds of other terms of address normally used for daily relations (like *Pak, mas, dik*). With the fading of this sense of comradeship, then, the old hierarchical relations were rejected and as a result, the prestige of the old leadership faded.

In Tangerang prison, this 'spirit of change' was manifest in two events. The first was the murder of a prisoner who was an informer named Silitonga; the second was the existence of an underground party organisation within the camp. The illegal organisation was exposed in an operation called Operation Kalong – an army Intelligence network under the leadership of Captain Suroso (who was later promoted after he succeeded in capturing Brigadier General Supardjo), specially formed to hunt down and capture 'G30S-PKI types'. About sixty cadres – most of them young – were severely tortured. The farming project was shut down, all the prisoners working on it were taken back into the prison, and for months there were punishments at Tangerang prison. Cell doors were locked continuously, no food parcels from family were allowed, and the prisoners had to survive on the government food ration budgeted at 25 cents a day per prisoner.

It was at this time, around late 1970 and early 1971 that the collective spirit and trust in organisations and their leadership among the young cadres was at its lowest ebb.

Unit XIV Bantalareja's history on the island of Buru began on August 17, 1971, two years after the first group of prisoners were sent to Buru in 1969. I have no idea what kind of entertainment the first units had during that time. In Unit IV Savanajaya, which was the unit closest to Unit XIV, there were already some *gamelan* instruments and *wayang kulit* puppets. According to Hersat Sudiyono, an inmate of Barracks IV in that unit (a former head of the Salatiga branch of

Taman Siswa and Secretary of the Central Java branch of Lekra), the 'Javanese artists' in this unit had already performed a short 3-4 hour *wayang* during the day in Indonesian. This was possible because a famous *dalang* (master puppeteer) from Purwadadi, Tristuti Rachmadi, was in that unit. There was also Joko Waluyo who played the drums, Hersat himself who was a skilled *gamelan* musician, and Sudarno As, an amateur *wayang* puppet-maker. Evidently, they were very busy experimenting with performances of the poetry of *suluk* (mood poems in the *wayang*) and the long narrative sections of the *wayang* not in Javanese, but in the national language, Indonesian. However, even with this expertise, the Javanese arts in that unit remained a spontaneous activity. There was never a fixed group with a name, and never any clear leadership.

It was different in Unit XIV Bantalareja, the so-called 'liberal' 'Jakarta' unit. The artistic life and Javanese entertainment that developed there included a band, a *keroncong* music group, an *Irama Melayu* music group and a *lenong* performance group. Their activities were not just spontaneous occurrences, but the groups were formed with proper leadership. As I mentioned, the band Bantala Nada was under the leadership of Martin Lapanguli, while Go Giok Liong led the keroncong group called Suara Bantala, 'Arab' (that was his nickname, I don't know his real name) led the Irama Melayu group called Irama Bantala, and Tahir Yahya led the lenong group called Lenong Bantala. A group of gamelan musicians, *wayang orang* and *ketoprak* performers soon built a complete set of *gamelan* instruments and called themselves Krida Bantala under the leadership of Mohidi and Warno Wamin.

The 'entertainment' group of Unit IV played at least once a month in the unit's 'arts building', with a program of dance and songs, alternating with special performances of Javanese traditional *ketoprak* or *wayang orang*. There was never any pro-contra discussion about this entertainment. It was clear that some of the more ideologically 'strict' prisoners rejected the presence of entertainment in the unit, but there was not much room for their views in the midst of the life of the 'liberal unit' of the young prisoners from Tangerang.

And this was how it came to be that the Bantala Nada band from Unit XIV Bantalareja was given 'performance duty' for a night of entertainment in Namlea, the capital of Buru. No other unit had formed such a band, and as I said earlier, the entertainment was to be a send-off for A.S. Rangkuti and a welcome for Samsi M.S.

A few days after Basuki Effendy and Lie were tortured for singing songs suspected of being 'indicators', Lieutenant A.S. Rangkuti visited Unit XIV. It wasn't clear whether he was coming on a routine inspection before finishing his duties and departing from Buru, or whether he was coming to take some of the stock that was the ration of Unit XIV. That's what the top brass all did when they went on leave or ended their tours of duty. Nothing strange about that! Same old stuff. As the saying goes, the growing bean does not leave the bean pole. From the Unit Commander down to the guards and even including the civilian head of the Unit XIV storehouse, that's what they did if they were going home on leave or going home for good: they asked the prisoners for things to take with them, a 'bonus'. And it was not even just the secular officials, the spiritual ones were just as bad. For instance, Pastor Matatula was so greedy that the prisoners called him 'Mata Ula' – Pastor snake eyes …

The size of the 'bonus' differed, of course, according to the rank and the greed of the official. The procedure for getting the 'bonus' also differed. Those in Command Headquarters would use the official chain of command from Unit Commander, to the coordinators of the barracks beneath him, and from the coordinators down to the 'inhabitants'. Yes, if they were asking for things, then they would flatter us with that term, 'inhabitant'. As for guards, if they felt this procedure was too long, they would go directly to the heads of the barracks, or even directly to the prisoners out working in the fields and 'threaten' them by throwing them some gunny sacks – the number of sacks depended on their level of greed.

'Fill it!' they would order.

The sack would be filled with corn, peanuts, soya beans, potatoes, cassava, eggplant – whatever was in the garden and could be sold in the market at Namlea or Ambon. Captain Ahmad Noor, the Unit Commander from Bantalareja during the time I was coordinator, got so fed up to see the guards competing in their greed, once said to me, 'They want to take everything from the prisoners. If you painted your shit they would take that too …'

While prisoners would fill the sacks, the Platoon Commander would look for a barracks head – any barracks head – and demand a *corvée* for 'ghost duty', to take the sacks in the dead of night to Sanleko, Jamilo or Marloso, where he would have arranged for some local people to provide 'storage'.

So it was. None of this is important to the story at hand about the band. What is relevant is that when A.S. Rangkuti came to visit our Unit XIV, he took the opportunity to summon Basuki Effendy who was working in the fields at the time. Since he had been punished for singing his song about a 'Comeback', along with Lie Bok Hoo for singing 'Run!', the two of them had been prohibited from working very far from the Commander's wisma and the guard's mess. Of course, Basuki approached the wisma with trepidation. Could they really have discovered some group of prisoners somewhere who could be linked to that song? Was he going to be taken to Command Headquarters? Was he going to get more punishment? Who knew? Whatever would happen, would happen.

As for us prisoners, we were resigned. What could we do? In this perfect state of total disempowerment, all we could do was go back to the one thing we possessed: Hope!

* * *

Later that evening, returning from roll call, Basuki came up to me.

'I'll come with you to the barracks', he said 'I have something important to talk about.'

What on earth could this be? I asked myself. But I noticed that he did not have a swollen face. He was not limping, and he did not have bruises and gashes from being beaten up.

When we got back to my 'allotment', Basuki started to talk at once. It turned out that nothing bad had happened to him. Instead, he was bringing good news. At least, I thought it was good news, and probably so did Basuki, especially when the person who brought the news was A.S. Rangkuti, the most powerful man in Buru, who had once been Basuki's 'fellow professional' as an actor in the world of the silver screen. Maybe the news A.S. Rangkuti brought if it came to pass, was a kind of salve to his conscience, the maximum possible from a high official towards a political prisoner who came from the same 'workgroup'. Perhaps it was also a kind of apology that the highest military official could never possibly utter to one of his prisoners, for the actions of the platoon commanders in Namlea and Bantalareja and one of his Unit Commanders, First Lieutenant

Sukirno, who punished prisoners based on convoluted accusations about the titles of two songs.

The fact that Basuki Effendy had been summoned by the Buru Commander as an 'old friend' and that he had sat at the same table with the Unit Commander while the guards in the mess awaited their orders, made Basuki's prestige in the unit soar. There were two reasons the Buru Commander A.S. Rangkuti, had summoned Basuki. Firstly, he had received notification from the Ministry of Social Affairs in Jakarta that the 'rehabilitation camp' in Buru was going to receive a donation of a complete set of musical instruments for modern music. The instruments had to be used and maintained, and not just stored in some storehouse to go rusty and broken. As the Buru Camp did not have one combined band, the instruments were going to be given to the Bantala Nada band of Unit XIV.

After the instruments were collected from Command Headquarters and brought to the Bantalareja Unit, the Bantala Nada band, under the leadership of Basuki Effendy, was often asked to perform to entertain other units. They would tour and be away for maybe a month at a time. So now a new group term arose, 'the artists' group', which was used scornfully. It was based on a sense of envy of the majority towards one particular social group. Members of 'artists group' did indeed become different from their fellows in the unit. For instance, they would smoke 'shag tobacco' and no longer wanted to smoke the cheap barracks tobacco cuts; they would use 'white folks' soap' when they bathed, and not straw or leaves to rub their bodies; and they would use proper toothpaste to clean their teeth, and not just soft sand scraped from ditches.

The second reason A.S. Rangkuti summoned Basuki Effendy was to ask him to write a short, clear report about the role of culture and the arts in the life of prisoners in the units. If he approved the report, then he would submit it for the design of program policy in Buru rehabilitation camp for the future.

'What do you think?' Basuki asked me.

I understood why he had come to me. Apart from the fact that we had known each other since junior high school days in Yogyakarta, even though our classes were two years apart, there was no other Lekra person in Bantalareja with experience running a cultural organisation. In the first month in Buru, in our unit there had also been S. Anantaguna, who apart from having a wealth of organisational experience, was also the same 'level' as Basuki, meaning they were both former Lekra leaders. But S. Anantaguna had been moved to Indrapura unit. Basuki saw there was no-one else in our unit apart from me, even though my 'former rank' – if we can think that Lekra had ranks like in the army – was not the same as his.

'I know', Basuki continued, 'that Rangkuti just wants to use me. But ...'

'Of course he does!' I answered. 'But why the but?' I mean, can you refuse? As a former actor himself, Rangkuti must remember the actor Chatir Harro miming singing in the film '*Untuk Sang Merah Putih*' but it was actually your voice. And don't forget that he came here not to chat with you as a fellow actor, but as the Unit Commander to give an order to a political prisoner.'

'But won't all the prisoners accuse me later on?'

'When's "later"? Who knows if we will even get the stuff? And if people accuse you, that is easily answered. Because firstly, this is a matter of responsibility between fellows, and secondly between fellows of the same age group. Not like you and Rangkuti now.'

'What do you mean?'

I went on to compare the situation of the artists in Jakarta and Yogyakarta during the WWII occupation of the Japanese fascist forces. There were cultural centres called *Keimin Bunka Shidosho* and propaganda groups called *Sendenbu* everywhere. The artists who gathered there were given the primary task of contributing to the victory of the war of Greater East Asia. But in fact, it encouraged the birth of artistic works that subtly conveyed messages of patriotism and nationalism. Apart from the more 'official' songs that Cornel Simanjuntak and Kusbini composed like *'Bekerja'* (Work) and *'Tonarigumi'*, they also managed to slip in more critical songs like *'Citra'* (Image) and *'Padi Menguning'* (Yellowing ricefields). And apart from all the short stories published in *Pandji Poestaka* in the Showa calendar (1943-45), in praise of our Japanese 'big brothers' and the kamikaze spirit, there was also Chairil Anwar who somehow managed to write stirring pieces like *'Semangat'* and Diponegoro (even though according to Basuki Resobowo, Chairil was called in to the Japanese secret police in Jakarta).

Apart from these stories about Indonesia during the Japanese occupation, I also pointed out the historical novels of Leon Uris like *Exodus* (1958) and *Battle Cry* (1953) that relate the fight of the Israelis to return to and build their 'Promised Land'. In the camps, there was open resistance and a secret one. On stage, they would rehearse choral singing and drama, but behind the stage they would be rehearsing battle and politics.

Finding opportunity wherever one can in adversity is the right of prisoners when all possibility of escape is closed to them. And it is there – where necessity is the mother of invention – that creativity in the arts can emerge and produce something interesting and challenging in the lives of prisoners.

'So apart from all that', I said to Basuki, wanting to draw this talk to a close, 'I think that people's urge to find entertainment is basic human nature and cannot be banned. Surely you remember back when we were in those tiny cramped Salemba prison cells, when we could hear Slamet Parto singing Javanese poetry. Then there was Mudiyoko, the former regent of Sukohardjo who was such a great storyteller, and Hadisuripto who after family visit days would do makeshift *wayang kulit* shadow performances.'

'Will you help me?' he asked.

'Of course, I will.' I said, and asked him in return, 'what do you choose? To leave your fellow inmates to hang themselves, drink poison, or chop each other up because of homosexual rivalries … because of despair? Or do we try to get through to them with any entertainment we can?'

End of conversation.

It turned out that Basuki meant could I help him from that very moment. He gave me a pen and an exercise book with the camp stamp, and asked me to write down for him an explanation about culture, along the lines the Camp Commander wanted. I was not sure whether this was because Basuki felt I could do this better than him, or whether this was insurance for later down the track when his 'fellows' would accuse him of 'working together' with the authorities.

So I took the pen and exercise book knowing full well what I was doing. But I did not think for a moment about the authorities. I looked to myself and to all my fellow prisoners. I wanted, together with them, via small alleys of culture in the units, to break through the grind of daily life with its dead ends of space and time. I wanted, together with them, every now and then to laugh and applaud, and for there to be a decrease in the statistics of suicide by hanging, poison and in the vicious fights everywhere in the units.

I filled the exercise book with ideas about culture and its role, along the lines of Lekra and Taman Siswa, which were ideas always in my head. All I did was replace words like 'the people' (*rakyat*) with 'political prisoners' or 'society', and replace 'people's culture' with 'the culture of Pancasila, or the Taman Siswa concept of 'nurture'. I merely asked Basuki to get a guarantee from the Unit Commander that the pen and exercise book that I placed beneath my pillow would not be seized and used against me as an accusation of encouraging 'a comeback' or 'others to run'.

Seven days later, the exercise book was in the hands of the Camp Commander at Command Headquarters. Not long after that, the Unit XIV Bantalareja was asked to send a workforce to pick up the band instruments from Command Headquarters. Around the middle of the following year, the instruments were taken back there along with three of our unit inmates who would be based there as core members of a music group. They were Basuki Effendy the singer and candidate for the group leader, Martin Lapanguli the violin player and music arranger, and Pardede who played the guitar. Some other artists were called from other units, in particular Subronto K. Atmodjo from Unit X Wanadharma, as a candidate for technical leader of music and who later was known as bandleader.

By this time the leadership of Buru Camp had passed from A.S. Rangkuti to Lieutenant Colonel Samsi M.S. The New Camp Commander brought in changes immediately. For instance, in using prison labour, he changed the work system from 'man-days' to a fixed contract basis that tended to be more liberal but was also more exhaustive. He also reorganised the arrangement of units, including putting together in one barracks near Command Headquarters those prisoners with particular skills. After the Command band group was formed, Pramoedya Ananta Toer was given special duty as a writer (the earlier attempt by Ibnu B.A. a prisoner in Unit I had been a failure); there was a *gamelan* and *wayang kulit* group led by the dalang Ki Tristuti Rahmadi Syuryaputra B.A.; a wood carving group led by someone I can't remember; an artists' group led by Sumardjo, who was an ex-member of the Young Artists of Indonesia (SIM, Seniman Indonesia Muda); and an engineers' group made up of many engineering graduates from Moscow and Beijing, led by Drs Paulus.

After Basuki Effendy and Martin Lapanguli left us, the Bantala Nada band from Unit XIV Bantalareja kept on going. It went back to using whatever old musical instruments it could find, and was led by Samsu Bahri who was also the unit coordinator.

Chapter 15

THE 'SAVANAJAYA FAMILY'

Savanajaya was the name of Unit IV, one of the oldest units for political prisoners in Buru, established in 1969. It was situated near Sanleko coast (3 kilometres), and named 'Savanajaya' because it was built on a 'savanna' plain of cogon grass. Unlike the units situated further upstream on the Wai Apo River (*'wai'* means river in the local language), which were built in cleared forest and scrub, the Savanajaya Unit below was built as an experiment, or so the story went. It was a trial to see if the area could be agriculturally productive like the units further up.

The upper units were green because apart from the more fertile soil, they also had water from the Wai Apo, which flowed the whole year round. The soil around Unit IV Savanajaya, on the other hand, had only about 15 centimetres of arable soil cover, and was dependent on the whims of the Wai Bini River. There were a few villages situated on the banks of this river (Sanleko, Walgan Lama, Marloso and Jamilo), but the villagers could not make a living from their farming. The Wai Bini would dry up if the dry season was long, and sometimes the dry season could last eight months. Furthermore, because the land was flat with little gradient, the river had a weak flow. When the rains did come, this meant it flooded.

There had been a plan to dam the Wai Bini from back in the time of the Ali Sastroamidjojo Cabinet [1953-55], but it was not until the time of the Buru's Rehabilitation Camp Commander Major Rusno that it was built (with forced labour). However, the dam often burst and the Wai Bini also often changed its course.

Even though this was the situation, not even two years after Savanajaya Unit was built, it was given a younger sibling located right beside it. The isolation Unit Jiku Kecil in Namlea was moved there and given a new name: Ancol Unit (after the seaside area of Jakarta) because it was on the coast. There were now three lower units on the flat coastal area: Savanajaya, Bantalareja and Ancol.

It was clear then that these coastal units were not built as an 'experiment' to open more agricultural land, but for strategic military reasons. Twelve thousand prisoners are no small force if they unite and rebel. The fact that the placement of these units had a strategic purpose became clear in 1972 when the project to build a proper road between the units commenced. This road was built to connect to the 'Great Post Road' (to use the analogy of the Great Post Road Daendels built in Java from Anyer to Panarukan in the early 19th century) running from Namlea to Savanajaya, which followed the shore of Kayeli Bay.

* * *

The official name of the entire Buru Camp was 'Rehabilitation Installation', known by its acronym *Inrehab*, and it housed 22 units of prisoners called '*tapol*' – short for *tahanan politik*. The camp as a whole was managed by a body in Jakarta called the Badan Pelaksana Resettlement Pulau Buru, or Body for Carrying Out the Buru island Resettlement, which was shortened to *Bapreru*. One of its units was the isolation unit, which was known as Unit Jiku Kecil, and after 1973

The 'Savanajaya Family'

became Unit Ancol. The total number of prisoners in all the units in Buru was 12,000, all of them men.

Unit IV Savanajaya started out as a unit for political prisoners, just like all the others. In 1972, though, it was vacated and the 550 inmates were moved to other units. Unit IV Savanajaya was then 'developed' into a village named Savanajaya Village. The area of wet ricefields was increased from about 60 hectares to more than 161 hectares, and the fields for crops increased from about 25 hectares to more than 112 hectares.

In this process of building the village and extending the farming land, our unit of XIV Bantalareja, as the neighbouring unit to Savanajaya, had to surrender some of its ricefields. Some went to Savanajaya, and some to the Ancol Unit. Our unit now had to break in new fields to the north up to the foot of Kakibotol hills, and to the northwest, by draining the sago swamp of Wai Tui.

Savanajaya Village was in actual fact a special unit among the prison units, because it housed prisoners with families. By 1974 there were about 200 families from various units. There were also one or two prisoners who had married local women and had asked permission to bring in their wives and children. The other families were made up of those whose wives and children in Java who 'had voluntarily requested the government' to 'be permitted' to follow their husbands and fathers. Some military commands in Central Java forced prisoners' wives (and their children) to join their husbands.

But before that, about a year before the wives and children arrived from Java, an official announcement was made in each unit. In my unit the Unit Commander First Lieutenant Moh. Nur made the announcement at roll call. He stated that the Buru Island Rehabilitation

Installation was going to receive a shipment of transmigrants – women from Kramat Tunggak prostitution area, who had undergone 'guidance'.

The reason for this was a humanitarian one, according to the second principle of the nation's five guiding pillars, Pancasila, and intended to make the society of Wai Apo complete. After all, the Unit Commander went on, using crude Javanese metaphors to refer to the sexual organs of women and men, humans are divided between those with 'cloven hoofs' and those with 'single hoofs'.

Not long after this news was broadcast, a group of spiritual leaders visited from Jakarta. One of them who came to Unit XIV Bantalareja as a Muslim leader had a bachelor's degree and was called A. Pranowo. He dared to tackle the plan head on. On the one hand, the government separated prisoners from their wives and children, whilst on the other, it wanted to link them up with prostitutes.

'They might be justifying this because of Pancasila, but it is completely against Islam', he said.

'And what would he know?' the prisoners whispered to each other in the prayer *mushola* when he preached this talk.

The young Pak Pranowo was not only sympathetic, but was also vocal and could always take a joke (where are you now, Pak?). To him, the sound of the cucakrowo birds that always called to each other greeting the dawn was just like the third verse of the Surat Al-Ikhlas proclaiming the oneness of God: *'Lam yalid walam yuulad, lam yalid walam yuulat …'*. However, the identical birdsong, to the ears of the prisoner Kromoredjo from Cilacap who had formerly been in the leadership of the Railway Workers Union and as a *romusha* had worked on building the Burma Road, sounded like a special call to the prisoners *'golek kéong, golek kéong'* (look for snails, look for snails).

The 'Savanajaya Family'

Sometimes, once a week on average, my unit would send a couple of prisoners to join those from other units on a secret snail-finding mission in the mangrove swamps near Sanleko beach. The reason was protein. During the occupation of the Japanese fascists, many people escaped death from malnutrition by eating snails. And now here we were, 'G30S-PKI' prisoners in the time of the New Order fascism, looking for snails so we could survive!

To cut a long story short, just as it was nonsense that all those wives and children had 'begged to be permitted' to follow their husbands and fathers, the official announcement from the Unit Commander – which had been roundly attacked by our spiritual leader – was also utter nonsense.

Every prisoner family in Savanajaya Village was given a three-roomed house with a dirt floor and a zinc roof, and wooden plank walls. Each family was given the right to use a 0.5-hectare plot of ricefield for their livelihood. And that was how it remained for about six years.

From the time it was opened in 1972 until the end of 1978, Savanajaya Village didn't have a single year of calm and peace. There was constant quarrelling between the wives and children and the officials. Torture and humiliation, sexual abuse and endless verbal abuse from the officials and guards would cause outbreaks of anger and continual protest from the women.

* * *

On November 15, 1978, according to the official letter from the Commander for the Restoration of Security and Order Operations (Pangkopkamtib) Number Skep-60/KOPKAM/XI/1978 dated November 7, 1978, the political prisoners with families living in

Savanajaya Village were declared to be free. The official letter also went on to say that their status was now not that of prisoners, but transmigrants at Savanajaya Village, Buru island. Although the official letter was worded in this way, it was not, in fact, a declaration of their freedom. The village was still guarded and the inhabitants were not allowed to leave the village without a permit from the military authority in the village. There was now a village head with the usual subordinate structure of neighbourhood heads who were appointed and 'chosen' from among the former prisoners, but their role was just the same as unit coordinators with their staff and barracks heads. They were no more than an extension of the authorities.

Apart from one or two 'cockroach' informers and others sucking up to the authorities, people in the village generally rejected the letter and its contents. As free citizens, they said, they should be free to choose where they wanted to live. They rejected this *fait accompli* of being declared transmigrants, and secondly of having to stay in Savanajaya Village on Buru island.

This was why, about a month later when Indonesia's Attorney General and staff visited the Buru 'Rehabilitation Installation' and Savanajaya Village, the people protested at the arts centre. They stated categorically that they were not prepared to be sent as transmigrants to any transmigration area at all. At that time there was a rumour going around that they might be moved to a transmigration site in Kalimantan. They demanded to be sent back to where they had come from, namely Java.

Feeling cornered by these demands and the villagers' protest, especially from the women, the Attorney General used his skilful manoeuvres to dodge responsibility. He hid behind meaningless pleasantries and oral instructions so that later he would not be answerable to any legal challenge. He would only be morally answerable to his God, but that is something no-one can control; and he would be morally answerable to his fellow humans, but he was part of the machine of power that held all the tools of enforcement.

The Attorney General's instruction, which was given via the village administration, was that there should be a process of registration of everyone in the village, whereby each could nominate if they wanted to return to Java or to stay on Buru. This registration was quickly carried out. The result was that two-thirds wanted to go back to Java, and one-third wanted to stay.

What followed was a long stretch of uncertainty and waiting with vague hope. Those families who had chosen to leave Buru felt even more anxiety-stricken. Some of the villagers who had already been infected with the 'cockroach' mentality and had become informers, started to harangue those who had almost given up hope, telling them to withdraw their demand to return to Java. A few families did give up, but not many.

Meanwhile, the living situation became even more difficult. A plague of insects destroyed the harvest. Some of the 'upper' units sent down work parties bearing food from their units, as much as they could spare, like cassava, corn and yam.

About eight months later came the instruction from the Commander for the Restoration of Security and Order Operations, sent via radiogram with the code Rdg. No. TR/407/Kopkam/VIII/1979, that (1) those ex-political prisoners who wanted to return to Java should immediately organise their travel and (2) those who wanted to stay should organise their local resident card, certificate of land title, and so forth.

It turned out that the radiogram was not just an empty promise. In October 1979, on the 14th as I recall, the group of about two-thirds of the families from Savanajaya departed – about 160 families – and returned to Java. The government covered one-third of the cost of their travel, and the remaining two-thirds the ex-prisoners had to find themselves. The cost for each family at that time, for travel by sea and land from Buru, Namlea and Ambon to Surabaya was one hundred and fifty rupiah.

For some unknown reason – maybe just an administrative mix-up, or for some political reason – the departure of ten families was refused by Regional Special Operations in Maluku. When these families and the village administration tried to find out why, they were given no explanation, and told they would simply have to wait. But waiting and waiting with no explanation or time limit is the same as letting a problem remain a problem when actually there is no longer any problem. In early January 1980, these ten families wrote two open letters. One letter they all signed and sent to the Head of the House of Representatives, General Daryatmo, and the second letter they sent to the Commander for the Restoration of Security and Order Operation. In early February 1980, an official reply came back from the Commission V of the House of Representatives. The letter stated that their petition had been received, and secondly that they promised to settle the problem at once.

On April 15, 1980, the waiting finally ended. A travel authorisation arrived from Maluku. The families were permitted to return to Java, but they had to cover the full cost themselves. Whether this was really the decision from 'Jakarta' or whether the Special Operations in Maluku were getting some 'benefit' out of it, who knows. Perhaps it was like the classic joke the Javanese *dalangs* tell in *wayang kulit* performance in the *goro-goro* section with the clowns.

The three clowns are taking their leave from Abiyasa at the Wukir Awawu hermitage. Abiyasa is wise and kind. Gareng, as the oldest of the three, goes up first, asking for Abiyasa's blessing and something for the journey. He gets one hundred rupiah. He calls his younger brother. 'Petruk, it's your turn now. Go and ask for a blessing. I already got money for all of us. Fifty rupiah to be split three ways.'

Sure enough, Petruk gets a blessing, but no money. He calls the youngest brother, Bagong. 'Gong. Go and ask for a blessing. We already got the money. Twenty-five rupiah to be split three ways.'

'You two can keep that twenty-five rupiah', Bagong replies. 'Grandfather Abiyasa already gave me some money. Two hundred rupiah ...'

'What! How did you get that?' Petruk says, amazed.

'Ha ha ... I used the back door ...' Bagong replies.

And so, whatever happened, on May 2, 1980 ten ex-political prisoners with their families who had been given this special treatment, arrived safely at the port of Tanjung Perak in Surabaya.

Those Who 'Did Not Wish to Return Home'

I am sure many readers do not know why I wrote the subheading above using inverted commas. Let me explain.

Formerly, around 1964, certain groups had memorised a poem by H.R. Bandaharo. It was said that the poem was composed during the violent conflict between the land-grabbing military and the farmers in North Sumatra. Two lines of the poem became a kind of battle cry:

> 'no-one wants to go home
> even though death awaits'

But seasons change and time moves on. Those who were before on top suddenly lived under the threat of death. It was not a matter of seasons and times, but the terrifying shadow could come like a ghost from one second to the next. For those already disappeared or shot, of course there was no more shadow of the fear of death. But for those in prison or in exile, things were different. They adapted those two lines to make their own battle cry, which you could hear in prison and in exile,

> 'everyone wants to go home
> even though death awaits'

The meaning was reversed from no-one wanting to go home, to everyone desperate to go home, but the odds were still the same: life. So it was with their 'guiding star' which was still the same: life.

So why were there some who 'did not want to go home?' How many, and who were they?

As I said above, it was about one-third of Savanajaya's population, so around 72 families decided to stay. Apart from them, there were another 90 or so 'bachelors' from other units who also declared that they wanted to stay in Buru. Most of them later lived in Savanajaya, but a few were spread between other units which were also converted into transmigration villages, and some others stayed in the town of Namlea. Apart from those who stayed in Namlea, the rest lived as farmers. Some families opened food stalls and bicycle repair shops, some became teachers, and other merchants or small businessmen.

Who were they and why did they not want to return home? Based on their own answers, they can be generally divided into four groups. (1) Those who were small farmers even before they were political prisoners – poor farmers or even labourers working for farmers. Because of the circumstances, they had lost all their possessions, including their house and land. (2) Those who had previously been small farmers, and had not lost all their possessions in Java, but came from areas where the land was infertile, for instance, the area of Gunung Kidul near Yogyakarta. Whereas in Buru they got a house, ricefields and two hectares of land, plus the loan of a cow as a work animal. (3) Those who had been influenced by the smooth words of others, and those who were afraid because of various kinds of intimidation from officials as well as the prisoner informers. (4) Those who felt they had been ostracised by the other political prisoners because they were known to be spies, informers or traitors.

This last group was the largest group among those who did not want to return home, or more correctly, who did not dare to go home. In actual fact, they lived with inner suffering, haunted by their own karma from the past. The lightest form of this suffering was a sense of shame among their old friends and acquaintances. But their worst suffering was their fear of reprisal from those who they had caused to suffer.

There was also another reason why the 'cockroach' prisoners preferred to stay in Buru. They still dreamed that the rulers would continue to use them, as was the case with the 'cockroaches' in Jakarta. But this dream merely caused competition between them. Their arse-licking of authorities led to an internal dog-eat-dog scenario. A few of the cockroaches I can mention from Savanajaya Village were Murtiono, Kustoyo, Ruslan, Jatmoko and Tony Halim.

Chapter 16

SALT TALES

One day, at the office of the Team for the Research and Investigation into Serious Human Rights Abuse on the Island of Buru, under the Indonesian National Commission for Human Rights, there arrived a thin but healthy old man from the pepper fields of Lampung in Sumatra. Like many of his fellows, he had come especially to tell some of his experience when he was held in exile.

'I was once extremely ill because of salt deficiency', he said. 'I thought I had not much longer to live. My fellows probably thought so too, and so someone would always look in on me. Some of them I knew, but some I did not.' He paused, and drew a deep breath, calming a strong inner emotion.

'One day', he went on 'someone came. I did not know him before that, but he gave me a fistful of salt'. He paused again in his telling, then, his eyes welled with tears, he said. 'It is because of that fistful of salt that I am here today before you …'

* * *

October 6, 1972. My fellow inmates and I from Unit XIV Bantalareja had been in the unit just over a year. We had already had two failed harvests. The insect pests devoured all our dry rice plants. We had planted five hectares of yams in plot number D, which we hoped would bring our greatest yield because of the sandy earth. But we got nothing.

The bugs had beaten us to it. We did not get a day off on 17 August, Independence Day. Nor did we even get any special 'extra' food on national or religious holidays like we used to get at Salemba prison. Our food ration for the midday and evening meal at the unit – there was no ration for breakfast – was three boiled yams for lunch and two in the evening. The yams I got for my ration were so hard from being eaten by insects, that they could not even be peeled. When I bit into them and chewed, they were sour.

The cassava plants in the 15 hectare plot G had all lost their leaves, and the roots had rotted in the earth when the plants were seven months old. The expected harvest in two months' time would also fail, as plot G was much lower than the other fields and with the heavy rain every day, it had been completely inundated.

Our unit could not possibly be self-sustaining. Anything we planted needed at least three to four months' time for harvest, and so we were totally dependent on two workers – 'liberated' from our work duties – who secretly chopped sago trees in the swamp. We hoped to get a minimum of ten tumang of sago at the end of each week. This was a calculation based on one sago tree producing 30-35 tumang, if indeed the sago tree was a good one and 'full'. One tree would take seven days to process.

That morning we went out for morning roll call as usual. But something was unusual that morning because the full contingent of unit authorities were present. This was not the usual routine. Usually, the master of ceremonies was there with the Platoon Commander, or sometimes just the guard from the guard post. But on this day it was the Unit Commander himself, and unusually, before the roll call took place, there was an announcement from the unit coordinator: Today, the prisoners in charge of the storeroom where all tools and equipment were kept must only take in the tools and not let them out of the storeroom. Today, all tools currently outside of the unit, in the sawmills and in the vegetable plots, must be returned to the storeroom.

This was strange! It meant we would not work today. And then what? What was going on? There were immediately a thousand unanswered questions in our heads. The order for the day came down from the Unit Commander: all prisoners were dismissed from roll call and had to return to their respective barracks. It was forbidden to visit any of the other barracks. You could only leave the fenced area with the permission of the guard post. At night, when going out of the barracks, for instance, to relieve yourself in the river, you had to carry a lamp and report first to the guard post. The coordinator was ordered to immediately call back in to the barracks any workers who were outside, and they had to bring all their tools with them. These included the prisoners working at the sawmill, the eucalyptus oil distillery, the animal cages, and those making palm sugar.

Prohibitions! We knew what that meant. Probably there would be severe prohibitions. We were prepared. But what the reasons were for all this, the Unit Commander was not saying.

My work duty at that time was in the barracks kitchen, together with Siswondo. It wasn't bad, I thought. I didn't have to just lie around in the barracks, talking about this and that when there was nothing new to talk about. The two of us started work in the kitchen at three in the morning, and would finish at four in the afternoon. Those on kitchen duty were assigned certain times – needless to say with the permission of the guards on post duty – when they could go out of the unit to collect firewood or vegetables. This meant going into the forest looking for eucalyptus that could be felled, then chopping it up and bringing it back to the barracks on a cart; or going into the forest looking for vegetables like bamboo shoot, ferns, or banana tree flowers. Of course the barracks head always whispered to us, 'try to find out some information from the Unit IV inmates about what is going on.'

The first, second and third days the strict prohibitions remained in place, and there were no signs of them being lifted. The guards actually increased their rounds to check the barracks. They were all wearing battle dress. So too the Unit Commander, his deputy and their staff – all in full battle dress. Every now and then a light aircraft would fly overhead and circle over the trees and the mangrove swamp around Bantalareja and Savanajaya. Lines of patrol guards would march through the units almost every day, from the upper units down to Sanleko beach, or the reverse direction. Sometimes we could hear rounds of shooting into the sky, accompanied by bloodthirsty yells. When the four of us with our cart full of firewood stopped beside the road, at full attention waiting for the patrol to pass, I noticed that their eyes were aflame with anger. Some of them were wearing a red scarf around their necks. It reminded me of the 'Ambonese soldiers', for that was what they were called, namely the Sulawesi Devotion of the People Brigade (KRIS, Kebaktian Rakyat Indonesia Sulawesi), which guarded the president and vice-president during the independence struggle when Yogyakarta was the capital of the republic. Their red kerchiefs also reminded me of the soldiers of the 'Dewan Revolusi' or 'Revolutionary Council' I came across when they were guarding the Jakarta headquarters of Indonesia's national radio RRI on Jalan Merdeka Barat and nearby on the evening of 1 October, 1965. They looked scary, for sure. But what was happening? I wondered.

* * *

Behind the row of five Barracks VI to X, within the barbed wire of course, was a well with a hand pump, which supplied water for the barracks. Not long after midday that day, Siswondo and I were waiting for our turn at the pump. There were two others with us from Barracks VI, one of them was Sumadi Peyek (are you still living at Cikajang Kebayaoran?). He was a former member of the High School Student Army (Tentara Peladjar known as TP), and like other TP members his voice was always optimistic and came out booming, even when he was trying to whisper.

'Where can he possibly run to now? The navy is standing by at Priok.'

'Who's that, Peyek?' Siswondo asked.

'Who do you think?' Peyek replied jokingly. 'This is general Hersri the gentleman from Yogyakarta ...' It wouldn't be Peyek if he didn't tease.

'Come on!' I protested at my name being used in one breath with 'the Yogyakarta general', for that was no other than General Soeharto, the mastermind of the whole catastrophe. But Peyek's retort worked to elicit information from Siswondo about the secret behind all the bans at the units.

'Ali Sadikin has taken over Jakarta!' he said firmly.

'What?' Siswondo replied. It wasn't clear whether it was an exclamation of astonishment or unanticipated joy.

I was silent. I did not dare to contradict. I doubted that it was true. Because nothing I had seen with my own eyes every day since these bans had begun suggested any fall of Soeharto.

'What do you think?' Siswondo whispered when we got back to the kitchen.

'I think we should be extremely careful', I said to him. 'I actually took Peyek's news as something to be spread by whispers just to cause trouble in our unit. Maybe also in other units, we do not know. So we should keep that secret to ourselves. What do you think?'

Siswondo sat on a kitchen bench, his feet dangling. He did not reply. He just nodded. His eyes blinked as he looked into the distance.

'What about if we ask Mus?' He meant Mustihar Umar.

'What for?'

'He could whisper to Sam about that news from Peyek?'

The Sam he meant was Samlawi, a young man from Serang, Banten like Mustihar. I knew Mustihar, but not Samlawi. Once a labourer at Tanjung Priok port in Jakarta, Mustihar, used to be a member of the Dock Workers Union (Serikat Buruh Pelabuhan dan Pelayaran). I don't know what Samlawi's activities were when he was still 'outside', but in the unit he was known as a champion of martial arts. He was called 'Champion of the West' because he came from the western tip of Java. He was also a pearl diver. He could dive to the bottom of the sea without an oxygen tank, using no breathing apparatus at all.

'Sam's nose is like gills' Mus once said proudly about this friend.

'Is he in the same barracks as Peyek? Let's wait and see if Peyek's news stops there, or if there is any follow-up.'

The next day Siswondo was given duties indoors. I went out to get vegetables. When I got to plot D, I met the unit coordinator not far from the cow stall. Maybe it was just chance, or maybe he was there deliberately to meet anyone who came, with the excuse that he had to look after the cows. He passed on some top-secret information, as he himself called it. This was further information that verified what Peyek had said yesterday, even though the unit coordinator did not once mention Peyek's name.

The previous evening, Suparno, a friend who worked at the Unit Commander's quarters, was dusting the Commander's desk.

Inadvertently he saw, but maybe the Commander had deliberately left it there for him to see, a radiogram from Command Headquarters on the desk. Because no-one was there, and the radiogram was just lying there, he could easily read it. The contents were clear: TOP SECRET STOP ON FIFTH OCTOBER SEVENTY TWO LT GEN ALI SADIKIN TOOK CONTROL OF THE CAPITAL STOP SITUATION UNDER CONTROL STOP AWAIT FURTHER INSTRUCTIONS STOP FULL BATTLE ALERT STOP.

After the briefing at the wisma, the coordinator said, he had tried fishing for the Commander's reaction.

'So are we having a party, Pak? How many cows are to be slaughtered?'

'What party are you talking about?'

And that was the top-secret information. The Unit Commander did not take the coordinator's bait. But the fishing line he had cast was not broken. The fisherman concluded: the fact that the bait was not taken did not mean it was the wrong bait, but it was because the water was too clear, and the fish afraid to take it.

By that evening the coordinator's top-secret information had become like an underground earth tremor. From barracks ten and six it spread to the eight other barracks. While the bait had not been taken in the wisma, in the barracks the hungry fish took it at once. In my barracks, the one most vocal in spreading the news and finding support for the next steps to take were Slamet Kondor and Susanto. Even Kadis and two of his young followers supported it, but still with a wait and see attitude. And that is how leaders play in times of peace. When it is a tailwind, they will find a place at the front, but when it is a headwind, they will find protection behind anything they can.

It was mainly the Salemba group that greeted this 'top info'. The Tangerang group were perhaps more jaded by their experience after suffering months of isolation after the Silitonga murder followed by the exposure of their illegal network by Operation Kalong led by Captain Suroso.

It was night. The unit was silent. In my barracks, the mosquito nets had long been let down. Mustihar wanted to go and have a pee at the back of the barracks. When he walked in front of my sleeping platform, he touched the tip of my foot. A sign! I slowly got up and went to join him for a pee.

'They're going to make a move tomorrow night', he whispered. 'Just when the barracks kitchen duty starts work. The leaders are our barracks and the one next door.'

'Kondor?' I said.

'Yes'.

'And from next door?'

'Jahar'.

'Do the other barracks know about it?'

'That's Sam's responsibility. He was the one who told us just this evening.'

*　*　*

Earlier in the day, Slamet Kondor had approached me. Maybe he thought I was one of Kadis's group, so he was not hesitant in telling me what was on his mind. I instinctively gathered that it was more a declaration of irritation and not at all a sign about a plan. It was like Heru Santoso when he wanted to escape from the barracks. He only made vague allusions. When Heru was caught after his escape, when we met again for the first time I asked 'Why didn't you tell us beforehand?' And he just sneered and said, 'I asked you lots of questions ... about how far you can walk in one hour, about the distance from here to Wabloi ... how could you not guess?'

'How long do we have to keep on waiting like this, Pak?' Slamet asked me.

'What do you mean?'

'In battle strategy, this means the enemy is quiet. We must take the initiative. We have to strike them! We can't all keep on quietly waiting!'

The tone of his voice rose, even though he was talking in a whisper. It was as though this was to do with a debt of history, where he was on the side of those drawing up the payment schedule, with the right to demand payment from anyone. Including me.

'With our bare hands?'

'Why not?' he answered, without thinking. He was showing off his courage as a former member of the security troops of Kramat-81. 'I'm ready, and I've got three with me. That's enough! Not counting two more from the guards' kitchen ... The enemy doesn't even number 30!'

'And the method?'

'We'll seize their weapons. Cut the telephone wires ...'

Inwardly, I smiled. It reminded me of the bravery of the communists, as mother had told me. 'Becoming a communist isn't easy, Son', she said to me one day. 'You have to have the courage to cut telephone wires and to sabotage train lines.'

My conversation with Slamet Kondor stopped right there because I did not make any further comment. Apart from the fact that I indeed did not know 'battle tactics', it was all a bit too difficult for me to digest. To fight one against five, maybe even one against ten holding guns and bayonets.

I thought that Slamet Kondor just needed someone to listen to his outpouring of frustration. At the most, he was only at the stage of exploring what kind of force he could amass if the time should come to carry out their plan.

The next night I slept fitfully under the mosquito net. Around 3 am, when I usually awoke for my kitchen duty with Siswondo, I saw two of my fellow prisoners sitting dangling their feet over the edge of their sleeping platform. It was Pak Mardjo, the head of the barracks, and Yuswadi. It was as though they were waiting for Siswondo and me.

I saw that Slamet Kondor's mosquito net, which was third away from me, was gaping open a bit. I thought his platform must be empty. But the sleeping platforms of his two or three comrades, who we thought were *the* ones, did not show any unusual signs.

'Is Mus awake already?' I asked.

'He's taking a pee out the back', the barracks head answered.

The previous night, after the roll call, Siswondo and I had asked the barracks head to appoint the two people who would help us on kitchen duty. He had appointed Mustihar and Yuswadi, as well as himself. He volunteered to help out.

After keeping watch the whole night long, calming Slamet Karyadi and his friends and stopping them from threatened suicide, towards dawn Mustihar, Yuswadi and Pak Mardji were now going to be executioners. They were going to kill three dogs. There were nine dogs in our barracks. Too many.

That day and night, our barracks, and a few others were going to have a party. Not a feast of freshly slaughtered beef, but a feast of dog taken from each of the barracks. Other barracks joined the initiative of our barracks. That was why some people were waking up early. On the one hand were those who were dreaming of a feast with beef, to celebrate the success of Ali Sadikin in Jakarta. On the other hand, there were those who were preparing a feast of dog to quell the group suicide threat.

In the lives of the political prisoners, dogs were like a metaphor. A symbol of devoted loyalty. Early that morning, a few dogs sacrificed their lives to save five hundred prisoners, their friends.

The threat of mass suicide passed.

That morning Slamet Kondor waited in vain for his two comrades. From the mess kitchen, no green light signal came either. The entire barracks was anxious and tense because of the strict conditions that were not being lifted at all. Our supply of sago was diminished. There was only enough sugar, salt and MSG for another two or three days at the most. The Buton traders who came regularly to collect sago from the barracks and trade it for spices, and especially for salt, had not appeared for two days. Maybe they were afraid because they had been scared off by the authorities, but also because they too were affected by the length of time the prohibitions were being so strictly implemented.

That evening, the barracks head passed on Siswondo's report to the inmates. Commencing tomorrow, the food from the kitchen would be without MSG and only a little salt would remain. Someone suggested copying what the locals do, and use a little water with ash from sago leaves, but the majority rejected this. 'Better without salt that to go back to primitive times', Rohiman shouted.

After conveying his announcement, the barracks head and Siswondo came over to me, bringing the kitchen report. I knew what he wanted. He wanted me to sneak into Savanajaya and look for help trading our sago for spices in Jamilo or Maloso. Or at least to borrow some salt from other barracks' kitchens, like the sawmill barracks, or the Wai Bini dam barracks. The person in charge of the dam for Savanajaya was Pak Gunadi, who was also from Yogyakarta, and his deputy was Anday Rachma, the younger brother of Y.T. Rachma, the foremost Lekra person in West Java. The person in charge of the kitchen at the sawmill barracks at Kakibotol Hill was Sudono Kusumo, a member of staff from Lekra headquarters. But all I could think of was how unfriendly Sudono had been when Heru and I went to him just to ask about sago trees, not even to ask for anything!

'I don't want to go around begging, Pak!' I said. 'Even if it is to ask for help. I think it will just make me anxious and hate my comrades. Like when the barracks gave Heru and me the task of looking for sago. Don't you remember? All we wanted was a little helpful advice. We were not asking them to give us anything … And do you still remember how the Salemba comrades yelled when they were asked for solidarity with their fellow inmates?

Siswondo laughed. 'There's only one solidarity left', they said, 'and that is to take something home to our wives and kids when we get out!'

'You see?' I said.

'So, what should we do?' the barracks head asked.

I sensed his anxiety. He too was hounded by fear. Fear that the barracks inmates could get sick through salt deficiency.

'I'd prefer that we try to make our own salt', I said.

'Make it?' he asked, surprised. Siswondo's eyes also widened. They were urban types. Maybe they had grown up in the village but were not interested in things outside of their own concerns.

'How?'

So I explained how village people made a kind of fine-grain salt, as I remembered seeing it and people talking about it when I was a boy in my village.

'If you release me from kitchen duty, I will go tomorrow.'

'To the beach?' The barracks head asked.

'The coast is too far', I replied. 'Also it is too exposed, and too easy to be spotted. I will have to stay close around here, in the mangrove swamp.'

'And then do you just boil the water? Are you sure it will work?'

'Well, I have never made salt in my life. It's just like when Heru and I were sent off on the sago-hunting expedition. But we didn't fail, did we? So … if you want to try something, you have to be sure. If you have doubts before you even start, how will you succeed?'

'You make it sound easy', Siswondo said.

'I've never actually done it, as I said. But that's what the people who make it say, and I have watched', I said, trying to convince them that this was better than going around begging for salt from other units. 'When we go to Sanleko, you can see how the beach in the hot sun has a thin line of salt left from the waves.'

'You're right. Alright then. Over to you.'

'I need one other person to help', I said. 'Penjol, if possible, and if he agrees.'

'I'll ask him. As for tools, you will have to ask Mus. He is the one in charge. There are a few tools we have not stored in the storeroom.'

The very next morning after roll call, Penjol and I left. We went eastwards towards the mangrove swamp at Ancol. We passed by the barracks garden at the edge of Walgan Lama and picked up a hoe, a scythe and an axe. We had brought four small pots with us from the kitchen.

We were already familiar with the Ancol swamp area. I had been sent there often to collect snails – or protein as he used to call them. The swamp snails lived collectively. With their comrades. They would crowd together at the bottom of holes under the mangroves and shrubs.

They also lived beneath the prickly palms, but we avoided them because the palm thorns were very sharp.

The method for catching snails was like catching the kind of fish called '*gogo*'. You would grope around in the water with your hands. But for snails you would also use your feet. When you felt the shell, you would dig around with your hands. If you were in the right place, then there would be dozens of snails crowding there playing dead. You just pulled them all up and put them in an 18-litre bucket. When we got 24 buckets full, we would crack the shells one by one using a hard piece of mangrove wood. That would then make two buckets full of de-shelled snails to take back to the barracks. The barracks kitchen would boil them just like that, or at the most, might add a bit of ground wild chilli. Without salt. The snails themselves were already salty. The end product would then be shared around for 'protein consumption' for 500 people. Each person would get one aluminium mug full.

The way I saw it, before we actually got to the worksite, we would boil the water from under the mangroves to make salt. But it turned out that the night before heavy rain had fallen and so the water was too muddy and flowing too fast. The two of us doubted whether the water was salty enough.

'This is swamp water, after all. Not sea water!' Penjol said.

'Yes, you're right', I said, as I dipped my finger in and licked it. The water was nowhere near as salty as the waves at Sanleko beach. And our arms and legs, having been in the water and then drying in the sun, had no trace of salt.

We walked further down. We arrived at another area with similar flora. But there was a kind of grass there with long stiff circular fronds. On the south coast of Yogyakarta, people call this grass '*gerinting*' grass. The land here was flatter and the earth whiter, and scattered around were mounds without any growth, just water-filled holes. The water was clear, so you could see the bottom of the holes clearly. There were tiny fish swimming around, no thicker than a reed. Mullet fish fry!

I remembered my friend Suyanto from the same cell block in Salemba. He came from Blitar and had worked for the regency level office of the Department of Agriculture and Fisheries. One Sunday afternoon when the leader of I Block was the journalist Djoni Hendra Sitompul, Suyanto had given a talk about ways of farming *mujair* (tilapia) and mullet fish. Both these fish, he said, can live in salt or freshwater, but the mullet always breeds in saltwater. Once the fry are big enough to fend for themselves against predators and big waves, they will find banks or go to mangrove swamps.

Penjol and I realised that this was our 'salt-making' place. It was mangrove swamp, but the mullet fry there told us it was near the sea, as did the dry *gerinting* grass.

Penjol found a protected raised spot, walled in by the scrub and mangroves. Using coral, he built four fire enclosures for our four pots and went to find firewood – mangrove and eucalyptus branches about an arm's length long. Eucalyptus burns easily because of the oil content and mangrove wood burns hot because it is a hardwood. I went digging in holes not far from the 'fish hole' because we agreed not to disturb the little fry. When I dug down as far as my knees, the water began to flow. We took it to boil in the four pots.

We boiled and we boiled.

We worked like that, every time the pot was almost dry, we would add more water and kept the fire burning hot. When the sun was already tilted just a quarter above the western horizon, and I was digging the hole a bit deeper, I heard Penjol call …

'Pak Her, Pak Her! We've got it! There's salt!'

I left my hoe beside the half-dug hole and ran over to the salt factory. We shook hands. I was relieved. Penjol was relieved.

'Thank God!' I said. 'We didn't fail. That's enough to take home today. We don't have to make a lot right now. Better to get back with this than miss the roll call and everyone will be in trouble …'

'Yes, tomorrow we're sure to get more!' Penjol said. 'We only started boiling around midday. But one last time, okay? Then let's stop …'

Penjol filled the pots one last time. I cleaned the tools and hid them where I thought they would be safe.

That evening was the first evening our barracks produced its own salt. We had taken back just one mug full. But that one mugful was a guarantee that we could make more. It was just a question of labour, work hours, and tools. By the third day, and thereafter we always managed to take home a potful of salt every day. We shared that among the other barracks. We would start with our own barracks, and then distribute evenly among the others.

Ketoprak Performance in Unit V Wanakarta

Around midday, on the second day, we were taking a rest. While watching the four fires, we ate the food we had brought with us from the barracks. Each of us had one mug of sago porridge and one tin plate with three pieces of boiled cassava. The cassava was thanks to Tasiyo who had gone to work for some local villagers in Badalale. That kampung was far away, about 6-7 kilometres behind the hills to the north. He left very early in the morning, and often did not take part in roll call. To hide his absence, one of the people on kitchen duty would stand in his place. He often came back late, carrying on his shoulders a sack full of cassava. Offering his services to local villagers in this way meant that he did all kinds of things, and it was never-ending. He would clear and scrub, hoe, look for cassava and potato seeds, and plant them. Tasiyo also introduced the villagers to planting peanuts and vegetables.

The people of Buru, at the time we arrived there, were not familiar with planting vegetables. As a result of not eating vegetables, skin diseases were common. They would just use powdered turmeric to treat it. Tasiyo taught them how to plant peanuts and vegetables, especially beans. When the vegetables had grown quite big, the next job was to keep the weeds away. They called it 'cleaning the grass'.

As we sat there taking our midday rest, we suddenly heard the sound of a low-flying plane. It sounded as though it was directly above our heads. It arrived so fast that we had no time to extinguish the fire. But I pulled Penjol into the bushes to hide. This was probably Penjol's first experience of being ambushed by a plane, but not mine. Back in the time of *doorstoot* (Dutch attacks), I used to sell cigarettes under a tamarind tree beside the road in front of the Brosot primary school. Back then, Brosot was on the front line of the Indonesian republican guerilla fighters after the area of Bantul in Yogyakarta had fallen to the Dutch. On the market days in Brosot (the Javanese days of Pon and Legi), there were often fighter plane ambushes. They would circle low in the sky above the village. I would copy the older boys by taking shelter under the tamarind trees, circling to keep out of sight and looking upwards. We would check the direction the plane was flying and its position in the sky. The plane would not go until it had scared enough people, so it would go only after it dropped its bomb on the market or had sprayed its 12.7 bullets everywhere. Once a bomb fell and destroyed the village mosque beside the railway line opposite the school.

Because of my childhood experience, I was not afraid or nervous when there was a fighter plane assault. The way I saw it, the most the plane could do was smash some roof tiles of the village mosque. The 12.7 bullets it sprayed, went all over the place and would only actually kill someone if 'their time had come'. The older boys in the fighting brigade said that the bullets could not penetrate tamarind trees, the trunk of which was so thick it took two of us to embrace it.

Actually, the fighter plane and sometimes a helicopter had been circling the forest and the swamp of Wai Apo for a few days, but this time it was swooping low over Wai Tui and Ancol. Could this be because of the smoke from our 'salt factory'? But the Buru fighter plane did not drop any bomb. Thank God! The only thing it dropped were pamphlets, and then it flew on. We picked up some of the pamphlets and took them back to the barracks.

Even though the plane had moved away, we did not re-light the fire straight away. We waited quite some time to make sure that the plane's visit would not be followed by a squad of guards or by the overseer, Amat Jawa, and the two of us would be suddenly ambushed.

We went back into the bushes and read the pamphlet. It was written by Brigadier General Wing Wirjawan, the Maluku head of Special Operations for the Commander for the Restoration of Security and Order Operations. It reminded the people of Buru of our status as prisoners because we were 'the group of people' who had attempted to 'eliminate the unitary republic Indonesia with its guiding Pancasila philosophy'; that Buru was a humanitarian project to 'restore us to the path of truth, to become Indonesian people of Pancasila'; and reminded them that 'the guards' duty is to help us to return to being good citizens'; therefore anyone who hindered the guards, was 'obstructing, interfering or sabotaging this humanitarian project.'

After going on with a thousand and one such reminders, there was a warning from the Head of the Body for the Administration of Buru Resettlement and Rehabilitation. 'If there is any such obstruction, then you already know the consequences. Do not even try to do anything that can hinder or interfere with the work of my staff in carrying out the noble duty of this humanitarian project. This is the last warning. Take heed.'

'What's all this about?' Penjol asked when we finished reading it.

'This is a good response to the news of Ali Sadikin's take over.'

'But here is only says: "In the recent events, you abused the opportunity, and you only brought harm to yourselves"', Penjol said. 'But what, and where?'

'The way I see it, it is very clear. Whatever happened, happened right here, not in Jakarta, and it was between prisoners and guards, not between Ali Sadikin and Soeharto.'

On the tenth day of the prohibitions, everything became clear. The big roll call bell was struck. All five hundred prisoners had to be present, except for the sick. All the unit authorities had to be present too, and the military had to wear the full battle dress. At this roll call, the Unit Commander made an announcement about the death of a guard, Serma Umar (later posthumously promoted to deputy second lieutenant), who was a guard in Unit XVI. When he was walking through the grounds of Unit V Wanakarta, some of the sawmill prisoners had attacked and hacked him from behind. When an immediate general roll call followed, it turned out that many prisoners did not appear, and were declared escapees. A mass hunt was still underway. That was the story about Unit V Wanakarta as our Unit Commander related it.

Now that the matter was clear (and actually this meant that the commandos now had the situation 'under control'), the Unit Commander read out to us the contents of the pamphlet and declared the end of the special regulations. All prisoners were now free to return to their appointed duties. The sectors working outside of the unit, like at the sawmill or the eucalyptus oil distillery, could return to their barracks. But the important point of the Unit Commander's 'message' was the warning, with threats of course. If any one of us ever saw a prisoner from another unit, whether during the day or night, come to the sheds or to our unit, then we had to report to the wisma or the mess at once. And anyone who disobeyed this would suffer severe consequences.

On the evening of the next day we heard more news about what had happened at Unit V Wanakarta from our fellow prisoners working outside in the fields. It was true that there were still three prisoners on the run. But at Unit V, after the body of Serma Umar was discovered (and this was not part of the news we got at our unit), all the prisoners there were summoned for roll call. They had to line up bare-chested. Armed guards surrounded the yard, their expressions ready to kill. There were machine guns at each corner. Then the guards from Unit XVI Indrakarya arrived, baying for blood. They joined the Unit V guards and started an orgy of revenge. The Unit Commander and his deputy did not dare come out of their rooms. The Commander of the Buru Camp, Lieutenant Colonel A.S. Rangkuti, along with his deputy and staff also did not dare intervene, or deliberately did nothing at all.

It was only the next morning that the guards could be brought under control. The Deputy Commander of the Buru Camp came by motorbike. The person who had the courage to step in was First Lieutenant Daim, the Commander of Unit XVI Indrakarya. Even though he was not from the same division as the division of guards at his unit, he dared take action, using his authority as their indirect superior. Not only was he brave enough to manage to stop the guards' frenzy, but he was also the one who ordered the people from the village compounds nearby to dig graves for the dead. He led the burial ceremony for the prisoners and read prayers for those killed during that night of torture.

There were nine prisoners killed in the yard. Two more died after lying in the unit polyclinic. One was captured alive, Samiyono, a young man from Pati in Central Java, and he was left in Java. He was probably the key figure of the incident. He was the one who was the fuse, from where the network of provocation was lit.

As a consequence, for a few months that unit was paralysed. Almost every inmate who had escaped death had to be treated in the polyclinic. All that day and night of October 5-6, 1972, the guards of Unit V Wanakarta and Unit XVI Indrakarya defended Serma Umar, their fellow soldier from the same corps, with uncontrolled frenzy. They used any hard implement they could find, from rifle butts to hoes, to smash the naked bodies of the prisoners kneeling in the yard. All the prisoners could do was try to protect their heads, or those in the rows behind others would put their heads under the feet of their fellows in the row in front.

There was the sound of bones being smashed by hard implements and the force of the soldiers' rage. Crack, crack, *ketoprak* as bones and skulls were bashed. Like the name of the traditional Javanese performance, *ketoprak*. And so the Unit V Wanakarta named this incident the 'Ketoprak incident at Unit Five', a name that will be forever remembered by all former prisoners at Buru.

This bloodthirsty 'ketoprak performance' was the background to the 'Bantalareja salt factory'. A while after this, the Unit Commander made Penjol the head of the squad in charge of salt and fish at the mouth of the Wai Bini river. I was made the head of the squad in charge of gathering sago with sixty workers from my unit. We no longer needed the guerilla tactics of salt making, and no longer needed the stealth of the 'swamp devils'.

The Bantalareja salt, like all salt that people make this way, tasted rather bitter. But it was also extra salty – salted with the tears of all the prisoners in the entire Buru Camp.

Part III

Buru People

Chapter 17

HERU SANTOSO

It was Irawan who introduced me to him, back when we were both in G Block at Salemba, and all I knew of him then was that he was a young, quiet type. He always looked and acted suspiciously towards everyone. He tended to be cold. I did not consider him anyone interesting to be embraced as a true friend. But I became more interested in him one day when there was trouble in the block.

At the time, several inmates had suddenly been summoned and told they had to move to a different cell block. Conversely, some inmates from other blocks were moved to ours. This kind of summons and move happened often, without our ever knowing what the reasons were. Maybe it was just a kind of Intelligence move, a strategy to create unease. In that way, the prisoners could be exhausted just through having one anxiety piled upon another, and have no time to plan this or that which would threaten the desired 'security'.

One of the people sent into our block was called Hariyudi, a former journalist for the Jakarta daily *Ekonomi Nasional*. He hadn't even put down his rolled-up mat and few possessions before Heru Santoso and Tukimin set upon him. They pushed him up against the wall and pounded his stomach and chest with their fists. There was nothing Hariyudi could do except hold his two arms close to his chest. He did not dare to shout or call for help. The whole thing stopped only when the head of the cell block, Ridwan Basyar, intervened.

'Heru! That's enough! And you, Min, Stop!' Ridwan said with the wise authority of an older man. 'You're both right. But that's enough now! You can go back to it when you're outside.' And he pulled Tukimin back.

'You'd better watch it! If you carry on what you've been up to, you're dead meat!' Tukimin shouted at the newcomer.

Tukimin was one of those in charge of work duties and security in the block. He was big in build and had a gold tooth, which made him look scary when he laughed.

'Friends', Heru said, 'what you see here is an informer. A cockroach. If we weren't inside, we'd kill him no trouble.'

Heru, the quiet young man who usually spoke only with his eyes, was suddenly roaring like a wild *reog* performer who feels his honour has been abused.

* * *

Things settled back down. Some were sleeping, and some were just sitting in their own allotted spaces, all with their own thoughts. While lying down I overheard my two neighbours, Retna Pracaya and Sudadi, whispering. One had been a high official in the Department for Marine Communications, who had been arrested because of his involvement in the Barisan Soekarno (Soekarno Front), and the other had been a member of the Communist Party's Jakarta City Body for Daily Government (BPH, Badan Pemerintah Harian). Even though he had been recalled and fired from the Communist Party because of an accusation of involvement with illicit land dealings, the New Order regime would not let him stay free. These two incomers, apart from their 'high' backgrounds, were also viewed with certain respect among the prisoners because they each received food parcels three times a week, with a good selection of healthy food. There was always cassava but also bread; always white rice and never cracked wheat; always clove cigarettes and good dark tobacco, not ordinary shag; not only peanuts with anchovy but also hot sauce with chicken liver; coffee and milk powder; as well as soap powder and bathroom soap.

'I feel sorry for Heru', Sudadi whispered.

'You know him?' His friend replied.

'We were together for quite a while. We were both held at the Jakarta district Military Command and then at the army Intelligence unit at Kebayoran. I helped him through, when he almost lost all hope.'

'What happened?'

'He's an only child, and now he's really totally alone. His father died in the battle of Surabaya. His mother, Bu Munapsiah, was the leader of the East Java Gerwani (Indonesian Women's Movement). She was sentenced to death because of the South Blitar incident. His wife was captured at the same time as him, but later released, so they said. When we were still being held at Kebayoran, Heru was called in and forced to sign divorce papers.'

'And he agreed?'

'How could he refuse? What did he have to offer? Especially when they said his wife was pregnant and was going to be married to her interrogator. The same one who interrogated Heru.'

'Who was that?'

'Rosadi'

'The bastard! Rosadi, the First Lieutenant of the round-up of communists, the Intelligence's Operation Kalong?'

I couldn't believe my ears. I remembered reading a snippet of news about the wedding of this First Lieutenant Rosadi from Operation

Kalong in the daily *Berita Yudha*. It was when I was still free, wandering around outside, and I happened to pass by the building where the reception was being held near Jalan Cikajang in Kebayoran Baru.

'Even though Heru's wife used to be an activist for CGMI (Consentrasi Gerakan Mahasiswa Indonesia, Indonesian Student Movement Concentration) together with him, she was the prima donna of the students in Surabaya, both because of her activities and her beauty. How could he have agreed to it?' Sudadi added, as though he too was regretting it.

'What if there's a pistol at your head? And didn't they say she was pregnant? Yes, what a bastard that officer with no officer code was. The Operation Kalong types and the others too, they're are all the same.'

From then on I paid more attention to Heru. Even though it was probably just sympathy after hearing how the cruelty of the authorities had made him so totally alone.

Heru shared a cell with Tukimin, a prisoner who never received any food parcels, and Ridwan Basyar, who was a top food-parcel recipient. I had known Ridwan from the time we were still in Colombo. He used to visit sometimes as Indonesia's representative for the sessions of the Asia-Africa Economics Bureau which was also based in Colombo. He was a prominent figure from the past who the Jakarta youth sent together with Kakung Gunadi to bring Bung Karno from Padang to Jakarta. However, because the situation in Jakarta at the time was too unsettled, and the primary purpose of their mission was to make sure that the Dutch did not ship Bung Karno off to Australia, they left him in South Sumatra with the youth there, like A.K. Gani and A.S. Sumadi. Bung Karno was in Padang because the Dutch had moved him there from Papat indeed with the intention of sending him by sea to Australia, one of the 'allies' that was distant from the Japanese invasion. But the looming shadow of the short soldiers from the north overwhelmed The Netherlands Indies KNIL forces who had no war experience. The front line of attack of the Japanese army had already reached Shonanto – their name for Singapore at the time – and Bung Karno, as a political prisoner, was left to escape to Padang and become a prisoner of the Japanese.

Maybe it was also because Ridwan Basyar had heard Heru's background story, that like me, he took him under his wing. The cell inhabited by the 'cell block deputy head' was at the 'front', near the entry to G block. It was the second cell, because the first one was always for the cell block's head who was then Djoni Hendra Sitompul, a prominent journalist who had been in the leadership of the Indonesian Journalists' Union (PWI, Persatuan Wartawan Indonesia).

G Block was made up not of separate cells, but one big space which in 'normal times' had been not a detention centre, but a workplace for prisoners who made shoes, fibre floor mats, and various other handicrafts.

Heru always wore shorts, a small towel around his neck, and went bare-chested. This was not because he did not have any shirt to wear, because I always saw him wearing a shirt at roll call, even though it was an old pale blue tetron one. I think he went bare-chested because this was a kind of ascetic practice for him. But his reason for doing it was different. He did it as a way to steel his body, not to seek spiritual power, or worse still as a way of slowly killing himself out of despair. Heru Santoso was not the type to be anxious and doubt the dawn. Quite the contrary! Undoubtedly because of his background in youth activities, he tended to be overly daring and did not think enough before he acted.

2 August, 1971. From very early in the morning, before we were loaded onto the trucks leaving Tangerang prison for Tanjung Priok harbour, the guards yelled summons and commands at us to move from this cell to that, from that block to this. For the whole week we had been constantly shaken by this kind of thing, to deliberately unsettle us. So, every morning, the minute we woke up, we immediately rolled up our mats and put our few clothes and possessions in our knapsacks, so that all we would have to do was put on our trousers and shirts. We waited in our places, to see what would happen. Those who had any leftover food shared it out with their cellmates. Those who had nothing just drank the warm water from the prison kitchen.

The roar of trucks competed with the sound of walkie-talkies and megaphones, and Lieutenant Sani Gonjo and his soldiers yelling and swearing at us … and this added to the tightness in my chest. In the midst of this early morning cacophony, Irawan came over to give me a message from Heru. Irawan had been in the same block as me since we had been moved from Salemba to Tangerang, along with Heru, Penjol and Slamet Kondor.

'Pak', he whispered, 'Heru's got the idea that we should revolt. We should all get prepared.'

I was so startled that I could not get a single word out of my mouth. Irawan looked at me, his eyes questioning.

'When the trucks start going but have not speeded up, just as we're going out the gate, we should all jump down and attack the guards.'

I made no comment. Heru's message was indeed an idea for action, but too late for comment. In my heart, I could only hope that Heru and his friends would change their minds after we had been rounded up in the yard. None of us knew how many guards and soldiers there would be, how they would be armed, what the prisoners' situation would be when loaded on the trucks, and thousands of other questions of course. I directed my own thinking not to jumping from the truck and overwhelming the guards together with them, but to save myself, and to the probability that I would be shot. Maybe I was a coward. But I did not want to die in a stupid way for something I was not sure of.

It turned out that they were able to assess the situation. Among the 850 prisoners, there were sixty-four who were paralysed or lame, and countless others who were physically weak and suffering from various sicknesses. The soldiers and guards wandering around the yard seemed to outnumber the prisoners, and that did not yet include the guards outside the prison walls. All of them were in full battle dress and armed to the teeth.

In the prison yard, we were rounded up and made to squat, and moved here and there as we awaited further instructions. After a while, we no longer felt the beating hot sun and our gnawing hunger. Irawan came over to me again.

'Pak', he said. 'When the trucks start going, we are all going to sing!'

I was speechless. These young guys just never stop! I thought.

'What songs?' I asked.

'You'll find out', he said, 'the truck in front will start.'

Oh, thank heavens! He did not repeat his call to violent revolt, and I did not remind him. They only wanted to call us to sing together all along the way, like the armed squads and youth groups the Japanese formed during the Japanese occupation who would sing as they marched off to battle practice. I was relieved that the singing they were planning was just moderate revolt, or maybe even more a way of cheering ourselves up? Who knows! But at least we could forget for a moment the searing heat of the sun, and the hunger pangs of our stomachs.

'It will be revolutionary songs, of course', Irawan said. 'The songs will pass from the truck at the front, all the way down the convoy. We have appointed a leader for each truck. In our truck, you will be the leader.'

And that is what happened. All along the way, from the exit of the Tangerang jail until the final bend as we entered Priok harbour, we sang nonstop, occasionally raising our fists in the air. There were popular oldies like '*Sorak-sorak Bergembira*' and '*Halo-Halo Bandung*', through to charged songs like 'The Internationale', '*Darah Rakyat*' and '*Nasakom Bersatu*'.

> *Acungkan tinju kita satu padu*
> *Bersatu bulat semangat kita*
> *Ayo terus maju*
> *Nasakom bersatu*
> *Singkirkan kepala batu*
> *Nasakom satu cita*
> *Tanah air pasti jaya*

> Raise your fist in the air
> Unite our resolve as one
> Forward now, together
> One in Nasakom
> (nationalism/religion/communism)
> Put obstinance aside
> With Nasakom our ideal
> Our country will be glorious

The roads were quiet that day. It seemed they had been closed to allow our convoys to pass – the trucks of prisoners and guards, the officials' jeeps, and dozens of Military Police motorbikes. We did not pass a single other motorised vehicle going either direction. Nor any becaks, bicycles or pedestrians!

All along the route – Jalan Tangerang – Grogol – S Parman – Gatot Subroto – Ahmad Yani – Yos Sudarso, the roads were completely silent. Every hundred metres or so, I could see from the truck as we sped past armed soldiers guarding the road. But they did not face the road, they had their backs to it. It reminded me of an illustration in the book *Babad Tanah Djawi* by R.D.S. Hadiwidjana, the headteacher of the *Normaalschool* in Ambarawa in Dutch times. In the chapter about the construction of the post road from Anyer to Panarukan, there was a picture of Governor-General Daendels and his entourage on horseback, making an inspection. The Javanese coolies were lined up in squatting position, and making the sign of homage with their two hands brought to the face. But they were not looking at the great man himself, rather they were facing the jungle beside the road.

So it was with these New Order soldiers. They paid more attention to threats of attack from 'remnants of G30S-PKI' behind the bushes along the bypass, than to the possibility of the prisoners jumping from the trucks, as Heru and friends had planned.

* * *

When I got to the unit, in accordance with the number on my shirt I was placed in Barracks IX. Our barracks head was Irawan, and Heru was his deputy who was also in charge of work duty. The person in charge of barracks welfare, Soleh Amar, had been a leader of Lekra in Semarang who was moved to Jakarta to lead the Union of Motor Vehicles Workers (SBKB, Seikat Buruh Kendaraan Bermotor), and when he had been in F Blok in Salemba he had been my teacher for Qur'an reading lessons. The unit coordinator – a title later changed to work organiser, was Suwardi Penjol, who was in charge of ten barracks heads in meetings with the Unit Commander and his staff. The leadership team, Irawan-Heru-Soleh Amat agreed that if the barracks heads were busy, then the deputy barracks heads were in charge of external matters and the head of social and economic affairs would be in charge of internal matters.

It appeared that when he was still in Tangerang jail and during the voyage to Buru on the *MV Tokala*, Heru, who was a Salemba prisoner, did not get swayed by the 'news' of our imminent release that the older prisoners were circulating. Instead, he spent his time gathering experience from the younger Tangerang prisoners about how to organise work projects, and what stand to take towards the authorities. Later, a few days after our arrival in the unit, he got additional information through listening to the whispering of the inmates in the neighbouring Unit IV Savanajaya, which bordered our unit.

The conclusion was just this: do not trust the authorities! Because of this, do not compromise. We should not believe that all the food supplies supposed to be for the prisoners for eight months during the settling in period will actually find their way into the barracks kitchens, and that the prisoners will enjoy all the produce of the gardens and ricefields. And so, therefore, we should not give all our labour and energy in working for the unit.

For the first five days, the entire labour force of prisoners was mobilised as one, and not divided into barracks workgroups. From the total of fifty people in each barracks, after subtracting two people for kitchen duty, ten were put on duty to carry the goods from the ship *Tokala* to the food and tools storerooms. The rest were all put on the same work duty, land clearing, clearing the forest outside the wire fences of the unit, and slashing the cogon grass in front of the barracks and the wisma to make a yard for roll call and ceremonies.

In five days, they had cleared space for two yards measuring two hectares. Now the yards just had to be tidied, and for this one person per barracks was allotted. The task of this tidying up was given to those who were elderly or physically weak, even though what was called 'tidying' was in practice still levelling the ground, pulling out the stumps of shrubs, and breaking up the roots and stalks of cogon grass which were sharp as nails. The rest of the labour was put on land clearing duty, felling trees and slashing, behind them came the hoers, and behind them those who broke up and smoothed the clods of earth from the hoes. Water buffalo and cattle were not used probably because there were too many stumps of big trees and shrubs.

This was when Penjol and the ten barracks heads came up with a different kind of work strategy. They asked that the Unit Commander work out a figure of a daily labour supply, which the coordinator and the barracks heads would then divide equally into ten. Each of the ten barracks would then have to provide one-tenth of this overall labour. Of course, the division was done after first subtracting those working on fixed duties, like the barracks kitchen, those working and serving in the kitchens of the wisma and mess, the smithy, and those caring for the cattle which were being groomed to drag the ploughs once the wet ricefields were made.

With this work organisation, the Unit Commander and staff, along with the guards, were not centralised, but had to go around checking all the different work areas. This was when our barracks started its 'labour conspiracy' for survival.

Heru was the pioneer – long before the other nine barracks – in adopting and employing Bung Karno's motto *'vivere pericoloso'*, take risks, live dangerously! There were two possible reasons why the *vivere pericoloso* spirit came a bit later to the other nine barracks. The first reason is that the young inmates in the other barracks were still affected by the trauma of the Tangerang Incident. As I have mentioned before, our unit was known in Buru as the Jakarta Raya unit, because the unit inmates had come from Tangerang and Salemba prisons in Jakarta. Secondly, because the young prisoners were still traumatised, the older prisoners from Salemba, who the Tangerang inmates called cowardly and indecisive 'aristocrat prisoners', had more influence.

On this particular evening, there were four workers not named when Heru called out the work duties for the next day. The way it worked in the unit was that in the evening after roll call, between the *maghrib* and *isha* prayers, the coordinator and the barracks heads held a briefing in the wisma to get instructions on the work to be done the following day. After the *isha* prayers, the barracks heads would convey the briefing instructions to the person in charge in the barracks, namely those managing labour assignments, and they, in turn, would then assign the work to the chosen inmates.

Only after the internal barracks meeting when we knew what our duty was the next day, would we immediately jump in under the mosquito net, not just to avoid the biting mosquitoes and sandflies, but because we were exhausted. On this particular evening, Heru came over to me.

'Pak, I am stealing four workers tomorrow', he whispered. 'Four to start with, while we take a look at things. If necessary we will add more later.'

'Who are they?'

'That's the problem. That's why I want to chat with you. Tasiyo and Bonar Siregar are both young, from Tangerang, agile and strong. They both have experience in work projects. We have asked Tasiyo to go and work for local people who are far from the unit, so he can make contacts. Siregar will survey the forest to find somewhere to make a barracks garden.'

What he meant by 'barracks garden' was of course not the official one owned by the authorities, but an 'internally owned' garden, which was the euphemism for a clandestine garden run by the prisoners themselves.

It was the produce of the 'internal gardens', mainly cassava and corn, that kept the prisoners going. This garden was therefore tended more intensively, was hidden in the middle of the forest far from the unit, and had a bamboo fence around it to protect it from wild pigs and deer. We also fenced it with closely planted banana trees, especially the type of banana tree called *kepok*, which has a shorter life span than other banana trees. We could eat the fruit, and the banana trunks were an effective fence against pigs and deer, and could also absorb bullets if worst came to worst.

'You and I will go to the swamp. Do a survey of sago', Heru said.

Oh no! I thought to myself. I had never once in my life entered a sago swamp. The only swamp I had ever seen was at Ambarawa in Java, the Rawa Bening, which was full of water hyacinth, and the Hikaduwa swamp in southern Sri Lanka, with fishermen on sampans casting their nets.

'Oh', I said 'but what does a sago tree even look like? And where is the sago swamp?'

'This is exactly why Irawan and I want to appoint you. First, because we trust you. Second, you're not weak, and you're still young. Third, many of the inmates in the 'central Java' Savanajaya Unit know you.'

The following morning, soon after roll call, Heru and I slipped away from the line heading out, crossed the Tui River, and entered the thick scrub, walking towards Gunung Kakibotol. We were each carrying an official work-issue sickle and a plastic bucket, and inside the bucket one mug of our daily lunch ration of cracked wheat and one kettle of drinking water.

Gunung Kakibotol or Kakibotol Mountain was actually just hills. A pair of hills, that reminded me of Gunung Sepikul in Yogyakarta, a pair of hills beside the main road from Bantul to Mangiran, which legend says was created by Semar's carrying pole when he was smoothing the Jamurdipa lands to make Java. At the top of one of the hills of Gunung Kakibotol was a small hamlet of just three houses, and at the top of the other was the sawmill run by the inmates of Unit IV Savanajaya. Their barracks were higher up than ours, and below the barracks was their kitchen.

'*Salam lekum*' I greeted in slang Betawi style, from the door of the kitchen.

'What the hell? You're taking a risk! The guards will see you …'

'So, the most they'll do is beat us up', Heru replied calmly while greeting them.

The greeting of fear had come from Bung Dono. His full name was Sudono Kusumo, who worked in the kitchen of the sawmill barracks. When we walked in he was making round sago cakes that we called '*roda bemo*' or 'mini-bus wheels' and water spinach soup that we called '*sayur penthil*' or 'nipple vegetables' because the chopped up tubular stems looked like nipples. Even though it was only this simple food, with the MSG and the coconut milk it smelt delicious to us. The barracks for specialised work and situated far from the units, like the sawmill, the eucalyptus oil distillery, and the extraction unit were known as being 'soft' places. Those who worked there were able to set aside part of what they produced, and they would sell it on the sly for their own purposes.

'Don', I said, 'we need your help'.

I had known Sudono for a long time. He had been head of the secretariat at the central Lekra office, and liked to think of himself as an artist even though I had never seen a single one of his paintings. He had once been sent to Japan to study staging and lighting, as part of the preparation for the performance of the dance-drama *'Djajalah Partai dan Neg'ri'* (Glorious Party and Nation) to mark the 45th anniversary of the Indonesian Communist Party on May 23, 1965.

'How? Be quick. It's not safe here.'

His fear had risen again. Heru hid a smile by pretending to turn to look outside.

'You don't believe me? This place is not safe!'

I thought that he was trying more to convince himself than us.

'Come on, where is anywhere safe for a political prisoner?', Heru said.

Right on! I thought to myself.

'You're newcomers at the unit. Down there is the road to the dock and to the units higher up. There are guards passing by all the time, and they like to call in here.'

'Okay, Don. We won't take long. But you know that none of us can rely on the unit storerooms and what the unit gardens and ricefields produce. So the two of us have come here. We want to know how to look for sago, where to find it, and how to get it from the tree …'

'How to cut sago?' Go by yourselves and look in the sago swamp over there!'

'That's just what we want to ask you', Heru joined in. 'Where is the sago swamp and how do we get there?'

'It's a long way … the inmates here cut sago over in Badalale.'

'Well, it's like this', Heru went on. 'You'll be through with your cooking soon and then you'll have to take food over there. We'll wait and come with you.'

'It's up to you if you want to wait. But I'll still be quite a while. And anyway, why do you have to go looking over there? Your own unit has the Tui swamp. That swamp is all sago. If you cut for a hundred years you couldn't finish it!'

'Where is Tui swamp, exactly?' I asked.

'Pak!' Heru called. He was standing in front of the door. 'Let's go!' he said impatiently. 'There's no point in this idle chat.'

'What do sago trees look like, anyway?' As I stood up I was still asking … so that my task would not be a complete waste of time, so at least I would know for sure what a sago tree looked like.

'It's like a coconut palm.' Dono replied. He pretended to be busy with his round sago cakes we called 'mini-bus wheels' in the cooker.

Heru and I quickly descended the slope of Gunung Kakibotol. We ducked under the shade of the cogon grass and the bushes. A strong stink was carried by the wind. In the middle of the rustling of the buds of the cogon grass and the stink of the corpse flower, there was suddenly a fragrance. We stopped immediately.

'That's bathroom soap'.

'Yes'.

Immediately we dived further in. We sat by the roots of some trees on the edge of a mud hole with blue water and a sour smell under the shade of waving fronds of a kind of palm. We did not yet know that this was, in fact, the young sago plant.

Not long after, we heard the voices of two or three guards getting closer. Loud and noisy. Maybe because that was the way they always talked, yelling at each other, or because of the echo in the middle of the forest. I had no idea what Heru was feeling. But I felt as though I was on the edge of a contest between life and death. If we were caught out on the road then probably the worst they would do is torture us mercilessly. But what if we were caught hiding like this? Or what if one of them just glanced and saw us, and thought we were deer or wild pig and then fired their pistol? Was I going to die just seven days after arriving in Buru?

We heard the sound of their steps as they walked up to Dono's kitchen. We hoped they were only dropping in to eat and drink and were not going hunting. They laughed and joked for a while. Heru closed his eyes tight, put his chin to his knees held tight by his hands. I wanted to hold my breath so that my beating chest would not make a noise like splashing water or rustling leaves. It seemed that I was waiting forever. The throb of my heart felt as though it was being squeezed by the voices of the soldiers and Dono chatting.

But at last the moment we were waiting for came. The foot of Gunung Kakibotol went quiet again. There was just the rustling of the wind among the buds of the cogon grass. The fragrance of the bathroom soap disappeared along with the wind and their steps. The stink of the corpse flower and the putrid swamp returned. But the stink was the fruit of life, not the fragrant smell that brought the threat of danger. I breathed it in deeply. Heru lifted his face. Without another word we started to walk, pushing our way between the bushes and the cogon grass. Every now and then I looked up at the sky to see the direction of the sun and also look for sago trees. What on earth did they look like?

'He's a bastard', Heru said at last.

'Yes, sure is. I just don't get it.'

'It's like he wasn't even talking to fellow prisoners.'

I remained quiet.

'That's why I said, "let's go". There was no point in continuing to talk to him. Apart from that, I might've lost control and bashed him! Tell us where the sago swamp is and what the tree looks like, that's all we wanted … and he wouldn't do it. What's it to him? And then he tells us to go and find the swamp in our own unit … Ah, he's just like an official. He's the Hariyudi type, I think!'

I did not reply. Secretly, I agreed with Heru. Also, his comparison with Hariyudi made me think. I myself did not have any strange or bad experience with Hariyudi. But Heru and Tukimin had their own reasons. On the other hand, with Dono I had had a strange experience that Heru had definitely not had.

It was back in early 1966. One day Dono came with Suroso to my home in Tebet Timur. After chatting about this and that, Dono finally got to the reason for his visit. He wanted to show his amulet of immunity in the midst of the political crisis disaster. It was more than just show. He also suggested that I get the same kind of magical amulet. He pulled out of his shirt pocket a sheet of small paper, the size of an identity card, which was the card for an informant issued by the Military Command V Jaya, complete with the stamp of the Military Commander and the signature of the officer from Section One, or the Intelligence Bureau.

'Get yourself a card like this', he said to me. 'You'll be safe!' he said proudly, with assurance.

He has been trapped into the Intel net, I thought. It is impossible that he knowingly and willingly set out to get this himself, as he was now recommending me to do. Impossible! I convinced myself. I still believed in him and Suroso. I glanced and saw Suroso giving him a look. Was it a warning to his friend that he had gone too far? Whatever it was, and impossible or true, that experience stuck in my memory. Now, here at the foot of the Kakibotol hills, that warning came back. Watch out! The friends and foes of yesterday are not always the friends and foes of today and tomorrow!

Like the Apostle Peter: Eating Insects

We walked on further into the thicket, carefully parting the thick cogon grass that was higher than us. The cogon leaves could slice your skin at a certain angle, like a blade. The newly emerging stumps were also just as sharp, like the roots of a certain kind of yam plant.

A bit further ahead of us we could see three trees standing tall like coconut palms. The trees were higher than coconut palms, though, the trunks were whiter and smoother, and the leaves greener. The fibre at the base of the fronts was also rather black, not brown like coconut frond fibre.

We stopped when we came beneath these mysterious trees. I tapped the trunk, as though calling a greeting, and looked at the tip of a branch. The leaves were blown by the strong, hot savanna wind. We were surrounded by a field of dense cogon grass, interspersed here and there with hardwood trees. They all had small leaves. A little further, in the direction of the mud hole where we had hidden, was a clump of wild banana trees. They too were stunted and had thin leaves, as though nature knew that where water is scarce, it is no place for large-leafed plants. They will be exhausted through being blown by the wind, and fall to the stone-hard earth.

'Heru', I said, 'Dono said that the sago tree looked like a coconut palm. Do you think this is it?'

Heru answered with a laugh.

'How would I know?' He went on with some questions. He sounded annoyed, probably because I mentioned the name Dono. But one thing was sure. We were absolutely exhausted. The sun was burning hot. The air in the dense cogon grass was close, and we were still feeling the tension from hiding from the guards at the base of Kakibotol.

The sun was now almost directly overhead. We sat on our buckets. I then told him what I suddenly remembered about sago. It was from back when I was in the third grade of primary school, and we had just got a book for reading Javanese. The title of the book was *Kembang Setaman* and if I am not wrong it was written by C. van Dijk and R. Samoed Sastrowardojo and the illustrations on every page of the book were by B. Margono. One of the chapters in the book was about the island of 'Papoewah' and it had illustrations too. One of them showed a pile of sago trunks, and another showed two 'Papoewans' in loincloths; one was sitting holding a split sago trunk while the other was standing beside fronds lying at an angle propped with a pole.

'Well, let's just cut one down right here', Heru said. 'What else can we do? After all, neither of us has a clue.'

'Okay, let's cut it.'

We agreed. And anyway there were no other trees anywhere that looked anything like a coconut palm and that could be cut down. So we slashed back the cogon grass around the tree, just enough for us to work and to get out of the way of the tree when it fell. After eating our midday ration of cracked wheat with wild turmeric root that was growing here and there, and having drunk some water and finished smoking a rolled cigarette, we got to work. We used our machetes to cut the 'sago' tree. Heru on one side, and me on the other.

It turned out that the bark of this 'sago' tree was incredibly hard, like coconut trees. Our machetes were supposed to be a good brand, known for being strong and sharp and good for this kind of work, but they were not living up to this reputation. Maybe they were not, actually, the German brand they claimed to be but army-made fakes? Our hands were soon blistered and bleeding, and the machete blades cracked and bent here and there.

That evening we went back to our barracks with the report that our work duty was not finished. The next day we asked the equipment store supervisor for an axe and two new machetes.

'Heru, listen. There is a sound like an echo', I said as I began to swing the axe against the trunk.

I stopped. The palms of my hands were sore and hot. I took off my singlet and ripped it in half to use as bandages. One for me and one for Heru. He took over with the axe. In the middle of the forest and savanna, you could hear the axe resounding everywhere.

'What if the guards hear?'

'Well?' Heru said. 'We've got this far. We can't leave it now. Later is for later', he said, between swinging the axe.

'I know. Where is there a prisoner who has a "later"? Now is only now! But what will we say if they get us? We have to have the same story.'

He was quiet a moment.

'We have been sent on kitchen duty to get firewood. What do you think?'

'Have you said anything to the kitchen head? What if they check?'

'Oh stop these what-ifs. I can do that too. What if those flies are not as smart as you?'

By 'flies' he meant the guards and army soldiers at the unit. Prisoners used the slang term 'flies' because they had green stripes and flocked to shit and corpses.

'Ah, you're crazy!'

'Well, am I right or not?' You want to go on with what-ifs?'

And in this frame of mind, Heru and I continued taking turns with the axe. It wasn't only the palms of our hands that blistered. The blisters on our backs from sunburn also started to burst, and stung from the salt of flowing sweat. But we kept on working. We were determined to fell the 'sago tree' by evening so that tomorrow we could start to press the sago. Oh, how happy we would be to bring some extra food to our fifty mates at the barracks!

Our shadows were at an angle of seven o'clock. That meant it was around four or three-thirty already.

'We have to start going back in a moment, Heru', I reminded him. 'So we're not late for roll call.'

'Ah we're nearly there', he said 'just a bit there, a bit here.'

'Crack!' Suddenly I heard the sound.

'Out of the way!' I yelled.

He ran back a few steps, looking up.

'Where?' he said. 'Look at the top. Only when it starts to rock do we have to …'

He went forward again swinging his axe. Harder now, with full force. This time from the opposite side. Just three strokes later we heard another crack. Heru stopped, walked back and looked up.

'Look. In which direction are the tips of the branches moving?'

I couldn't see. The tips were moving, swayed back and forth by the wind. Maybe this was also why the trunk, which was almost cut right through, remained balanced. Back in my village when I was a child, I used to watch people cutting down coconut trees. It was never just two people, but always a group of between seven and ten. Before they started to cut the trunk, one of them would climb to the top of the trunk and strip it of anything that would be caught by the wind; not only the fronds, but also any coconuts, blossoms and very young coconuts still in their sheaths. Then they would take a very long rope made from plaited bamboo, connect one end tightly to the tip of the tree and let the other end hang loose to the ground. Later they would all pull on the rope when the first cracking sound was heard. At the same time, one of them would give the *coup de grace* with a swing of his axe. That way, they could control the direction the tree would fall, and it would not be blown by the wind.

'Look!' Heru said. 'It's going to fall towards Kakibotol. We should get over here.'

The trunk started to lean. The tip was twisting, teased by the fronds, before it crashed down about five steps in front of the base. The earth shook and the savanna air filled with the hum of the vibration. It did not fall in the direction of Kakibotol. The wind had turned it in the direction of the water hole. The power of the wind was amazing! Heru and I just gaped, speechless.

'Just imagine if we'd been in the wrong place!'

'Yes. No primitive native would ever be as stupid as us …'

That evening we took back our work report to the barracks. We had felled the 'sago tree'. Tomorrow we would split it, pound the sago inside, and begin to press it. For that, we asked our friends for a log of hard *doran* wood used for hoes as a scraper, and I surrendered another of my singlets to use as a sieve. Luckily, in the last batch of food parcels sent to Tangerang jail, I had received a few clothes from my younger brother. He had probably heard from his officer colleagues involved in 'Operation Whale' that a new batch of prisoners was about to be sent to Buru, and that I was among them.

The next day we cut the doran wood into a few pieces each about one and a half metres in length. After, with great difficulty, we managed to split the sago trunk which had an incredibly thick bark, and then we began pounding and pressing. We got the rinsing water from the pond where we had hidden three days before. But we could see from the few drips coming through the singlet sieve that the water had not changed colour. It did not look white as it should from being mixed with the pounded sago. Over and over again we did it, but with no result. There was no starch in the bucket. Was the tree too old? Were we not pounding it fine enough? Was the singlet too fine to use as a sieve? All kinds of questions arose, without us knowing the answer to a single one.

We had run out of ideas and sat dejected on the cool split log. Suddenly we were startled by a local villager. We had no idea where he had appeared from, but there he was suddenly standing by the stump. He was wearing only a loincloth and had a machete at his waist. In his right hand, he was carrying a staff. His mouth was red from chewing betel nut, and around his forehead he wore rings of rattan.

We looked at each other. Apart from being startled, the two of us were confused because we did not know what language to use to talk to him. Meanwhile, it was he who began the communication. Heru and I listened to him, and guessed at what he was saying from his tone and his gestures, and also from a few words of Ambon-Malay he used here and there. There was *beta (I), ose (you) dorang (you, a group) torang (all of us) kamu orang (all of you), seng (no, not)* and various other words. This is more or less how the conversation went.

'How dare you cut down a tree? All the trees here belong to the king Kayeli. I am the one allowed to cut it down. If I wanted, I could kill you both. Just like that. Or you can pay *manu*.'

Then he listed some things: so many machetes; so many axes, so many pigs, so many pieces of cloth ... What he meant by *'manu'* was a barter price.

'We are both prisoners', Heru said, paying no attention as to whether he understood or not.

'We are prisoners of the king of the unit. You [*ose*] are a soldier of the king Kayeli. We are not soldiers. We are just slaves. Slaves of the soldiers of the unit. If you want *manu* you have to ask the Unit Commander. If you want to kill, you should kill the Unit Commander, not us ...'

We were quiet. We did not know what else to say. I was laughing to myself. But then I suddenly had a strange idea. Wouldn't it be wonderful if Basuki Effendy were here with us? He was the actor and film director, and a friend of all the inmates of Purwadji barracks. Probably he would get an idea of writing a scenario. It would be like cowboys and Indians, but with a peaceful and friendly approach. No pillage and plunder and shootouts with the Indians always portrayed as barbarians who should be wiped out.

After a while, we invited the man to sit. We smoked rolled cigarettes together. I looked for some wide leaves and divided our two cups of cracked wheat into three portions, and we ate together.

After eating, drinking and smoking, he became our friend. Not, of course, because of the cracked wheat, water and cigarettes, but mainly because we truly did relate to him with openness. His name was Mahele and he lived in Walgan Lama. We learned from him why the 'sago' tree bark was so hard and why the flesh inside was not producing any starch. The tree that looked like a coconut palm and which we had worked on for four days was not a sago tree at all, but an areca palm tree. It was an old tree, which was why it had no flowers or fruit.

Come back tomorrow earlier in the morning, Mahele seemed to be saying, by pointing at the sun, and saying over and over the word for 'horizon'. 'You come here and I will take you to the Tui swamp where the sago forest is.'

That evening we went back to the camp bearing the story of our four-day long failure. But we also brought some hope and clarity. We promised that in one week our barracks would already have some supplementary food. Ambonese sago! This had been even more valuable as a food-parcel commodity than cracked wheat back in jail in Jakarta!

They accepted both our report and our promise. No-one thought that we had actually spent four days just loafing. Our hands were bloody and our backs covered with blisters. At the same time, the two of us also knew just how hard our fellows had to work out in the fields and under the constant threat of torture. Bung Tasleman and Bung Haryo, the heads of barracks number five and three, had been tortured by being made to stand with their eyes open staring at the sky in front of the wisma from morning until evening roll call. They had been caught attempting to take a sack of bean seeds from the food storehouse – rather than take stuff during the day when they would be the target of the head of the storehouse, Dullah, and the guards, they stole at night, and bartered their booty in the kampungs of Marloso and Jamilo.

'Bung Sis!' Heru said to Siswondo, the head of the kitchen. 'Try to give us an extra ration of cracked wheat for Mahale. If that's impossible, then take his share from our ration.'

'Ah, that's no problem', Siswondo said. 'If it's just one mugful, I can scrape around at the bottom of the drum.'

'And salt, please', I added.

I thought that apart from the cracked wheat, salt would also be good for cementing our friendship with Mahale. Later we would find out that for the local population of Buru who were still extremely dependent on what nature had to offer, salt had a high exchange value. Salt was still something rare, so they used to flavour their food with the ash from sago leaves.

'But be careful, Heru!' Irawan warned. 'Are you sure it's not a trap? Tomorrow Mahale will turn up with his "friend" who will take both of you off to the unit?'

'That's right.' I said. 'But even if what you say is true, what can we do about it? That's the risk we take. We'll be as careful as we can. We'll spy from a distance first, and we won't arrive until he gets there first.'

The next day we proceeded with extra caution, trusting Mahale. He arrived, like the day before, with his spear in his hand and machete at his waist. He was also carrying some strips of branches of bamban wood, some sago palm leaves, and two tools that were shaped like axes but with short wooden handles, about two hand-widths long, and topped with the bark of wild pandan. This was the tool used to pound the *ela* or sago 'meat'. The sago trunk, after being split in two, was not just beaten as we had done at the foot of Kakibotol. It was hit using this particular tool, and with a movement like someone hoeing. The tool had a beautiful name, *nani*. The sago fronds were used to make a sieve for the pounded *ela*. This sieve also had a beautiful name, *sani*.

I have no idea what Heru was thinking or feeling. But as for me, I was amazed and thrilled to be entering a new world of adventure. The water in the sago swamp was clear and blue, and flowed calmly. Only the sour swampy smell was strong.

Sago trees turned out to grow in clusters, because they grow from seeds that fall around the trunks. They are not like coconut palms which grow separately. The trunk of the sago tree is no different to a coconut palm. Not very tall, but thick and full. The trunk is between 10-12 metres high. The fronds have soft thorns at their point, and the backs and base of the fronds have tiny long thorns. The tips of the branches with flowers and fruit attract special bees, as well as birds including wild doves.

The Tui swamp was not a breeding ground for crocodiles, but it was a place where large lizards and wild pigs looked for food, namely the sago bee larva which proliferated in the rotting residue from pounding the sago. The sago swamp was really a natural source of food, where nature offered exchange. Among the paths in the sago grove, local sago pounders and middlemen would meet to do their open-air trading.

The paths in the sago swamp were made from the bark of sago trees, also called *ela*, sliced long like bamboo, and placed rounded side up on top of a base made from sago or coconut fronds. To make the undersurface sit on the water, the fronds would not be stripped. The paths then were like floating bridges. When walking, to keep from putting a heavy weight on them, you had to walk almost on tiptoe, like a slow jog.

* * *

That day, Mahele taught us the ABC of the culture of making 'white gold'. How to know which sago tree had contents and was ready to be felled, and which trees were filled only with water and should not be felled. A tree should be felled only when it held at least thirty *tumang* of sago. A tumang is a cylindrical container for sago starch made of sago leaves, and when full it weighs about 2.5 kilograms. There is customary law to govern these things, which the king and his officers implement. Local customary law also stipulates that for every sago tree felled, whether or not it is then pounded for the sago, a person must pay a fee of seven or eight *tumang* of sago to the king.

Mahele also showed us how to fell a tree, split it, and pound the sago, and how to make the sieves and the *kole-kole* or long vats made from whole sago branches, to carry away the sago fluid after sieving the starch. Like villagers in Java when they cut down a coconut palm, the feller will cut the tip of some plant growing nearby and then put it in the stump of the tree he has felled, as a symbol of taking responsibility for caring for the balance of life. The people in Buru did the same. Also, when someone hungry passes by a cassava field, he or she may pull out and eat some cassava root, but the customary sanctions teach: you must replant the stem of the plant where you took out that living thing.

After all that work, except for making the *kole-kole*, we rested. Mahele said he had to go for a while. Heru learned how to make the *tumang* sago containers, and I plaited some coconut fronds to make a roof for shade.

Heru chuckled.

'All of our factory knowledge and city skills aren't worth much here, are they?' he said.

'What do you mean?'

'Just yesterday we were almost dead from working for four days straight. We used T-shirts and buckets for sieves and containers and did not even get a drop. And now? Our tools are fronds and leaves, and we can even make *tumang*. We use the diameter of our heads as a measure for the circumference, and two stretches of our hand for the length. No need to worry about finding tape measures!

I chuckled too. Maybe this is what is meant when we say that comparing one civilisation with another should not be to judge them and slot them into categories – modern for one, primitive for another; refined for one, and crude for another; glorious for one, and despised for another.

When Mahele returned, he carried two packets wrapped in bamban leaves containing *midong* (larva of the sago tree beetle), *ela* mushrooms, and wild chillies. We stopped work and waited while Mahele prepared this extra food. He found reeds and pierced the sago-leaf wrapped midong and roasted them like satay. The mushrooms and chillies, after giving them a little salt, he wrapped in bamban leaves and roasted them too.

'Delicious!' Heru said, tapping Mahele on the back. 'This is protein, Mahele, protein!'

Heru was right. The mushrooms and the larva were sources of protein. Mushrooms, like all fungi, even poisonous ones, everyone finds delicious. And the midong, like all kinds of larvae, was creamy and fatty. The prisoners always called any kind of fatty and hearty food protein. Back in Tangerang prison, we never got any protein at all except for what arrived in food parcels. After we arrived in Buru at the unit, we found protein in fungi on the cogon grass (which we called *bakso* because it was round and tough), in rats we managed to catch when out clearing the cogon grass, in snails, or in the worms we found in banana tree trunks.

Mahele gave a big smile when Heru tapped him on the back. His black eyes shone in his peaceful way.

Back when I was still studying and teaching I often heard and also repeated the slogan ' back to nature', namely about when Europe was searching for new values from the neglected values of ancient Greek and Roman civilisation. Was this too the secret of Mahale's peace and that of my fellow human beings in the Buru interior? In relying on nature, they did not surrender and they did not plunder it.

That evening we returned to the barracks in victory. We now possessed skills and the essence of the beauty of life of the simple 'Mahale' folk.

* * *

I wasn't Heru's work partner for long. That time of being the 'Two "Her" devils' (Heru and Hersri) of Tui swamp, as our fellow unit inmates called us, was short. Each evening we brought back two 18-litre buckets full of wet sago, and four *tumang* of dry sago once a week. But about two months later I was pulled back to general work duty, and replaced with two younger workers who could be ordered around, Syamsudin Gobel and Bogel. Syamsudin Gobel was from Gorontalo and had been a member of People's Youth (Pemuda Rakyat), and was the nephew of the Gobel who used to be the 'transistor king' of Cawang, the owner of the radio factory. Bogel was the youngest political prisoner. He had been picked up when he was only 13 and taken to Buru as a hostage for his father who had gone on the run and was never captured. Who knows what his real name was – nobody cared, because we liked using the friendly nickname 'Bogel', which in Javanese means blunt or having a rounded tip, and in Batawi slang means a boy who is circumcised when he is too old.

Having three to do the sago work made sense. Two workers to do the pounding, and one to do the pressing. Because with one pounder and one presser, the person doing the pounding could never keep up with the one doing the pressing.

From then on, Heru and his two workmates always came back late to the barracks. Heru himself often came back later than Bogel and Gobel, entering the barracks after evening roll call, so that when the roll call took place, the head of the barracks had to hide his absence by 'borrowing someone' from the kitchen. Because of this, some of the inmates began to suspect that Heru was hiding some of the *tumang* of sago meant for the barracks for himself and the other two. Indeed, sago traders from Buton sometimes came to the swamp bringing various things to trade, like loincloths, singlets, black tobacco, thread, salt, monosodium glutamate, coconut and other things. Even though Heru's sleeping area in the barracks was right next to me, now he also rarely spoke to me. But we could only really meet in the late evening and at night after everyone was asleep.

'Pak!' he called one evening. He was behind his mosquito net, and I was behind mine. 'How many kilometres can a person walk in a day?'

This was a strange question. When you were a prisoner, you could not walk wherever you wanted, so why ask how many kilometres in a day? And when did a prisoner ever walk for one whole day, unless herded by a guard? But strangely, I gave him a straight answer, even though it was no more than directly responding to his words. This was because of my naivety and the absolute trust I had in him.

'That's a difficult question', I replied. 'But I'll tell you about my experience as a boy. Maybe this'll be useful as a guide. When I was in high school I always walked to school. The school was in Jalan Terban Taman opposite Panti Rapih hospital, and I lived in the kampung of Panembahan, south of the northern Alun-alun square. It was a distance of about four kilometres, and it usually took me one hour or a bit more. So I would say a person walks on an average one kilometre per fifteen minutes.'

Heru was quiet. He seemed to be paying careful attention.

'But that was when I was a high-school student, and walking on city pavements', I went on. 'Now it would be different. Apart from the fact that my steps are wider, I am walking on earth, and sometimes in the swamps where we have to jog.'

Heru still made no response.

'So I would say that here, probably you would cover a kilometre in ten minutes. Maybe even less …'

'So that means a least 60 kilometres in one day?' Heru said.

'More or less' I said. 'So where would that be from here?'

'Rana Lake, if you went inland. If you went south to the coast, Leksula is 80 kilometres. Maybe you could get to Leksula if you had a compass to take shortcuts. You could go via the swamps, couldn't you?' he tried to sound convincing.

'You could take short cuts if you really knew the direction. If not, it would be even further …'

That evening, our conversation went on like that, and I never gave it another thought, especially because Heru did not seem to be open to talking. The other inmates were becoming increasingly suspicious of him. The sago production was declining. The three of them were producing less than Heru and I had produced when it was just the two of us. At the end of the week sometimes they did not bring back any dry sago at all! They had various reasons. They had changed the work area. They were still surveying trees, they still had to make the *kole* pipes, they had not found a tree that was 'full', and so on. Gobel and Bogel, maybe at Heru's instigation, were not forthcoming about what was really going on in the swamp. Meanwhile, Irawan did not step in and pull Heru back from working in the swamp and replace him with someone else. Maybe because he felt protective towards him as one of his own kind, and wanted to hide the flaws of the young group in front of the older ones.

There was something else odd about Heru's behaviour. The others in the barracks just didn't get it, or if they did, they paid no attention because they thought it was not important. Stomachs racked with hunger and bodies threatened daily with torture will ignore all kinds of small things. As for me, I saw Heru's strange behaviour merely as some kind of joke I did not quite understand.

It was to do with the coolie hats all prisoners had been issued with a few hours before we left Tangerang prison. Apart from the coolie hat, we had also received one plastic bucket, one mug, one aluminium spoon, one mat and one pillow, and one set of khaki clothes stamped with our deportation number. Those of us who worked out in the fields did not always wear our coolie hats because they got in the way when you were wielding the hoe. But Heru and Bonar Siregar always wore theirs, from morning roll call when they went out to work until evening roll call when both the sun and the prisoners were getting ready to sleep.

Heru's and Siregar's joke, which I did not understand, was that on the band of their hats on their foreheads, they had written their names. Heru had written La Heru and Siregar had written La Regar. I had no idea what it meant. 'La' is a prefix used by Buton people for men (while 'Wa' is used for women).

I knew this from my childhood. Back in Yogya during the time fighting for independence, there was a theatre director I admired from the Petera group (Penghibur Tentara dan Rakyat, Entertainers of the Army and the People), from the Regional Struggle Bureau XXV Yogyakarta, whose name was Dahlan La Nisi. He was from Buton. Other actors and actresses included Sasmito, Sudjadi and

Rukinah, who later became stars of the *ketoprak* group Krida Mardi, and a woman of mixed Indonesian-European blood from Gandekan kampung called Norma, who was also a *keroncong* singer. I have no idea where she ended up. Dahlan La Nisi himself vanished after the Madiun incident of 1948.

Anyway, back to the coolie hats of La Heru and La Regar. The others paid no attention. I thought it was funny. Just a childish attempt to show how they had 'integrated' with the traders and middlemen who they considered to be 'advanced' elements of the local society.

There was one time, for three consecutive days – and it had to have been during our first four months at Buru – when Unit XV Indrapura, whose fields have been cleared from bamboo, had their harvest. Their crop was dry rice. It was a celebration because they had succeeded in growing dry rice, and because it was the very first harvest. Our unit, meanwhile, whose fields were cleared from cogon grass and scrub, went hungry for almost two years. The commander of Unit XV asked us to help them with their harvest. Maybe he had a glimmer of pity for the 500 hungry prisoners in the unit neighbouring his, but it is more likely that he wanted to show off to his superiors and to the Unit Commander of our unit. There was First Lieutenant Sukirno in Bantalareja who had failed, and here was First Lieutenant Suyadi from Indrapura who was champion!

So all of us, the entire workforce from our unit, was called back in to help with the harvest of our neighbouring unit. Of course, that included Heru and Siregar, who had been secretly relieved of their general work duties. For those three days, we were together again. Not just together in the ricefield, but we were also side by side cutting the rice plants, me, Heru, Irawan, Penjol, Aziz, Purwadji, Mustihar, and a few other young ones from our gang in the last days at Tangerang, during the voyage on the *Tokala*, and for the seven days in the transit unit at Jiku Kecil. Like the others, every now and then we would stop to take a quick break.

'Look out, protein!' someone shouted.

This was a sign that there was a rat around, and for us to stop working in a line and quickly form a circle, cutting as we pushed forward. Together we would encircle and catch the rat. When we caught it, we would bash it on the ground and throw it into a plastic bucket. Then we would go back to our previous work formation in rows while waiting for someone to make the next 'protein' call. Later, during lunch break, we would skin the unfortunate rats and roast them on a fire to eat with the bland daily food ration.

But Heru was different. Apart from hunting rats, he would ask us to hunt for grasshoppers and locusts, and give them to him.

He only wanted a special kind of insect – the ones that were green and quite large, with red eyes and the tips of their legs yellowish. They are known to frequent ricefields. He did not want any that had short bodies and were brown in colour.

'What about these grasshoppers, Heru? do you want these?' Irawan asked.

The ones he was talking about were the ones called *walang wadung* which are cannibals, with triangular heads, one pair of serrated legs at the front, and long thin bodies covered by their wings. The female is savage. After mating, she eats the male. This insect likes to eat leaves that are bitter, like guava for instance.

Every time Heru was given someone's insect catch, or got his own, he would immediately clean off the wings and legs, and eat it raw.

'You're mad!' Purwadji said to him. 'How can you eat raw insects?'
'Not even crazy Pardjo P.A. does that!'

'Pardjo P.A. is still green. Heru here is just stupid!'

'Ah, shut up! Haven't you ever read about the apostles? It says that once when Peter was being chased, he ate insects.'

'That's just because there was nothing else to eat!' Aziz put in his two cents' worth. 'We've still got other stuff. Even if it's only cassava.'

'Well we have for now', Heru said. 'But who knows tomorrow? If there's no food tomorrow, you will not be prepared. But I am getting into practice, right now.'

Penjol roared with laughter.

'Is that really true' he asked me, 'that story from the Bible?'

I was silent.

'Now have any of you ever read the book by Nguyen Ngok that Shannu translated, titled *Kampung Nan Pantung Menyerah* (The Village That Never Gave Up)?'

'I have!' chimed the reply.

'So, was it true or not, that they shot at helicopters using catapults?'

They all laughed at my answer. But, I thought, every question always demands an answer. Giving the right answer is the problem. Truth in a proverb will not be found by chewing on it. Like Heru chewing his insects. But maybe the truth will be found in Mahale's way of looking for sago starch. By pressing, and pressing again, then sieving with a sieve that is both strong and soft. Even though it is only made from leaves …

* * *

After the first four months, Unit XV Indrapura celebrated its first harvest of 35 hectares of dry ricefields and 10 hectares of corn and peanuts. The area of our fields of wet rice and crops was just as large, but only five hectares of dry rice plants, located across from the wisma, looked green, but were not all that healthy. All the rest of our fields, including seven hectares of corn, had been devastated by locusts. There was only around six hectares of cassava at the far end of our land that we held out any hopes for, but we still had to wait another four to five months before we could dig them up. The only plants that had succeeded was an area of about one and a half hectares of cucumber. But who can live off cucumber, even if you eat as much as you want?

That night, around midnight, at the barracks we were startled by a strange noise. In the middle of the silence of the night and the omnipresent threat of torture, we woke with a sense of dread. There was the sound of boots marching, coming ever closer. The thudding sound seemed to be surrounding us outside the barbed-wire fence. But we had no idea what it was. We could only be alert and wait. Wait for our last moments. And be alert because we did not want to be sleepy. Towards dawn, the noise stopped.

There was absolutely no announcement during roll call. Not from the wisma commander, not from the mess guards. It seemed impossible that they had not heard. Were they just like us? Also afraid, thinking it was the noise of marching prisoners on the rise? The morning roll call went by in a mood of dread, suspicion, and also alert. It was only after dawn and when the view of the fields slowly revealed itself that the frightening riddle of the night before was solved. The entire field was completely bare. When we went to work it turned out that the only thing left were a few remaining stalks, and countless caterpillars looking for places to hide among the grass and the cracks in the earth.

The caterpillars had eaten the entire 35 hectares of plants. We did not know, neither did the agriculture officer, know what alias the thug bug went under. Where had these caterpillars come from, what wings did the insects have, and on which leaves did they lay their eggs? It reminded me of the plague of rats in Gunung Kidul in Yogyakarta around 1956. People said that the rats came from the coast, and were brought in on the waves, one wave upon another. The farmers said that the rats were the transformed spirit army of the Queen of the South Seas.

But which spirit was it that produced these Bantalareja caterpillars that brought not prosperity, but misfortune? Some prisoners whose anti-American sentiment was still strong started heaping the blame on America. This superpower, they said, not only spreads germs with its bombs showered on Vietnam, but also spread pests in rice seed and fertiliser that they produce and export to third world countries. The name of the rice-husk pest was also strange: soldier worm!

The sound of the pest army that attacked the unit like an army of pests that we had heard the night before was terrifying. It was just as impressive as Sarwo Eddie's 'Sky Army' when they parachuted from behind the clouds to attack the communists armed only with hoes and sickles in the ricefields and fields of Central Java and Bali.

Now the caterpillars were lounging around covering the now-bare field, climbing the ridges of the paths, and hiding in the cracks of the earth and in the odd remaining clusters and pits of the corn leaves. Because they were immune to sprays of powerful insecticide, that morning our job was to pick them off one by one. Put them in buckets and burn them in piles.

In the eyes of prisoners starved of food, all living creatures are protein. This word becomes a pretext to change anything into something edible. So too with any kind of plant and root. So there arose a saying among the prisoners, 'anything with legs is edible, except for tables and chairs'. For instance, why not try the roots of flowering plants like the corpse flower plant (which looks like a small Raffelesia)? So we peeled it, sliced it very thinly and soaked it for three days and nights, sprinkled it with ash and dried it in the sun. Once dry and washed again, we boiled it and tried to eat it. But it was so poisonous that even before we swallowed, it made our lips and tongues swell and stiffen.

So when the prisoners gathered the 'soldier worms', they immediately tried to cook them, dry-frying them in tins out in the field.

'Let's crush these soldiers' Rohiman said.

'We can't crush the real soldiers, so let's do it with these worms', Mustihar added.

He took a mouthful, but immediately his face screwed and he vomited.

'Goddam!'

'What do they taste like, Roh?'

'Like earth and leaves …'

'Just swallow it, Roh. You'll turn into a cow. When your teats appear, we'll milk you …'

'Cut it out. Are you queer?'

We had not lost our ability to joke and tease, even when we were starving and had no idea when we would get any decent food, and under the constant threat of torture. Or maybe it was because of that that the instinct for survival emerged in joking about our own fate. If a day went by and we did not hear one of our fellows being hit as he walked past the guard post, then someone would ask, 'Why is it so quiet today?' When Pardjo P.A. came back exhausted from working in the fields and was ordered to sing some songs, this was not an order praising his voice and so cheering him up. No, it was a sadistic teasing that made his sensitive nature suffer all the more. And when Tika bin Dina, a skinny, sick prisoner from Kramat Pulo Jakarta, collapsed and died one day out in heavy rain while clearing a field of cogon grass, it was the first death in the first month after our arrival in the unit. Torture was part of our breathing.

* * *

Amidst the gnawing hunger of his fellow prisoners in the unit, along with the terror of yelled abuse, bashing, and warning shots that made the atmosphere unbearable, Heru Santoso exercised the one and only right left to a prisoner. The right to escape. He convinced Bonar Siregar to join him in this gamble with fate, to breathe the fresh air of freedom.

It was evening before roll call. The tools had all been returned to the storehouse. After roll call, the coordinator and the ten barracks heads had their briefing at the wisma for work duties the next day. Irawan was no longer our barracks head. He had been replaced by Soleh Amat, my former Qur'anic reading teacher at Salemba jail. The unit coordinator had also been changed. It was no longer Suwardi Penjol, but (let's call him) Samodra. He was not a former member of the League of Indonesian Youth and High School Students (IPPI, Ikatan Pemuda Peladjar Indonesia) or the Indonesian Student Movement Concentration (CGMI, Consentrasi Gerakan Mahasiswa Indonesia), but from Pemuda Rakyat (People's Youth), which was stronger in its Communist Party affiliation. Samodra also could not really be grouped in with the 'young' prisoners, even though he was not really old enough to be in the 'old' group either. He was a figure in the middle between the two. Maybe, on the one hand, the change was made because both Penjol and Irawan were suffering from malaria, but on the other also it was a sign that the domination of the 'young group' was beginning to fade, while the 'old group' had not yet restored their status. Soleh Amat approached me. He looked worried.

'It's serious, Pak', he whispered. 'What do you think?'

'About what?'

'It's the tool storehouse. The tools from our barracks have not all been returned, even though Dullah checked them before roll call.'

Dullah was the civilian staff under the Unit Commander, in charge of the storehouse.

'What tools?'

'Machetes, small saws and hammers. Two of each. One axe and one adze. None of them are the tools we need in the fields.'

'So who borrowed them then?'

'Leman said it was Siregar. But I think it was Siregar and Heru.'

I was silent. My breathing seemed to stop. I thought the barracks head was right. This also was the answer to the Buton joke on their hats, La Regar and La Heru. I immediately suspected that the two of them had escaped.

'Gobel!'

Gobel was sleeping in his place, which was just two from mine. He was pretending to have his eyes closed, his arm resting on his pillow. He got up and sat beside us.

'When did you and Heru stop working earlier today? I asked him.

'Heru did not work together with us today, Pak. Before we got to Tui he went off, to survey a new workplace at Walgan, he said.'

Our conversation was interrupted. The bell for roll call ordered us all to gather at once in the yard. While walking there, the barracks head and I made an agreement. We would stick to Gobel's explanation as an alibi. We had only to take responsibility for 'stealing' two workers from general work duty to go and find sago in Tui swamp.

Perhaps they were lost and did not know the way back. We would mention no names except for Heru and Siregar, nor would we make any mention of our 'internal garden'. If we were accused of sabotaging the barracks work project, we would turn this around and say no, actually we were determined to make our barracks project a success. That is why we had to ensure that the inmates were not too hungry, after the harvest that we had been so eagerly awaiting had been ruined by the plague of insects.

Roll call proceeded as normal. Of course with the normal tension and anxiety. After roll call we were all allowed to go back to the barracks except for the barracks head. As we walked back, there was no sound of talking, only the whispers of one or two. I felt that the eyes of the entire unit were throwing daggers on our barracks. Nobody knew what had happened, except for the fact that Heru and Siregar had been reported missing. Nobody knew what punishment the unit authorities would mete out to all of us. It would certainly be to all of us. Because we knew perfectly well the 'train-carriage law' and the 'cluster law' that was the quota of the political prisoners of G30S-PKI.

Suddenly the roll call bell rang again. This time louder, faster, and for longer. It was as though the iron bell made from an old bomb casing was yelling its anger. We got back into line in the yard, as we had just been, according to our barracks and the numbers on our shirts. In front of us, the unit authorities stood in line. The head of our barracks stood between the Deputy Unit Commander and the Platoon Commander. A few guards stood behind them, and the others stood surrounding the yard. They were all in full battle dress.

The sun had already gone down behind the trees. Only a few remaining reddish rays illuminated the roof of the Unit Commander's wisma. The yard was busy with the noise of the barracks heads getting their lines in order, tidying the rows at the side and at the back, and counting, all according to usual marching orders. Then, one by one, from barracks number 1 through to number 10, the heads reported the count to the Platoon Commander, who was head of the roll call. After receiving their reports, the roll call commander did not do the usual 'at ease' call. The order he yelled, in an angry tone, was for us to remain in line, to take off all our clothes except for our underpants, and to stand again, at attention.

'Who sleeps to the right of Heru and Siregar?' boomed the commander.

Alibasah and I raised our hands. I did not understand why he said only 'to the right'. Do people when they sleep face the right more than the left? Or had they already studied the layout of the barracks and checked against their data, so that only Alibasah and I were called out, and not Gobel and Jamhari who slept to the left of Heru and Siregar.

'Step forward', came the order.

The two of us jogged up, soldier style when summoned by the sergeant, and stood like statues in front of him. Our barracks head was ordered to stand between us. The Platoon Commander then gave orders: we could not move, and had to stand there bare-chested in the yard until Heru and Siregar returned.

'Understand?'

We were silent. I don't know why. Because of fear? Because of the cold, that made it hard to move our jaws? Because we did not know Indonesian military custom which is the opposite of Javanese morality? Javanese morality tells us not to respond to angry people, except if you want to also be consumed by the fire of anger. To do that is a sign of stupidity and low character. As in these lines from a Javanese poem:

dedalane guna lawan sekti,
wani ngolah lihur wekasane
bapang den singkiri,
ana catur mungkur.

The path to inner power and victory
is to dare to accept loss
avoid obstacles
turn your back on gossip

Bang! Bang! Bang! Suddenly we were startled by pistol shots from the guard commander. The birds and bats in the trees screeched and flew off, scared.

'Do you understand?' He repeated.

'Understand!' Now we got it. We repeated like parrots.

The Platoon Commander turned and faced the three of us.

'You, you, and you!' he yelled pointing at Alibasah, Soleh Amat and me. 'Time for a bath!' and he jerked his pointing finger at the ditch that surrounded the yard.

I had not even had time to digest how to carry out this order before two soldiers came up and dragged us off one by one. They threw us down face forward into the cold, stagnant water in the ditch. Alibasah was at the top, then Soleh Amat in the middle, and then me. Six soldiers stood on the edge of the ditch, two each standing on top of the three of us, one on the left and one on the right. They were holding their unsheathed bayonets in their hands, ready to strike at a moment's notice.

The ditch around the yard, apart from being drainage for rain, was also the drain for kitchen waste and the wisma bathroom. The water was a filthy bluish colour, the stink unbelievable, and it was about knee-high in depth. The three of us had to lie there, with our mouths just above the water. Sometimes face down, sometimes made to turn on our backs. If any part of our body emerged out of the water, a soldier's boot from the edge of the ditch would trample it back down. Where does the power of torture come from? Was this the 'bath', or was there still worse 'bathing' to come? A blood bath? A shower of bullets? Why bath? In Hitler's time, there was the same term. But there the prisoners were given a cake of soap, put into a locked room, and showered with gas ...

A few pressure lamps were placed here and there in the yard. There was no sound except for whispers of the top brass and the unit guards, interspersed with the yells of Alibasah and Soleh Amat.

'Enough, Pak, enough.'

'I've done nothing wrong, Pak.'

'I don't know anything, Pak!'

'I'm cold Pak. Have mercy!'

I kept my mouth tightly shut. I even locked my jaw. Not only to stifle the anger inside of me from leaking out, but also to fight against the cold that penetrated to my very bone marrow. But even more than that, I shut up because of my own sense of pride about self-worth and my resistance. I was utterly and completely aware. I would not stoop to call out or beg from those low, arrogant tyrants, drunk on power. I just wanted to survive. If I was going to die, please let not a single word of weakness come from me. I did not even think of how cold all the others were, standing in their underpants like statues in the yard, and how hard it was for them to bear the mosquitoes and gnats swarming over their bodies.

It got late. The air got colder. My head began to freeze, and my body became heavy. My eyes and ears took in everything as though it was a dream. The sound of the owl hooting sadly in the tree, the sound of the flapping wings of the bats, and the buzzing of the crickets … it was all like a haunting hallucination.

Around midnight, some guards came from the direction of Kakibotol. It seemed they had been the ones sent to search for Heru and Siregar. They immediately reported to the Unit Commander, and were surrounded by the Platoon Commander, Deputy Platoon Commander and the unit staff. I could only hear their whispers.

Suddenly we heard the order of the Platoon Commander as it resounded in the wall of forest.

'Back to barracks. Quick smart.'

The others all grabbed their clothes that were lying beside where they stood, and quickly dispersed, half running, leaving the yard. Even Alibasah and Soleh Amat! They picked themselves out of the ditch and ran off after the others. But I couldn't move anything except my shaking hand, which was holding up my weight to keep my mouth and nostrils out of the filthy water. Mustihar Umar, my barracks mate who was lame and therefore did not run off as fast as the others, seemed to notice that I could not move. Perhaps he thought I was dead and stiff after being submerged half the night in stagnant water.

'Sis! It's Pak Hersri!' he called to Siswando, who was from our barracks and worked in the kitchen.

The two of them came over to me, got my hands, and pulled me up out of the ditch. Supporting me, one on the left and one on the right, they dragged me, running as fast as they could, to the well behind the barracks. They poured warm water over me, bucket after bucket, until they saw I could move a little, and my lips moved.

'Enough', I said. 'Thank you'.

They led me to my sleeping place, and dried me with my one and only official prison-issue towel, then they rubbed my body with lots of eucalyptus oil.

'Try to sleep Pak, Mustihar said, lowering my mosquito net.

Siswondo took Heru's pillow, and his own, and used them to cover my body. Someone else, I don't know who, lent me a black and white striped cotton blanket. Then they went to their sleeping places, and fell asleep like the others who had already done so, because they had to get whatever energy they could to work in the morning.

I shut my eyes and tried to sleep. Even though I no longer felt stiff, my ears seemed to be ringing. My head was jumping about all over the place. I thought of Siswondo who had left his pregnant wife behind when he was captured. Was she still working in the kitchen of the Indonesian Research Institute (LIPI, Lembaga Ilmu Pengetahuan Indonesia) in Jl Teuku Umar? Or had she been picked up and taken who knows where? And what of their first child who was then still unborn? Was it a girl or a boy? During our rest times, Siswondo would wonder about these things. And Mustihar Umar? A young man from Serang who worked at the port of Tanjung Priok, and was strong. He had a disability, one leg was longer than the other, which was a condition he was born with. But rather than be angry about it, he joked about his disability. When the two of us were given work duty to carry goods, we would work as a pair. I chose to be behind, and him in front.

'Hey,' he said, 'what are you up to?' He thought that I was also limping, copying him.

'Well, they say that if you are carrying goods on a pole like this, working as a pair, then you have to have equal steps and rhythm', I said.

'Bullshit! Do you know, Pak, how my leg got to be like this?'
'Nope. Tell me'
'Well. It was back when I was big in my mother's belly. My old man got the idea he wanted to ripen me up. What an idea! Poor Mum. So as soon as he got in, I gave him a kick. And that's how I got to be like this.'

I was amazed at Alibasah and Soleh Amat. I was younger than them. Alibasah was skinnier and weaker than me. Why had they been able to get up from the ditch and run after the others the minute the order was given to return to barracks? Whereas I had to be dragged by two friends? Was it because during half the night of being submerged they had cried out and wriggled around, so their bodies kept warm? Whereas I had stayed still and kept my mouth shut, and as a result, my body had gone cold and stiff? Was it because of my own pride? The Javanese saying is true. 'Pride is the doorway to disaster.' But anyway, I would stick with my pride and oppose that saying rather than kowtow to those vile cretins.

Maybe I did finally fall asleep, because I was startled when the barracks head shook me awake. The kitchen behind our barracks was already up and running. I could hear the sound of the drums being filled with water and the firewood being thrown. It was around three in the morning, before dawn.

'Pak', Soleh Asmat said. 'We've been summoned to the wisma'.

Tarmo, a fellow inmate who worked at the wisma, was standing at the barracks doorway with a kerosene lamp, waiting for us,

'What'll we say?'

'Just keep to what we said earlier, right?' I replied. 'Don't make any new story. They'll think we're inconsistent and will torture us no end.'

'Okay. And as for you?'

'We will observe their line of questioning and the way they're thinking. If you want to add anything, add it only as a possibility, not as a new admission. Don't forget to emphasise the superstitions about the local spirits. All the soldiers are superstitious. Say that maybe our two friends have been hidden by the local spirits or even been eaten …'

'Pak Soleh!' Tarmo's voice came from the door. Hurry up! They're flashing signals with a torch from the guard post.'

When we went into the front room of the wisma, we faced a long table where they were sitting in a line. The Deputy Unit Commander, the head of the storehouse, the head of farming, the head of health, and the guards' commander. The Unit Commander himself was not there, maybe he preferred to sleep in his room. As I faced them, I was flanked by two guards and the head of our barracks. There was one pressure lamp on the table. I suddenly realised that Abibasah had not been called in as well. Why was that? Was it because his position as head of the Catholic group in the unit acted as a kind of shield? Or what kind of magic amulet did he have?

But I had no moment to think about that. The model of interrogation of the 'G30S-PKI' political prisoners in Jakarta headquarters, here in the jungle, and from years past until now, was just the same. We were immediately showered with questions and abuse interspersed with beating, curses, threats, and physical abuse. The ones questioning and the ones beating took turns, even fighting over their turn. It was not only the Deputy Unit Commander and the Platoon Commander who did the interrogation, the heads of farming and health were also interrogators. The whole point of the interrogation was the same for all of them: not to find out the truth of what happened, but to force their interpretation of what happened.

We were lucky, I thought, that at least on that table there was none of the usual torture equipment like the barbed whip, car batteries connected to rings and copper wire. But what about chairs and rifle butts? These can become torture tools when they turn their sadistic creativity to it. Even though, after some interrogation, one of them threatened he would go and get the electric shock equipment from the Commander's room. Oh well! If that was to be, then so be it. Let there be light! But, come on, Hersri. Face it with the one and only force you have. Hope!

And with that inner voice of mine, I sat calmly facing that row of executioners. Why shake? Shouldn't my life story have come to an end earlier that night? If, when I had been lying in that ditch, the guards standing on me had just thrust their bayonets. Deliberately, because of their hatred of those 'communist devils', or even not deliberately, but just because of the biting cold?

There had never been a single story of interrogation of a political 'G30S-PKI' prisoner without physical and mental torture. Towards dawn, the head of farming slapped Soleh Amal's face with his sandal, and then spat in his face. I was relieved that Soleh kept firm. He did not swerve from our story of yesterday evening. But the store's keeper brought new evidence, namely that the missing tools were not tools for getting sago. The guards who had been searching, who were sitting on either side of us, also said that they had found no trace of the two prisoners entering the Tui swamp. The reason Soleh Amat gave for 'stealing' workers for extra duties, namely that rather than sabotaging the project he was rescuing it, seemed to make sense to the Deputy Commander of the unit, Deputy Second Lieutenant Tuwuh. Soleh's alibi about the threat of angering the local spirits who had hidden or even eaten Heru and Siregar also seemed to hit the target, for the Platoon Commander fired back like a boomerang.

'Don't you mess with the spirits', he yelled.

'No Sir. But how could they not be angry when we fell their trees, and go into their sago groves?' Soleh said, emphasising the inclusive word for we, '*kita*', meaning all of us, including you.

The interrogators turned their focus to me. Not to 'examine' but to force my assent to anything they said. Heru and Siregar had vanished from the unit to escape. Not for any barracks duty of collecting sago. That was their conclusion that I had to prove right.

'Your barracks head is a liar', the Platoon Commander said.

'Lousy liar', chimed in the head of health.

'Lying son of a bitch', added Tuwuh.

Actually, their conclusion was not wrong. I too had the same suspicion. Heru's roll of possessions, which was always on his pillow, was nowhere to be seen. There was only his set of deportation clothes under his pillow. His toothbrush, which he always tucked into the plank of wood above his bed, was not there. That was proof for me. He was a city boy, educated. Like me, he could go a few days without bathing, but he had to brush his teeth, or rub them with soft sand or dry grass when bathing in the river.

Even so, there was no way I was going to support their conclusion. I backed up the barracks head who had put the blame on the local spirits. I reminded them of their own story about when one of the unit buffaloes had gone missing. The animal stall minders had found the bones by chance when they were looking for grass in Jamilo. Actually, they had stolen the buffalo to sell to the people of Jamilo who had slaughtered and eaten it. But the story that they circulated around the unit was about the local spirits who had wanted a sacrifice.

Needless to say, the soldiers could cover up their own lie in front of other people. Especially in front of powerless prisoners. But deep inside, I believe, they felt stung by their own lies.

Supporting the conclusion that Heru and Siregar had escaped, I thought, would only cause new problems even more complicated and dangerous. I have no idea where my clarity and speed of thinking came from that dawn. Maybe I had a new breath of life after nearly dying the night before, and my hatred towards my captors had reached its limit. What I was dreading, and what I had to completely deflect, came with the next accusation.

'You sleep on Heru's right', Tuwuh said. 'He must have talked about his escape plans with you.'

'But how?' I said. 'If you are going to escape, why would you tell someone who is not involved in your escape?'

The head of farming thumped the table. He was a big man, with long curly hair, and looked more like a thug than a farming expert.

'Or was it you, all along, who planned all this! Answer!'

Before I could answer, and not knowing what to answer, the guard sitting on my left caught a small cricket. Without me suspecting anything, he put it in my left ear. I immediately jumped around slapping my ear. My vision went black, there was a noise like a thousand roars in my ear canal, and I lost my balance. My body felt as though it was gliding. I could see their faces grinning, as they laughed.

'Go to the clinic!' yelled the head of health.

I did as he said. Ran to the barracks clinic, which was not far behind the wisma.

'Bung Sarjono!' I yelled as I banged on the door. I paid no attention to the one or two inmates who were lying inside. Sarjono, a prisoner who was also a nurse, opened the door.

'What's up?'

'A cricket in my ear!'

He made me sit on the chair where he received patients. Then he took some tweezers and a lantern to look in my ear.

'It's in deep. I can't get it out', he said after trying for a while with the tweezers. 'I will give you some drops. It'll die by itself.'

'Anything! Anything but this madness.'

I felt some cold drops enter my ear. The noise of a thousand thunders stopped immediately. But my left ear felt completely blocked.

Clutching my stiff ear, I went back to the wisma. They were all still sitting there in their places, except for Soleh Amat who was gone.

'Back to barracks!' ordered Tuwuh when I got to the doorway.

When I got back to the barracks, the others were already awake, waiting for the morning roll call bell, and of course also waiting for me. They greeted me, asking questions, how was the interrogation, and all the usual things that everyone always wanted to know of a fellow inmate who had been interrogated. We all came to the same conclusion. Heru and Siregar had exercised their right to make an attempt at escape. But because we all knew, or at least felt that there were various political 'factions', as people said there were in the other units, too, the sense of watching one another became intense and disturbing.

That day, life went on as usual even though we were haunted by extra tension. The guards scrutinised the borrowing of tools from the tool store, and were out on guard in every work area. The workforce in every barracks was reduced by two so that those two people could join the guards searching for the vanished La Heru and La Regar.

On the evening of the third day, the tension lessened somewhat. The barracks head, when he returned from the briefing session, brought some news. The barracks head had been changed, at the order of the commander. Sumardjo, who had previously been our barracks inmate in charge of making sure everyone got a fair share of any extra food and so forth, now replaced Soleh Amat as barracks head, He told us what a magic man from Jamilo had told the commander who had called him in to the wisma earlier that day. There was no point in searching for Heru and Siregar anymore. They had been hidden by the spirits, and at a certain time they would return.

We felt so relieved to hear that news. We had been saved by superstition. This marked the lessening of scrutiny and sanctions. The evening roll call had not been as full of swearing and threats as usual, but had been a talk by the Platoon Commander about the local spirits and their taboos. We were warned not to fool around with the spirits, never to violate their taboos, and never to enter places we did not know.

The crafty move by Soleh Amat – who had been my Qur'an teacher in prison, and formerly the head of the Semarang branch of Lekra, had succeeded, it seemed. After the evening roll call, the mood in the barracks started to relax. Not only in our barracks, but we heard the same from the neighbouring barracks. The prisoners were joking and laughing again. The incident of the disappearance of Heru and Siregar was no longer at the front of their minds, but they began chatting amongst themselves, careful of course as always to take note of the 'prevailing winds'.

The world of superstition that the soldiers and the authorities inhabited was actually not the natural world of the prisoners. Not a single one of us believed that the spirits had hidden Heru and Siregar. It was no longer a problem to us that the two had escaped. But what was a problem among us, rightly or wrongly, were the actions or steps of a faction. Some praised the escape as a daring deed, because that was a prisoner's right: others saw is as a personal act of adventure and irresponsibility towards other prisoners. There were some who had freed themselves of socialist ways, and were swept up in dreams of being safe. They busied themselves with a thousand and one questions: how far had the escapees got; how many kilometres from the coast was it until you reached international sea waters? Which land was closest to Buru, and so on, and so on. The end of all this wondering was to play guessing games: who was behind Heru's revolutionary deed or adventure? Yes, Heru himself. Because in the plot of this escape story, Siregar was just a kind of background figure.

'Ah, it's clear! Who else? Hersri was behind all this!'

I was shocked to hear the voice. It was uttered by someone in the barracks next door. Loud. Extremely loud, and with total certainty. I approached him through the back door.

'Bung', I said. You said that I was behind Heru's escape? Isn't that right? Are you joking or what?'

He was silent.

'This is not a joking matter. Why did you blurt that out? Is that your own conclusion, or are you broadcasting the view of the wisma?'

'No, Pak, No! Truly. It is just my own idea', he answered nervously.

'Right. You said it's your own idea, and that's right. So why do you have to go broadcasting it so that other barracks can hear it? Even the guards, perhaps.

Have you thought of the consequences?'

He did not reply.

'You remember this!' I wanted to end my words, and also shut him up. 'If your conclusion gets to the wisma, then it won't just be me who is tortured. All of us will be. Including you!'

I went back to my barracks. My fellow inmates greeted me with tense expressions. I saw the barracks head, Pak Soleh, Pak Mus and Pak Sis sitting together as a group.

The barracks head shook my hand. Then he stood in front of the barracks table. With a low voice, he made an announcement.

'Friends! We must not go around making our own conclusions about the disappearance of Heru and Siregar. We must follow and endorse what the commandant briefed us with earlier this evening. The spirits are still hiding Heru and Siregar. So now let's all get a good night's sleep ...'

* * *

Gradually, life in the unit returned to normal, as it had been before the incident of the disappearance of La Heru and La Regar. Dullah, the head of stores, was once again in charge of the collection and return of tools and equipment to the storeroom without guard supervision. The guards no longer watched the whole day in the work areas, but there could be sudden patrols and roll calls at any time.

We created a series of signals that we would send along the line, to let others know if a patrol was sighted. The role of those working in the wisma and on kitchen duty was important as the first source. If they noticed a patrol getting prepared, they would send a sign to the friends working in the vicinity of the wisma or the mess. We would change these code words regularly so they would not be detected. The code words might be 'fly' or 'bee' or 'bird' and so on, or sometimes 'water' and associated words like 'kettle', 'drink' and so forth.

About a month later, at evening roll call the commander announced that there was an important news item. Heru and Siregar had been captured, and they were now undergoing interrogation at Namlea. Just like that! The evening roll call was dismissed with no further ado. Nothing happened to Soleh Amat, no-one was called into the wisma to be accused of involvement in the 'Heru Incident'. Not even me. This was a sign that neither Heru nor Siregar had 'sung' when being interrogated, and so the provocateurs among the prisoners themselves gained no ground.

About three days later, the peace that was beginning to be restored in the unit was rocked once again. We were startled by the tolling of the roll call bell. This was an extraordinary roll call. It was still the middle of the day.

What was it this time? We were all asking. Everyone immediately looked tense. Torture again? Sweeping? Were some of us going to be sent off to Jiku Kecil? There were a thousand and one questions in our heads. Had they 'sung' after all? Maybe some provocateurs had sent an anonymous letter, looking for bait? We hurried to the yard. My anxiety returned. My heart was beating fast. I was not free of the effect of that provocation made by the inmate from the next door barracks, saying that I was the mastermind of the 'incident'. I was also still wondering about puzzles of my own. Why had Akibasah not been interrogated that night together with Soleh and me? Was there some secret connection there? I was worried that there was a group that deliberately wanted to make me the sacrificial victim of their fear.

But some of my own anxiety, and certainly too that of everyone, was answered when we got closer to the yard. There in front of the wisma stood Heru and Siregar. They were wearing shorts, and no shirts. Their hands were behind their backs, and they were staring at the sky. 'Thank God, it is light punishment! Only being made to stare at the sun,' Rohiman whispered.

We all lined up in our usual lines, according to our barracks and the numbers on our shirts. In the corner of the yard, in front of our barracks, the unit authorities stood in a line. There was an officer from Namlea, I do not know who, standing in the middle of them.

The heads of our lines, as usual, reported their groups to their respective guard commander, who then, in turn, reported to the Unit Commander, who then, in turn, reported to the officer from Namlea. Then the order came to be 'at ease' while we listened to the sermon from the Namlea officer.

'For the speech, at ease …!' The guard commander bellowed.

We did the military 'at ease' position. Two legs parallel and a little apart, two hands together behind the back, and face looking directly at the speech-giver. You must not look left or right, and not whisper. And hold back any coughs or sneezes!

I would know immediately if my throbbing anxiety were proven right. I believed in Heru Santoso. He was not a squealer type who liked to bite and was clever at chirruping away about rubbish. But what about Bonar Siregar? He and I had not known each other before. This was a factor, but even if he did have a cockroach mentality, it would not be just me who would suffer from his bite. We would all suffer.

We all felt relieved only when the sign for the end of roll call was given. We were then ordered to immediately return to our workplaces, without any order for someone to remain behind in the yard. The roll call had been called deliberately to make an example of Heru and Siregar and as a show for us. It was also an opportunity for indoctrination about the magical power of Pancasila, the generous New Order government, the wise and fatherly General Soeharto, the humanitarian project of Buru to educate political prisoners to become people who would be useful to the nation and the homeland, Indonesia that allowed no place for those who were anti-God, and all kinds of other bits and pieces which the prisoners had long since memorised.

Things returned to how they were at the previous extraordinary roll call, there was no directive that there was going to be any sweeping or interrogation in the unit. My faith in Heru and Siregar increased. They were both true and trusted friends who had the courage to take all the risk on their own shoulders. More than that, there were also signs that the command Intelligence had not got wind of the political factions at Bantalareja. This meant that the seed of provocation that the head of farming and some of those in the neighbouring barracks had thrown, had not found fertile ground.

That evening Heru and Siregar were taken back to Namlea. They were not returned to the unit, but were sent to Jiku Kecil for incarceration. From that time, I did not see Heru again. I merely got scraps of news about them, especially about Heru, which little birds told me. I heard he had been severely tortured. Our unit coordinator even spread the news that their fingers had been chopped off, that they had been locked in isolation cells, and given chicken feed, along with various other stories of cruelty. The coordinator – and others – did not seem to realise that telling these exaggerated stories merely helped the Intelligence spread terror, as a deliberate way of spreading angst and psychosis among the prisoners in the entire unit. They could strengthen their power even further on top of fear.

Around the end of 1973, Jiku Kecil Unit was moved to the territory of unit Bantalareja, in the tidal area of the mangrove swamp. Bantalareja unit provided them with a place for ricefields about seven hectares in area. Because of its position, the newly moved Jiku Kecil was thereafter called 'Ancol Unit', named after the area near the coast in Jakarta. The complex of buildings there comprised just one barracks, which was built by labour from Bantalareja and some from the special skills Command Headquarters section.

Jiku Kecil was now Ancol, and no longer far away isolated in Namlea, but close. Its land bordered that of Bantalareja. Even so, the move and this change did not wipe its role as the 'punishment unit', but it did lessen its secrecy. The Ancol inmates were allowed to do work duty, and even to visit other units. And conversely, units from other units could go to 'Ancol' which was no longer 'Jiku Kecil'.

One night there was a cultural night in our unit, Bantalareja. It was probably early 1974. This was still some time before all units were 'regrouped', as they called it when two units were created, Indrapura and Giripura, and I was moved into Indrapura in May 1974. I can't remember why the cultural night was held. Maybe it was to 'welcome' some big shot visitors from Jakarta, the *'santiaji* team' who came about once a year, or some visitors from the Red Cross and Indonesian and international journalists. Lieutenant Colonel Samsi M.S. wanted to show off his humanitarian wisdom in managing the 'Rehabilitation Post'.

Under Lieutenant Colonel Samri's leadership, the work system, previously calculated per 'man-days', was changed to a per-job package; the word *'tapol'* or political prisoner was no longer used, and replaced with *'warga'* for inhabitant; the military-style line up for roll call was changed to a checking-off system where groups of five at a time would check off their attendance; barracks and individuals were permitted to earn money for themselves; there were 'co-operative' shops in the units, and TVs were installed; prisoners could visit other units and non-prisoners could visit; performers and entertainers were allowed to perform on stage, and all kinds of other bits and pieces of 'perestroika'. It was all intended to foster a spirit of *laissez faire, laisser-passer*, or what's yours is yours and what's mine is mine, and to destroy the communal spirit of 'all together now, heave-ho!' or working together as a group, *gotong royong*.

The cultural night at Indrapura was held in this new political atmosphere. Not only the local people could attend, but also our fellows from Desa Savanajaya, together with their wives and children, and this even extended to our fellow 'inhabitants' from Ancol.

That was when I met Heru again after we had been separated for about two years. All this time I had only ever heard stories of his escape with Siregar as rumour, which was probably blown up in the retelling. I had never heard the real story directly from the actors. That is why I was not interested in watching the performances that night. I spent the entire night just with him, from sunset until dawn when the performances finished. He listened to stories about his unit of Bantalareja, from the moment of his disappearance, and I listened to the story about him and Siregar from when they left the unit. When they were no longer Heru Santoso and Bonar Siregar, but traders from Buton called La Heru and La Regar who had had an accident at sea.

* * *

'So you were eating all those raw insects as practice for you and Siregar?'

He laughed.

'I really was mad with you back then, Heru! Why didn't you say something?'

'Should I have spelt out everything to you in detail, crystal clear?'

He said this while laughing, teasing me. This was Heru's way. If he was talking to someone he trusted, he would always joke, even though it was a serious matter.

'So I could be deaf in both ears?' I said

He laughed.

'I'm sorry, Pak. But actually, it was you who was not getting the message. I don't know how many times I chatted to you about various things. About getting direction from the stars, and knowing the time, about the topography of the land and the people, about how far a person can walk in a day, about how long a person can survive if they are fasting ... Don't you remember?'

Yes, he was right. One night I had chatted with him about a political activist called Sirimavo who had managed to maintain a fast for nine days, without eating or drinking at all. The Asia-Africa Writers' Bureau at the time, together with the association of Sri Lankan writers, has helped negotiate by softening the stance of the two opposing forces.

'As if I had to spell it out! "Pak, I want to escape." That would have been impossible.'

'Yes. I was not very intuitive at reading the signs. But now, tell me the story.'

* * *

'Maybe we were wrong from the start. Or at least, I was wrong.' Heru began. 'Yes, I was wrong. I take full responsibility.

As it happened, we did not head south, but went to the north Buru coast. I preferred the north to the south, because the north was more open and explored. This is my tendency to find the easier way. To go right, to use the old jargon. Actually, this was the model of G30S too, look for the short cut! They were not patient with the revolutionary process, so they negated the whole thing by gambling with a putsch. Even though, since we started going to the Tui swamp I had often heard about the illegal Filipino timber industry entering Buru forests in the north.

My idea of going north was from looking at a map. North of Buru are the islands of Obi and Sula, which are closer to the coast than any islands near the southern coast. To the east, there is Ambon and Seram, which are closer still. But from the point of view of security, I thought Obi and Sula were better as a temporary place to stay. Ambon is already a military operation region. And Seram? So many of the guards and migrants in north Buru come from there.

Actually, I had not thought about our final destination. All I could think about was leaving Buru as fast as we could, and getting rid of all traces. Only then, after however long it took, we would get as far away from the Pattimura Division territory as we could. We hoped maybe we could get a ride on a Bugis boat and go to Australia, or to eastern Indonesia or to north Sulawesi.

'Do you remember that I mentioned Leksula that night we talked? The place about 80 kilometres from here? But Leksula is in the south, whereas I had changed direction to the north. Our final target was Wamlana, and good luck if we could reach Bara Bay. That evening, we reached Wai Blau. We stopped there the night, and on the next day went on to Wai Putih. We had to leave Wai Blau because it was too close to Namlea. Too much of a risk. Even Hasan, the prisoner in Savanajaya who does acupuncture, has some patients in Wai Blau. I did not trust him as he is too close to the soldiers.

'The first quarrel between Siregar and I had begun. I wanted to continue and stop only when we reached Wamlana, but Siregar wanted to stop. I wanted our stop in Wai Putih to be only temporary, but Siregar changed what we had already agreed. He said we did not have to keep going to Wamlana.

"Why do we have to go to Wamlana?" he said. "Let's start from here. The quicker we leave Buru the better. You said that yourself, right?"

'I did not answer him. I had no reason to contradict him. That was my first mistake with him. Not that I did not answer, but that I so easily just gave in to what he wanted.

'On the coasts everywhere in Java, where the beach is sloping, there are many fishing boats pulled up. I figured it would be the same outside of Java. The beach would be lined by coconut trees, set further back behind them would be one or two villages of local fishermen, and behind that would be bushes and forest. This layout seemed to make Siregar's suggestion sensible. So my initial reluctance to accept his suggestion vanished. We stopped at Wai Putih, did not continue our journey to Wamlana, and agreed to start our grand plan right there. I responded to the security fear in my head with an inner voice: "Be extra careful!" This was to calm me down, but also to cheer myself up after giving in to Siregar.

'Together we built a shack, like the shelter we made at the place where we pounded sago. It was for protection from the hot sun by day and the dew at night. It was pretty well hidden behind the bushes, but not too far from the beach. That way we could watch the activities of the fishermen, and also anyone going past on the beach. We took note of their boats, which ones had owners and which ones were always left on the beach. Wai Putih beach was pretty lively. Once it was light, many eucalyptus pickers went by, men and women. They carried tall baskets on their backs. This meant that there must be an open eucalyptus plantation not far away, and a eucalyptus oil distillery. That meant there was money around. And wherever there was money, there were always soldiers seeing where they could get a share.'

'On the second day hiding there, I said to Siregar, "Gar, it's very dangerous here. Wouldn't it be better to go further on?"

'I surprised even myself. This time, I was asking. I wasn't inviting, or even giving a decision. It was like a game of chess, and I had lost the first move. Siregar had taken his opportunity and kept moving forward.'

'"Why", he said. "It's dangerous everywhere. What's important is to be careful, like you said. And we have agreed that in two or three days we will go down to the beach, right?"'

'I did not answer. Again, he had beaten me.'

'"Tonight we'll go and check on the boats", he said, with a tone like an order. It was as though he sensed that I was now in a weak position.

'I was silent, giving in. Not really giving in, actually, I just had lost the argument. Now I felt I was following him, not the other way around like when we first started out from the unit. The two of us had not forged a strong unity, but we were also not strong individually. I was now more relying on him. Like some appendage following him, waiting for the time to strike, and there was no more negotiation on this.'

'Our stock of rice and dried fish was enough for the two of us for 20-30 days. So back when you all at the barracks were asking why the sago production was declining, actually I must own up about it now. I was using it all for our escape plan.'

Heru interrupted his story. 'Pak Hersri', he said to me. 'When the time is right, I want you to tell all this to the others. Tell them we are sorry, and ask for their understanding. But please too, we ask that they understand that it was not like some people said, that we escaped as an irresponsible adventure. It was not like that! Or at least I can swear that was not in my head. What I was thinking back then was please let me get to some other place safely, so that there I can speak up. There I can yell to the world, in the name of all of us, about what is really going on in Buru.'

He went back to his story.

'That night, once the beach and the surroundings were quiet, we came out from behind the bushes. Under the light of the stars, we went down to the beach, and took a good look at the boats with no owners, one by one. It turned out that they were all damaged. Some had cracks in the side, some had broken keels, some had holes in the hull, some had smashed rudders or outriggers.

We chose one of the better ones among these rejects. Around midnight, when the Milky Way was still overhead, we pushed the boat up into the trees. We did not have to worry about our footprints and the mark the hull had left on the sand. Towards dawn, they would be washed away when the tide came in.

But we had to postpone our plan to take to the sea in two or three days. The boat had leaks here and there, on the sides and in the hull. We had to find some eucalyptus bark and palm fibre to fix the holes and cracks. The bark of the eucalyptus tree absorbs water, swells when it is wet, and can also withstand salt water. This is why eucalyptus logs are good for building boats and masts. Palm fibre, apart from being resistant to salt water, can also stop the sand, which, like a sieve, can close the cavities in the holes after they are caulked.

Because of all this, it became urgent to meet and get to know the eucalyptus-leaf pickers. We needed their help to locate palms for the palm fibre, and eucalyptus trees. Perhaps because we were in such dire straits and tempted by hope for the future, both of us were more wishful thinking than really thinking things through. Well, I don't know about Siregar, but I myself suddenly felt naive. The eucalyptus workers on Wai Putih beach, who we had only known for a couple of days, I saw as figures of the working class there right before us with all the aspects of the typical proletariat. Class! An abstraction. No longer a group, a concrete group of workers. I immediately 'fell' for them. Because they were friendly. We felt so calm and safe that we thought we no longer had to hide from them anymore. But we kept quiet about who we really were.

We felt that in them we had found allies who would become our protection at a certain time. For instance, they would tell us if they heard news about the search for us, or if they saw guards doing their rounds. I was so naive and arrogant because of their friendliness. I made this conclusion as though it was the result of support from a front opposing militarism. At the very least we felt that we had succeeded in neutralising them, in the middle of the contradiction between us on the one hand, and the military on the other.

All we needed to do now, my simple thinking went, was to remain suspicious of the bosses in charge of the barrels and coconuts, and the brokers. And their own guards, including security guards and soldiers. In short, the old slogan, the 'seven village devils'. But as for the workers, if they were not yet comrades in arms, at least they could be friends in the struggle confronting those devils. As for us, my arrogant thinking went, we now had friends who offered us hope.

On the seventh night, after we finished fixing the boat and when the offshore wind was blowing and the fishermen were going out to sea, we joined them in their preparations. So they would not easily recognise us, we prepared our boat a little further away from them. We put our tools, food and drinking water, rice and cooked fish, inside the boat. We attached our sail that we had made from fertiliser sacks, and the two of us took the oars. I was at the bow, Siregar at the stern.'

"Oeeeee"

'Suddenly we heard them shouting at us. We had not even pushed off into the water. There were between ten and twenty people.'

"Who are you?"

"Where are you from?"

'They called the same thing, over and over.

The fishermen, it turned out, knew exactly who owned which boat. Even though our boat was one of theirs, they knew at once that we were not one of them. We were foreigners! Did this fishing area belong to certain bosses? Like in Java, where the beaches have all been divided up like that? If that was the case, they would not let us go out to sea, not one little bit. Because this area was for their own livelihood.

Siregar and I paid no notice. We rowed and we rowed, steering to catch the wind in our sail. Suddenly I was startled to feel water inside, lapping against my feet. The boat had a leak! The water was coming in fast. There was nothing we could do but jump out and swim to shore pushing the boat.

We went back and hid in the bushes. I stopped counting the days after that as we spent them fixing the boat. Our sense of being safe behind the shield of the friendly eucalyptus workers gave us some calm to work. We compensated for our lack of experience in shipbuilding with care in our work. We caulked not only the holes and the cracks, but covered everything with new boards. In short, we finished our work of patching. We were certain that the boat would not leak again, as it had the first time. As the saying goes, a donkey does not stumble twice on the same stone.

One night we went back to the sea. We deliberately went later than the fishermen, to avoid the noise of their shouting. The sky had been overcast since evening. Neither of us had any marine knowledge. The fishermen would know immediately whether it was going to rain or not, and whether there was going to be a storm or not. I was not afraid of the rain, actually. But what if there was a storm? The boat did not have a rudder. It had a sail. But would the mast on this old boat be strong enough? And what about our homemade fertiliser-sack sail? This was the second mistake, which I should have taken into account from the start. If people want to call me an adventurer, well maybe in this particular instance they are right. But not from the point of view of escape. Anyway, as I said, it was all my own responsibility.

Siregar looked at the horizon. There were flashes of lightning. Actually, this is something normal at sea. But I sensed his anxiety, even though he did not want to say it, let alone start abusing or blaming me. That is the sign of a good friend. He knew that all of this was the risk of the choice that we had made.

We kept rowing. We were driven by the wind that got stronger and more erratic. We were probably a hundred or two hundred metres from the shore when a huge wave struck the boat. I did not know what really happened. Suddenly the boat was half full of water. Siregar tried to bail out the water with a bucket. I pulled down the sail. Then we threw everything overboard, except for our work tools. But all this was in vain. Water was coming in faster than we could bail it out, and pulling down the sail made no difference. The water carried everything off, including our tools. The side of the boat was split and gaping wide. We swam to shore.

When we got back to our hut we had nothing but the wet clothes on our backs and the determination to survive. We lay down on some leaves on the ground, close to each other to keep warm. While we waited for dawn, I closed my eyes. I took stock of myself. This was yet another mistake. I had never imagined this sense of isolation in nature. Even if we had not lost all our tools, I would never have imagined stealing another boat. No. The one and only way we could survive was living from nature and isolation in the jungle, like the Japanese soldiers who stayed in their bunkers when the Pacific war ended. I had no regrets. This was the risk I had taken. I would not give myself up and go back to the unit. That would betray my conscience, and betray my comrades.

At this difficult time, we did not want to make it even more difficult for each other. Siregar seemed to know his place. He went back to relying on me. No problems arose between the two of us. We survived in the jungle for about seven days. We moved our hut further inland, because we were not going to look for a boat and gaze at the sea. We lived by stealing coconuts, and used these to barter for other things from a eucalyptus worker who became close to us. I felt more confident that we would be able to survive in the jungle until at some stage all our traces would be gone. But Siregar seemed to come to a different conclusion.'

"Are you asleep?" he asked me one night. Like me, he seemed preoccupied.

"How can I sleep?"

"What are you thinking about?"

I did not reply.

"You see? That's why we should talk."

"See what?"

'Suddenly I felt something was coming to spoil our seven days of peace. But whatever that was, I had to face it. Not turn a blind eye to it and avoid it. That night we finally talked about what we were feeling.'

"We've managed to survive now for seven days and nights: I said. I wanted to hold firm to my position of continuing to hide in the jungle. 'The coconuts are not going to run out. Not in ten years! And I'm sure that before ten years are up we'll get out of here.'

"So, you want to go to sea again?"

'Who knows? Maybe we can find a contact with a Buton or Bugis trader, or someone. La Ode, our friend, can help us.'

"I had the same idea!" He said. I also thought we could find a contact through La Ode, But not a Buton trader, or any trader, and we don't have to wait until who knows when."

"What do you mean?"

"Well". He looked me directly in the eye. "We can ask La Ode to take us to his boss. We could ask to work as eucalyptus gatherers," he said with assurance.

I went silent. I held my breath so that I would not hit him. There was just the two of us. What would be the point of us fighting? So I chose not to reply. I would let my emotion calm down first, and think about his idea, which had taken me by surprise. Even this, I thought, was also capitulation.

"What do you think?" he pressed me.

"I never thought you would think like that", I said. "So give me time to think about it. Two or three days."

He went silent now.

"Back in the unit we were tortured", he said after a bit, "we were hungry, the military ran our lives. But even that was better than this. There we had lots of other people around us. Now? Here we are in the jungle, just the two of us. I think we'll go mad!" He was really grumbling now.

"I just told you, give me two or three days!" I snapped.

He went quiet.

The next three days were full of tension. The two of us still did the 'three together', as the Lekra slogan went: work together – stealing coconuts, bartering them, and cooking together – eat together and sleep together. We even bathed together. But inside, now we were separate. There was no more togetherness. We worked together, but there was no longer a spirit of cooperation. So we rarely talked. How could we talk, if there are just two people, one way over there, and the other over here? We were each resolute in our own selves.

On the third day, Siregar held me to my word. He had kept careful count of the days. This was a sign that he could not bear living in the forest, and that he was not willing to have the same position as me.

"This is what I think", he said to me that morning. "I think our journey together ends here. You can keep on living in the forest, but I can't. I am going to ask La Ode to take me to his boss. I want to work with them."

I looked at Siregar's face. He really meant it. My mouth went dry. I was confused. Then my Javanese nature came to the fore, overcoming all rational considerations. My Javanese nature did not want to persist stubbornly. I felt that Siregar's Batak nature was putting pressure on me. Would I be compromising? Well, not exactly. Because I would be capitulating to Siregar's ideas of capitulation. Confronted by him, I could not wrestle or flex muscles.

"Very well", I said, sourly. "I'll do what you want. Just as long as you are prepared to face the consequences. Are you?"

"Why not? he said boastfully. We've got this far, haven't we?"

We came out of the forest. We waited for La Ode to pass by, as usual. When he heard our request, La Ode laughed. He said he had got two new friends. Siregar and I continued to introduce ourselves as La Heru and La Regar, from Buton, who had been away from Buton for so long that we had forgotten how to speak the language. Then we had had an accident at sea, when we were entering Buru looking to trade in eucalyptus oil.

La Ode took us to meet his foreman who he said also came from Buton. My heart skipped a beat when I saw from a distance the person he called his foreman, but there was no way to slip away now. He was wearing a security guard uniform! He greeted us without pleasantries, but was also direct and honest. He told La Ode to go off and work, and took us to meet his boss, because anything to do with recruitment was not his business. It was only the boss who could decide.

We were taken to him.

Even before we exchanged greetings, I sniffed danger. It was not difficult to see the suspicion in his eyes as he gave us the once over. Together with the foreman, he took us to the house. He said it was because he wanted to know more about us, because he had been ordered not to take any new employees without knowing where they had come from.

"We're caught", Siregar whispered.

'It's a bit late for you to realise that!' I said. I had sensed immediately, from when we first met the security guard, that we were now prisoners again.

"You were right", Siregar said.

'Remember. Keep your word. Do not betray your friends or yourself!' I said.

The 'house' was not where the head of production lived. It was an army post. We sat down at a long desk, with the foreman on one side and the boss on the other. In front of us was a square table, and the post commander sat there on a chair facing us. He seemed to be a corporal, judging from the rank on his arm. There was a blackboard hanging on the coconut-frond wall behind him, with a few bits of paper stuck here and two copies of enlarged passport photos, about the size of a postcard. Heru Santoso and Bonar Siregar, the writing said under the photos.

'That very day were we taken to Namlea.'

And that was the story that Heru told me that night when the two of us sat together.

'Pak Hersri! Are you still listening to my story?'

'Stop talking in your sleep', I said. 'The night is yet young.'

*　*　*

The audience was applauding and whistling the performance on the stage at the cultural centre. Bung Dasul, dressed in women's clothes as Miss Dakocan 'of beauty rare' in golliwog style, was on stage holding a microphone, swaying her hips artfully. Accompanied by the Buru Rehabilitation Centre Command Headquarters band – alias Bandko – under the leadership of Subronto K. Atmodjo, Miss Dakocan sang Javanese songs made popular by the singer Waljinah, like *'Kecik-Kecik'*, *'Walang Kekek'* and *'Ngalamuning Ati'*.

'Pak', Heru said. 'It actually started out as something small, the plan with Siregar. But no matter how small it was, I discovered all kinds of mistakes that arose because of my own stupidity. Just in that small thing, escaping from the unit.'

'So many mistakes? What else was there, apart from what you just told me?'

'Well, say there are two men. One a Javanese, one a Batak. You could say they come from two opposite ends of the magnetic field. They are both attracted to each other and repel each other. It would be different if they were both Javanese, or both Batak, but say one was male and one female. That's one thing. The second thing is that I also remembered the Javanese saying that you once told me when we were at Tui swamp.'

'What saying was that?'

'*Loro ganjil, telu ganep.* Two is odd, three is even. An egg has the potential to hatch if three elements are present. The yolk, the white, and the shell. That's why the Javanese have the word '*tigan*' (three) for egg. You were right, Pak. There should have been three of us, so there would have been a middle line when there was pulling and pushing between the Heru pole and the Siregar pole.'

'Three? And who would have been the third?'

'You!'

'You think I would have wanted that? I'm not so sure!'

Heru laughed. I laughed. We were smothered in the warm embrace of two brothers or two lifelong friends.

The cultural centre was now lively with the sound of the performers singing the 'going home' song. '*Sayonara! Sayonara! Sampai berjumpa pula …*'

***

'Two is Odd, Three is Even'

In late 1978, about two or three weeks before the announcement was made in the unit of who had won the 'lottery' of being selected for return to Java, I already knew my name would be on the list. My late mother had told me in a dream. 'Winning the lottery' was our term for those who were to be released from Buru and 're-socialised in Java', because who 'won' and who 'lost' seemed to be entirely some haphazard determination from the top.

[I then immediately began to approach those in charge to see if my name could be replaced with Heru's, as he was seriously ill in hospital with cirrhosis of the liver. All my efforts were in vain. Before I left, I went to visit Heru in hospital.]

'Heru', I said, taking hold of his cold hand.

This was my last day in the unit, and in Buru. The head of my barracks, Sabri Martoatmojo, had given me the opportunity to go and say goodbye to Heru in Savanajaya hospital.

'I'm so sorry, Heru. I've completely failed. I hope you understand.'

Heru was too ill to get off the bed. His stomach was all swollen. His face was green, and his eyes dim.

'Of course, I understand', he said. His voice was weak. 'You've done everything you can. Thank you.'

He squeezed my hand. His eyes glazed.

'I am ready for whatever happens', he said. 'Truly. I have been prepared for the worst from the start'. He stopped a moment. His lips quivered. 'That's the same with you, right?'

I squeezed his hand back, and could only utter his name.

'Do not worry about me, Pak', he said. 'You should be looking to the future now. You still have so much to do. More than ever. Go now, and have a light heart.'

I embraced him. And my tears fell on his skinny chest.

'I'll keep trying from Jakarta, Heru.'

'Well, good if you succeed. But don't hold out too much hope. So you won't be consumed by sadness if you fail.'

I did not reply.

'I am resigned to accept whatever happens. So you should be too. So we both are not burdened. Come on! *Ayo*.'

'Ayo', the calling word to go. Not the closing word '*sudah*'. Heru did not know the word *sudah*.

I let him go from my embrace and looked at his face. He was smiling. Nodding.

'Leave with a light heart, Pak. Travel safely.'

I took his extended hand.

'Do you remember our promise, Pak?'

'Yes'.

'Three is even'.

'Three is even'.

When I turned back at the doorway to look at him, he was still smiling. His eyes were glistening with tears. But ever so slowly he raised his right arm and made a fist. It was as though he wanted to give me a final eternal message. Be resolute!

* * *

It was not even a month since I had returned to Jakarta. It was early January 1979. Our efforts through the Cathedral Foundation to get Heru back to Java had not produced any results. Meanwhile, I was still going through the hoops of all the administration required for my 're-socialisation' in society. I needed a letter stating my previous place of residence, a letter of 'good behaviour', a letter requesting an identity card, and all kinds of other letters, and they always asked for more paperwork. Every dealing with bureaucracy took forever, because of all the bits of paper that had to be signed by both civilian and military officials, from those at the bottom like neighbourhood heads, through to regional level, like the mayor.

Every official would open a big book before affixing their signature to the paper at hand. In New Order times this was for slipping in the 'administration cost'. That's right! Indeed, there is nothing free in this world. You have to pay even to breathe, Pramoedya Ananta Toer said, by paying tax to the state. The 'administration cost' was an 'extra' tax for the common people, including former political prisoners.

When I suddenly got a summons from the Cathedral Foundation to come to their office at Banteng Square, my heart leapt with joy. But when I got there, it turned out not to be news of Heru's return to Java. There was another letter from Suwardi Penjol. It was short and to the point:

> Pak Hersi,
>
> About three weeks after the ship *Gunung Jati* sailed, Mas Heru died.
>
> He was buried at Air Mendidih, in the graveyard of the comrades in Unit I. Not long before he died, Mas Heru was moved from Savanajaya hospital to Mako hospital.
>
> Greetings
> *Penjol*

I was not shocked by what I read, but full of regret. Because death had taken Heru quicker than I wanted. I sent my reply to Penjol via the Cathedral Foundation immediately:

> Brother,
>
> Thank you for your letter. Please ask those who are organising Heru's grave to write this on his gravestone:
>
>> Heru Santoso, my little brother and friend,
>> Farewell!
>> Three is even: Birth – Life – Death
>> One: strength of character
>> Two: dreams of the future
>> Three: loyalty
>> Your promise, my promise, our promise

Part IV

Life after Buru

Chapter 18

THE PURGATORY ISLAND OF BURU TWENTY YEARS LATER

A dialogue between the ego and alter ego:

'Bang Sobron!' I said one day on the phone. 'I'm just calling to say goodbye. I'm off to the holy land!'

'Oh yeah? Really?' I could tell by the tone of his voice that he was surprised.

'Why would I waste money on an expensive international call just to lie to you?'

'Oops, sorry. Alhamdullilah. Good. That's really good. You've got my support. I hope all goes well, and you're showered with blessings.'

'Thanks. But I mean my holy land. Not Rome or Mecca!'

'Ah. So where is that, then?'

'Buru! For us, Buru is Purgatory Island.'

'Come on! Are you trying to be Dante or something?'

Buru island, from the start, was probably known only as a speck on the map of the Moluccas, even though that speck was drawn a bit bigger than Bali, or even the 'mother of the Moluccas', Ambon. From the pre-WWII days, Buru and Ambon were known as the primary sources of eucalyptus oil. The sago that was known in the markets in Java as 'Ambonese sago' was in actual fact mostly from Buru island, from the swamps of Tui which in the 'political prisoner time' became part of the area of Unit XIV Bantalareja – where I had once spent a few years, and this sago was said by the locals to be the most delicious.

Despite the sago trade, Buru island was isolated and relatively unknown in the wider world because its open land, apart from the valley of Wai Apu, was unbearably hot and therefore difficult for farming, and its forests and scrubland were poor in animals to hunt, and in fruit or wild roots. Because of this, there were no monkeys there, and few snakes. Buru's distance from other islands and the fact that the local population was sparse and culturally backward were also contributing factors. But precisely because of all these factors, Indonesia's New Order regime had cunningly chosen this island as the place of exile for prisoners. Buru turned into the former Ceylon of the East India Company, or the 'Digul' of the Netherlands East Indies.

So it was. Three years after the New Order came to power, Buru island was opened as a 'Closed Island' for prisoners. There, from 1969-76 the New Order regime exiled no fewer than 11,948 political prisoners from the incident called 'G30S-PKI'. And from then on, Buru became known and infamous over the entire archipelago. The name 'Buru' was synonymous with 'Digul' or 'Ceylon' as a place for getting rid of rebels, murderers and communists! In the old East India Company days, the verb was 'Ceyloned'. In the colonial Netherlands East Indies days it was 'Diguled', and now in the New Order days it was 'Burued'. They all meant the same thing: 'exiled' or 'thrown out'.

So behind the sound of the word 'Buru' there developed a kind of magical power, what van Ophuijsen called 'language magic'. There is magic with terrifying black power, as with the word 'Buru', and there is magic that is wonderful and white, like 'sago princess' – which is what I imagined when I cut sago for the first time in the still, mystical environment of Tui swamp. I can, therefore, understand why today in Java, former political prisoners try to lessen the black magical power of the word 'Buru'. It is a sign that the traumatic atmosphere of their time as political prisoners has not disappeared. You could even say, to use Freudian language, that the trauma has seeped into their subconscious. Among ex-prisoners, the word 'Buru' is unspoken, and replaced with 'Malvinas' – the small cluster of islands on the east coast of South America.

New Order types, especially the bosses like Soeharto-Sudomo-Sumitro, of course never thought that the political prisoners would manage to survive. Even though they were exploited in merciless forced labour, sometimes from four in the morning until midnight. They had to live in below bare-minimum conditions on a malaria-infested island. The Buru prisoners even had a name for the malaria fever shakes – namely 'riding a Honda motorbike'. Another example of language magic.

I remember clearly when the soldiers ordered us to jog from the Namlea dam to the transit unit of Jiku Kecil. All along the way, for the whole five kilometres, as we passed the thatched houses of the locals, we would see pairs of eyes staring at us in fear.

In my ears – to this very day – I hear the shrill voice of the Platoon Commander guard who was herding us from the village of Sanleko to the location of Unit XIV Bantalareja.

'Take a good look. This is where you all are going to live and work. Forever, until you die, one by one.'

We had to expire. In the name of the humanitarianism of the Holy Pancasila. Because of this, we had to expire not before a firing squad or on the gallows, but through torture, forced labour, hunger and the savagery of nature. But it turned out they miscalculated. The prisoners remained defiant. More than that, they even transformed themselves, like *wayang* characters. The baby Bandung Bandawasa or Gathutkaca, for instance, who is thrown into the bubbling lava of volcano crater and emerges as a young man with 'muscles and bones of iron'. To the political prisoners, Buru was like Purgatory. This was where they were made 'clean' and therefore 'strong'.

The prisoners did not just submit obediently to 'decisions of fate'. They even challenged them. Like Iqbal's famous lines, which I quote:

> You created the night, I made the lamp
> You created the clay, I made the cup
> You created the deserts, mountains and valleys
> And I made the flower beds, orchards and fields
> It is I who grinds a mirror out of stone
> And brews elixir from poison

Buru turned out not to follow the plan. What they planned was to dig a grave for the communists. But what grew was ricefields and crops, meranti and eucalyptus trees, sago and sugar cane. Buru did not turn into the corpse-stinking kingdom of Durga, the goddess of death. On the contrary, it quickly became the indispensable backbone of the Maluku province, 'How long has Buru been this busy?' I asked Pak Alex, a teacher at the Catholic junior high school in Namlea.

'Since 1969, when the political prisoners from Java began coming here. Then it really took off ten years later, after the prisoners had been released and many transmigrants were brought here.'

The answer rolled off his tongue. There was no fear and nothing fabricated, I got the same answer and in the same tone from Pak Patty, the postmaster at Namlea post office; also from Agus the room boy at the Duta Nusantara Hotel in Namlea; Aunty Lily, the owner of Lily karaoke restaurant in Namlea; and from anyone I met on the road and asked the same question.

Before the political prisoner era, the only agriculture was dry farming on the newly cleared forest in the Island of Buru. There were no fixed agricultural fields, let alone irrigated ricefields. In 1977, during the time of the political prisoners, there were 1,766,4846 hectares of wet ricefields. Now (in 1990) with transmigration, this has risen to 2,544 hectares and rice production is around 44,040 tons per year. Before the political prisoner time (pre-1969) there was no transport of any kind. By 1970 there was only one jeep, which was the transport for the Buru Camp Commander (Major Rusno, and later Lieutenant Colonel Rangkuti). By the 'end of the political prisoner era' (1980) there were dozens of Daihatsu public transport vans in the town of Namlea. (A driver on the Jiku Kecil-Namlea route said there were as many as 200). Back then, the furthest distance one of the Daihatsu vans would reach was Siahomi, which was 15 kilometres. By 1990, the furthest destinations the vans travelled to were Tifu, 68 kilometres away, and Wainibe, 77 kilometres. I have no idea how many hundreds of kilometres are covered by public transport now. No-one can give me a clear answer.

* * *

Since the prisoner days, Buru has become a major source of rice and 'red gold' – which is what the unit authorities used to call the red meranti timber back then. But the bad image of Buru still sticks, as a logical consequence of their plans, and it is not easy to get rid of it. 'That's a big mistake', the Coordinator of Buru's local government said. 'Buru should now be promoted as the rice-producing island for the province of Maluku.'

Actually, towards the end of the 'prisoner period', in the late 1970s when the prisoners were 'sent back to Java' – except for those who chose to stay, or were coerced into staying – this development was already anticipated. This is why Brigadier General Wing Wirjawan, the Maluku area Special Operations Commander for the Restoration of Security and Public Order who was concurrently the Head of Operations for the Administration of Buru Resettlement and Rehabilitation, did not fully support the central government's policy about release. He agreed with changing the status of the prisoners from 'prisoner' to 'citizen', and with the policy of 'returning them to society'. But as for returning them to Java? Wait a minute! Or, more likely, no! He made no bones about this, and even supported the 'Jakarta plan' announced a year or so before some prisoners' families came to Buru, of bringing prostitutes from Jakarta to Buru as transmigrants. Yes, prostitutes – and not the female political prisoners in Plantungan jail in Central Java. Thanks to the efforts of the Church and the Mosque, that 'Jakarta plan' came to nothing.

So, it was no coincidence that in the second year of repatriating prisoners to Java in the late 1970s, their ships crossed with the first batch of incoming transmigrants.

It was of course part of the program of wiping the black image of Buru island that in mid-January 1998, a harvest celebration was held at Command Headquarters Unit. In the end 'only' a minister came. But if Jakarta had not then been in the midst of the fever of the monetary crisis, and had Soeharto not been seriously ill, it was said that Soeharto himself would have led the ceremony.

It was the harvest of 50 hectares of irrigated ricefields at Command Headquarters Unit. And this was in the midst of a severe drought that had affected all units, leaving all the ricefields dry and untended. There had been no rain for eight months. This was not some comedy show to inspire belly laughs from the farmers, but an irony of life that would inspire protest, if the people dared.

* * *

It was November 21, 1997 and I was now in the metropolitan city of Jakarta. I called an old friend, a kind of head or *demang* of the area of Ragungan in South Jakarta. Back when we were young, we studied Javanese martial arts together with the masters at the Mataram *silat* school, Gajah Permada.

'Hi Pak Demang', I said, 'I'm back here in your town. Just calling to say goodbye.'

'What? And where are you going now, Lurah?' My friend and his crowd liked to tease me with the title of '*lurah*' (village head) and call me 'the lurah of Kokengen', the town in Holland where I had lived with my late wife.

'To Malvinas', I answered.

'What?' I could hear his shock. 'Are you mad? It's not the right time yet. Not yet!'

'And when is the right time, then?'

'Later ... wait a while longer!' He said, in a more soothing tone.

'Wait, wait. But until when?' I could hear my voice getting bitter.

'Well, there's no definite time. But everything is still murky. Just use your intuition.'

'Well, if I use my intuition, my intuition tells me "what are you waiting for, Bung?"'

'Ah, that's you. You always were someone who liked to 'live dangerously', like Bung Karno.'

And eventually, off we went, me and Willy van Rooijen, a journalist from *Onze Wereld*. As an ex-political prisoner, I needed someone to go with me on my pilgrimage to the 'holy land'. In April of 1997, the Indonesian daily newspaper *Kompas* had managed to enter Buru without any special permission. But that was *Kompas*, I thought, the most prestigious newspaper in the entire country, and a national newspaper at that. As for us? We were just tourists with Dutch passports. One was a white woman, a full-blooded Dutchwoman. I was a black Dutchman born in Yogyakarta (as it stated in my passport), and I had only to open my mouth and out came my heavily Javanese-inflected Indonesian. On top of that, The Netherlands was known as the country most vocal in talking about human rights issues in Indonesia. Even though it was just talk. Anyway, because of this, Willy's role in our journey to Malvinas was crucial (thank you, Willy!).

Knowing about the recent *Kompas* visit there, we thought there would be no special rules applying to us. After all, weren't we both tourists? And there were no restrictions on tourists wandering around there. But, who knows. Maybe the 'crocodiles' of Wai Apo estuary would snatch us, secretly? (Crocodiles always take their prey stealthily). Because of this, I wanted to copy the legendary Javanese hero Jaka Tingkir who, when crossing the Kedhung Srengene, on his mission to infiltrate the Demak kingdom, asked the help of crocodiles. I needed a crocodile too. Joko Tingkir's boat was pulled by forty crocodiles. I needed only one. But my crocodile had white skin! It was a magical crocodile among all the black ones. Like the words in the story of Aji Saka – the white crocodile cannot be defeated, only pushed back into the sea for a while.

* * *

When we arrived at the airport in Ambon, we took a taxi directly to the Ambon diocese presbytery. There we met with the Bishop, Monsignor Andreas Sol (who was 83), and the Emeritus Bishop for Amboina. Monsignor Sol was born in Amsterdam in 1915, and had lived in Ambon for all of his life as an ordained priest, from parish priest (1946) through to his ordination as a Bishop (1964) right until the present when we were meeting him, in 1998. He had spent more than two-thirds of his life in Maluku. He was one witness to the 'political prisoners' era.

The Monsignor told us two interesting stories. The first was about the *'sopi* hero'. This was a young sergeant who liked to get drunk on *sopi*, Dutch gin. He was killed in a fight with a fellow platoon guard, and yet was given full military honours at his funeral as a hero. The second story was about two nuns in Namlea, Sister Cecilia and Sister Francisca who the political prisoners called the 'Commander and Deputy Commander of Unit XXI'. No-one knows how the figure 'XXI' came about, as the numbered units only went from I to XVIII, and then there was Ancol Unit, R unit, S Unit and T Unit. But the two sisters were called 'commander' and 'deputy commander' because of their courage in defending the interests of the prisoners (both of them have since died in Makassar). Then there was Father Rovink who was made *persona-non-grata* in Indonesia and has since died in Latin America.

Monsignor Sol had an anonymous handwritten manuscript written by a political prisoner and dated May 20, 1978. The manuscript was titled *Dari Masa ke Masa* (From Era to Era), had 388 pages and was unfinished. How it got to the Bishop's library must be a story in itself, but it was kept there with hundreds of documents and about 1200 books in a collection I called the 'Monsignor Sol Library'. The real name of the library is the RUMPHIUS library of the Diocese of Amboina, housed in a 2x3-metre space, and since its establishment in 1961 has been managed personally by Monsignor Sol himself.

Willy and I went to meet Monsignor Sol to ask for his protection, for in our minds' protection (both spiritual and secular) is the primary function of religious leaders and also secular leaders in general. The kind of protection we were hoping for from Monsignor Sol was something concrete, namely a letter for the priests or sisters in Namlea, just a page, which would state that the Church in Namlea would offer us protection during our visit there. The letter might be small, but to its recipients, its aura was big.

Our primary aim (well, mainly my primary aim) was to visit the units once again, especially the units IV, XIV and XV where I had stayed and with which I was familiar. Even though there were still some of my friends living there, it did not enter my head to stay in one of the houses in the units. Particularly as I was coming with a white-skinned person who could barely speak any Indonesian and was carrying cameras, recording equipment, notebooks and pens! I thought this would only attract attention, which, if news spread, could easily turn into suspicion. On top of that, I remembered that in Savanajaya Village (which used to be Unit IV Savanajaya) there were some former political prisoners living there who had previously been informers. This included Masri, Kartijo and his wife, (not their real names) and one or two others.

The Purgatory Island of Buru

* * *

To cut a long story short, without any bureaucratic ado, unlike the unusual situation in Indonesia when there are any dealings involving paper, we received a letter of protection. It was not as magically powerful as the legendary Kalimasada letter of course, but was probably just as prestigious as an ambassador's letter of credence. To us, the letter felt like an amulet. The other amulets we were carrying were a few copies of a novel written by the Dutch writer Beb Vuyk who once lived in Namlea. Who knows, maybe the magic of these amulets would be like a king's regalia that we would use every now and then, when necessary? Beb Vuyk and her book could be used as an alibi if there were people overly curious as to why we were travelling around Buru. It was the same when I first re-entered Indonesia from Holland. I stopped by at Penyengat Island in Riau. There I visited the ruins and the graves of the Malay kings of Riau-Johor, especially the grave of Raja Ali Haji, the famous author of the poetic Malay work *Gurindam Dua Belas*.

Monsignor Sol gave us a piece of advice, namely not to say that we were journalists, but tourists. Even though that was actually rather odd – coming all that way from Holland, why were we not travelling somewhere like Lake Toba but rather to Buru island with its black history? The black marker-stones, like ancient inscriptions of the time of New Order 'slavery' in Buru, were still there in Namlea and at the units. It is clear that apart from being objects of big news (and therefore sensitive to army ears), their presence meant they were certainly not tourist objects! Especially when you think that tourism is limited to beautiful scenery, ancient temples, objects of refinement, exotic cultures and so on. But mindful of Monsignor Sol's advice, I was now wary of us wandering around carrying cameras and recording equipment. However, like soldiers marching off to war, we had to carry our weapons. Whether we would use them later would depend on the situation we found. We did decide, most reluctantly, to leave behind the big video camera – which later I deeply regretted. Firstly, so as not to attract too much suspicion, and secondly so as not to create a distance between me and my friends still living in the units.

* * *

In actual fact, you can also travel from Ambon to Namlea by plane, a Cessna 212, but because there are so few passengers, the schedule is unreliable. Even if it had been reliable, I preferred to travel by sea. Firstly, because this was not so far from my experience in the early 1970s when I was taken as a political prisoner from Tanjung Priok in Jakarta to Namlea; secondly, I could enjoy the view of the sea and the experience of being among all the other passengers on the ferry; and thirdly because the two of us were tourists, but tourists with thin wallets.

We got to Galala harbour in Ambon in the evening, where the Ambon-Namlea ferry departed from, and departed the following morning at about seven in the morning. The route is covered by two ferries, Kerapu I and Kerapu II, departing on alternate days. The ticket cost Rp 9,600 plus another Rp 4,000 to hire a mattress. What is called a 'mattress' is actually a wide wooden platform, bunks, covered with plastic the thickness of a tarpaulin, with each person getting a space of around 50 x 200 cm, side by side. On top of this, each passenger had to pay the harbour toll of Rp 200. If you wanted to sleep in a cabin (200 x 300 cm) then you did not have to pay for the 'mattress'. You paid Rp 40,000 for the cabin. There were four cabins for the crew, which they rented out to passengers. Each cabin had one set of bunks that had real kapok mattresses and pillows.

It was crowded and noisy on the ferry. Most of the passengers were traders or farmers (transmigrants), a few looked like civil servants, and there were passengers who were going on to other islands. The traders and the farmers carried all kinds of stuff from Ambon; also produce, livestock and forest products (including live parrots) from Buru. Just before the ferry departed, the atmosphere was chaotic, with all the food sellers yelling along with those selling cigarettes, drinks and fruit. The sellers were very young kids, teenagers and young women. A beer-bottleful of eucalyptus oil cost Rp 13,000, a small bottle of drinking water cost Rp 1,500, boiled eggs were Rp 1,500 for two, and salak fruit cost Rp 500 each. When the ferry was rocked by the sea and all the passengers were lying down, from my sleeping place I could smell an incredible mixture of aromas: durian, eucalyptus, smelly clothes, stinking toilets, and the acrid smell of sweat.

'Ambon is the hottest island!' the words of the taxi driver earlier rang in my ears. There was pride in his voice to say that Ambon was more something than anywhere else. But I remembered the Island of Buru years ago during the dry season when it was between 34-36 degrees Celsius. One stroke of the hoe was not enough to even crack the earth. Instead, it made a loud clang like two pieces of metal hitting each other, and sent a kind of electric shock from the fist right up to the arm.

* * *

The Kerapu II ferry entered Kayeki Bay at six in the morning. I woke up Willy. She quickly grabbed her camera. She focused on the bustle of the passengers, the sunrise, the brown, dry eucalyptus-covered hills behind Namlea. The shining mosque dome flashed beside the shore. I had seen that mosque for the first time when I arrived on the *MV Tokala* – the ship commissioned by the army to carry 850 prisoners – when I arrived on August 12, 1971. Back then, near the mosque there was a food stall selling Javanese food, its wooden walls painted green, reminding me of the food stall that sold satay on Semarang in front of the Sobokarti building where wayang orang was performed.

It was at that food stall that my closest friend, Heru, had bought some palm sugar and Bugis tobacco, using the 150 rupiah I had in my pocket – which was in the last food parcel I received at Tangerang prison from my family. Across from that food stall was the office of the local official, the *camat*, which was next door to the office of the headquarters of the Command for the Rehabilitation Camp of Buru. They were the only buildings with wooden walls and zinc roofs. The local people's houses here and there had walls made of coconut palm fronds and the roofs were made of sago leaves. Behind the houses of the locals and the port was the Namlea market, where the main article of trade was sago. Back then, money was not very important for trading because most buying and selling was still done by barter.

In front of the offices ran a long road, the main artery of Namlea. It was a dirt road paved with coral, and went past the Catholic presbytery and church all the way to the village of Jiku Kecil. That was where the transit unit for political prisoners was, before they were herded to go to their respective units. Later on, the transit unit was used as a camp within the camp, to inflict severe punishment on prisoners who had disobeyed the rules. As a punishment unit, it became known as the Jiku Kecil Unit. Even today, that name still gives me shivers, just as the name 'Nusakambangan' used to do in my imagination when I was a boy. That was the island where 'evil people' were exiled, including my uncle who had become an 'evil person' to the colonial Dutch East Indies government for printing and distributing counterfeit money. The island was also, in Javanese lore, the last resting place of the spirits who guarded the magical Wijayakusuma flower, the emblem of the kings of Yogyakarta and Solo.

* * *

It was with these images in my mind that I disembarked from the Kerapu II ferry. I led the tourist Willy van Rooijen to the presbytery to have an audience with the Namlea priest, to find a hotel and then to go and see some of the units where there were still former prisoners. I was carrying my knapsack, ready to walk as I had done twenty years before. The difference was that now I was not carrying a rolled-up mat and pillow, the ration given to every prisoner when the *Tokala* was still at sea between Jakarta and Namlea. My knapsack was also now Italian-made, not the handmade gunnysack one made in Tangerang prison.

Whatever I had imagined turned out to be different in reality. The old port, which had received 11,948 prisoners over the years 1969-76 was over to the right. All that remained of it were a few black poles which were bathed in the morning mist and rocked by the waves as though being patted to tell their story about the thousands of events they had witnessed.

Namlea now was not the Namlea of twenty years ago. The military headquarters had moved to Mako, a market and fish market had been built behind the house where Beb Vuyk had lived, all the roads and alleyways were now asphalted. There was not a thatched house to be seen among the TV antennae, the parabolas, the hotels and banks.

The Kerapa II laid anchor and was tethered at Namlea port. The harbour was small but wide, clean and looked brand new. The guard boxes at the gate seemed to be empty. I could not see a single person in a soldier's uniform. Nor on the ferry. There had been four or five people wearing uniforms on the ferry, but these had been the crew and immigration officials. There had also been a few young men of sturdy build and with crew cuts. Probably they were Intelligence. But did I have to worry about 'possibilities'? Wasn't I aware that what I was doing was also toying with danger? But then again maybe they were just ordinary young people who had missed out on being accepted as military trainees. I remembered my conversation with a village boy in Walgan Baru more than 20 years ago in the work fields of Unit XV Indrapura. His name was Jagad and his ambition was to be a prison guard, because 'prison guards have power over the prisoners'. One of those young men on the ferry who looked like Intelligence had approached me and asked a few questions. He tried to find out who the 'white woman' was who was 'sleeping with me' in Mualim's cabin.

'Does Missus have a husband?' he asked. 'What work does she do?'

'Oh, I'm sorry!' I replied. 'I could tell you her name. But I don't have the right to tell you anything more about her. You must ask her yourself. It is better for her, and you too will get clearer information.'

He left me without another word. I followed him with my eyes as he went over and sat beside Willy who was reading *Index on Censorship*. But he just turned and glanced at her and was not brave enough to speak to her. I continued my conversation with Alexander Untailawan, a teacher at the Savio Catholic School in Namlea, who was travelling with his family to Seram. I learnt from him that Namlea now (1998) had two junior high schools (one state, one Catholic), one Senior Economy High School (Al Hilal) and two state high schools. In the 'units area', there was Mako state junior high school, the Savanajaya state junior high school, the Mako Indonesian Teachers Association [Persatuan Guru Republic Indonesia, PGRI] junior high school, the PGRI junior high school for Units XVII, Tsanawiyah Unit XVII, and Tsanawiyah Unit V, and an Institute for Village Security [Lembaga Keamanan Masyarakat Desa, LKMD] high school for Unit XVI that was being prepared to become a state-run school. I also learned from him that the teachers' salaries were often sent late, and that one month's salary – if they ever received it – lasted only ten days. I also heard from him how the teachers looked for other work on the side, and as a result the quality of their teaching declined. Another problem was the teaching material – the textbooks for the social sciences from Jakarta were obligatory, even though they were not relevant to the situation of students in the outer regions.

I couldn't see my crew-cut friend. Maybe he was off in some corner with his mobile phone (which I had noticed in his pocket), busily telephoning ahead to the military headquarters in Mako. I imagined a motorboat chasing us, and taking us back to Ambon!

Ah, stop worrying! I said to myself. Whatever happens, happens. If he is indeed from Intelligence, isn't that just part of his duty? To spy on people, ask them leading questions, report, arrest, frighten, and even maybe do a bit of torturing? Whatever happened later, let me face it later. Isn't that how it should be in response to the New Order regime? No point in diving overboard just because of the threat of 'maybe's'.

And in this frame of mind, I enjoyed the voyage of Kerapu II, rocked through the night by the waves of the Maluku Sea. There were flickerings of light on the horizon, from ships passing to and fro, the black of the sea with its white foam as the sea parted for Kerapu II, and the stars shone in the sky.

***

Namlea harbour is situated around three to four kilometres from the centre of the town. Passengers, motorbikes and cars fought for noise and the road. The people meeting the boat and the taxi drivers at the entrance to the port all contributed to the hectic atmosphere.

Someone of stocky build, a Javanese face, wearing a white shirt, long trousers and (even at that hour of the morning!) dark sunglasses, came up to us. For a second, my heart missed a beat. He was holding car keys in one hand, and the other hand was hidden in his trousers pocket. Was it a pistol? Or a mobile phone?

'Taxi, Pak?'

'Where is the presbytery, Wisma Kartini?' I replied with a question of my own, doing my best to give the impression, 'We are people of the Church'.

'It's a long way, Pak.'

A long way? Oh, come on, I said to myself. He just wants to charge for a long ride. The port was indeed not the old one, but I still thought that it could not be far from the centre of town. But I did not dare contradict him. I had to pretend that this was my first visit to Namlea.

'How many kilometres?' Willy asked.

'About four or five', he answered.

'How much for the taxi ride there?'

'Five thousand rupiah.'

'Five thousand!' Willy responded. But she got my signal and did not bargain.

We were already in the taxi, heading for Wisma Kartini. It felt like it was taking far too long to travel a distance of only five kilometres. Was this driver really a taxi driver or someone from Intelligence, I kept asking myself. We went past the old port. The Javanese food stall that used to be there twenty years ago had gone. The old storehouses used for the Buru Camp supplies and equipment where we had often had to work in the past were still there, intact.

The taxi now followed the main road. If we kept going straight, then turned left and went up the hill a bit, we would arrive at Jiku Kecil. That meant military headquarters.

Hey Hersri. Stop being afraid, I heard my alter ego say. Isn't this what you wanted – to go to Purgatory Island? The holy land? Bow your head so that this pilgrimage of yours is not in vain. Be resolute about what cleansing means, and where you want to go when this cleansing is done.

Yes, why was I worried, I asked myself? Hadn't I already experienced everything here on this island except death? Do you remember when Heru and Siregar tried to escape from the unit? And you were made to lie in the gutter, from sunset until midnight, under the threat of bayonets and machine-gun spray? Did you not then bravely stand right at the threshold of death, and keep your mouth closed?

Yes, that is right. My ego said to my alter ego. I am ready. Here I am, you guys! Arrest me, if you want to arrest me again. I am still handy with a hoe and sieve.

The 'Daihatsu' we were riding in was heading to Mako. It was an open van, the means of public transport. Was 'Mako' the same as it was during the 'prisoners' era? Situated on the banks of the Ari Apo River, between the large units of Unit I Wanapura and Unit II Wanareja, at one point the road crossed the river and headed towards the units further up. The function assigned to Mako now was the same as in the prisoner days before, namely as Command Headquarters (Markas Komando). The difference was only in the explanation. In the prisoner time, Mako had authority over the Buru 'Rehabilitation Post', whereas, in the transmigration period, it had authority over the territory that was called 'Military District'. The Commander's rank was the same. It was still Lieutenant Commander, as it had been in the prisoner time, and the same as regional military posts (Kodim) all over Indonesia.

When I heard the word 'Mako' still being used twenty years later, I got a shock. Especially because it turned out it was not the only term to be perpetuated. There were other terms, like 'unit', which had not been changed to 'village', *'corvée'* had not been changed to 'voluntary work' or *'gotong royong'* – as in the fascist-military Japanese occupation, even though where the terms had been changed it was still just euphemisms to cover hypocrisy.

To people who did not themselves directly experience the time twenty years previously, when those terms were first fashioned and applied, maybe they had no connotations whatsoever. Among the transmigrants who live around the Wai Apo valley, and even more so their children, who began to be brought to the Island of Buru in waves starting in 1979, they just accept the terms as something pre-existing, There was no 'what's in a name' to them. Maybe this was also true for those former prisoners who chose to become 'transmigrants'. They had melted into the expression 'poison disappears through familiarity'. Or, more than that, they were like fish in an aquarium, unaware of their environment, and even perhaps of their own existence.

It was different for me. I had been out of that aquarium for twenty years. So when I now looked at it once again, my gaze came from a point and attitude of distance. I not only personally experienced the time when those terms were first applied, but now I was feeling directly how those terms were 'being translated' into daily life, and this made questions arise in me. Is the continuation of these terms from the prisoners' era a sign that the breath of militarism has become ingrained in the subculture of society?

* * *

The Daihatsu we were riding in departed from the main stop, in front of the Namlea market. The yellow vans were all lined up waiting for passengers to go in various directions. There was a noisy clamour of the brokers shouting for passengers.

These hustlers, like public transport hustlers everywhere, were aggressive characters. Maybe this was the nature of their work, but it may also be because of the violence of life in this period of New Order bankruptcy of the late 1990s. In this world of brokers and hustlers, the philosophy of 'free-for-all liberalism' is brazen. They fight with each other in the volume and shrillness of their voices, yelling their routes. From the nearest: Namlea-Dermaga (four kilometres), to the more distant and the furthest, Namlea-Mako (45 kilometres), Namlea-Tifu and Namlea-Wai Nébé (68 kilometres). They compete for passengers. Willy and I fought for a place to sit. There were fifteen people, including the driver and the conductor, all crammed into the Daihatsu. Three in the front, and twelve in the back. Six on one side, and five on the other. The conductor in front of the door.

There were three young men of high-school age, dressed in neat, clean town clothes. But they seemed to be shy and would just steal glances at us. I did not know what they were thinking about Willy. I didn't really pay much attention. But I did feel it when they stole glances at me. It felt as though I was under a spotlight. Did I look so strange? Was it my glasses? My shoes? Or was it my sweat that stank of Dutch cheese?

* * *

It was quiet in the Daihatsu. The passengers made no noise. It was as though everyone was pressed by their own private unuttered questions. Only the driver kept on doing his work driving the rumbling van. I felt confused. According to our scenario, I was the guide of a white tourist who couldn't speak 'the lingo'. Communication between the two of us could be any language except Indonesian. But if they heard us speaking in a foreign language, I thought, then this distance between us and them that was like silence would become even worse. That would be bad for them and us. On our side, we would look even more like white lambs in the middle of a pen of black goats. On their side, it would only increase their curiosity about us. That feeling, especially if combined with a sense of envy, can have bad consequences. In Javanese, we have a saying, *sadawa-dawané lurung, isih luwih dawa gurung*, however long the road, the windpipe is longer still. Or *sejengkal jadi sehasta*, a span of the hand becomes a cubit, as the Malay saying goes. In other words, stories get embellished in the telling. They become exaggerated and distorted as they are spread, and this story could be spread to the ears of the Military Command, back there on the banks of the Wai Apo River.

While I busied myself with my silence, suddenly I heard Willy's voice break the ice.

'Where are you going to, Pak?'

She was talking to a thin man sitting to her left. He looked to me as though he was more than sixty. He had a cloth covering on his head, and his mouth was red from chewing betel. He had a boy aged about seven on his lap. Probably his grandson, I thought. He is a Buru native, I thought. He reminded me of the head of the community of Walgan

Baru near my unit, Unit XV Indrapura. He had been already humped with age and poverty, but had a pretty young wife, which made him the envy of the prisoners.

'Oh, you can speak Indonesian!', some of the passengers immediately responded. The three young men whispered to each other. Their expressions softened.

'Just a little', Willy said.

I heard them then chatting about various things. The town of Namlea which was so busy now, with its shops all full of different goods which were too expensive for the local people. The amount of pension a junior high-school teacher earned (he used to be a teacher in a Christian junior high school) which was not enough to support a family. The number of foreign-owned timber mills in the interior. There were two national logging companies operating there, PT Jayanti and PT Gema Sanubari. Lake Rana, which is an interesting place to visit not only for the beautiful view, but also because the inhabitants there have fair skin.

'I live there myself. My wife has fair skin. Just like you, Madam', he said with pride.

How could there be white-skinned people there?

'Can you get to Rana by motorised transport?' I interrupted.

'Yes, you can!' answered a man sitting in the corner. He was at least as thin as Mr Retired- Junior-High-School-Teacher. His face and skin were wrinkled, blackened by the sun. His clothes, hair and moustache were tangled. His eyes were slightly slanted, and flashed resilience to his precarious life.

'Yes you can', he went on. 'But not directly, Pak. The public transport goes as far as Wai Nébé, then you have to charter transport to Rana.'

'Can you charter there?' Willy asked.

'Yes, Madam', Mr Retired Teacher replied. 'There are many Daihatsus at Wai Nébé. Then there are also the company drivers who will take you for a price.'

'And where are you from, Pak?' the man in the corner asked me.

'From Yogya', I said.

'Yogya!' His eyes brightened. 'I'm from Yogya too!' he said, swapping places with another passenger.

I did not believe he was from Yogyakarta. I thought he was of Chinese-Buton origin, and probably working in sago or eucalyptus. Just show me someone from Yogyakarta who would want to go far away to work, as far as this arid land of the Island of Buru? Watch out, Hersri! Maybe this is a trap, I warned myself.

* * *

I was suddenly reminded of an experience from the mid-1950s when I was living at the village of Ngalihan in Karangmaja, in the regency of Playen. It was one of the poorest villages in the area of Gunung Kidul, Yogyakarta. The village of Ngalihan, apart from being the poorest village, was at the time just recovering from a plague of poisonous snakes and an infestation of huge rats. Because food was so scarce, and the rampaging rats so prevalent, it was not only the crops that were devoured by the rats. They also attacked animals, babies and even adults. Many people wrapped their feet up in anything they could find at night. But even with these conditions, the people were resigned. They believed that the rats were not just rats. They were the army of the Queen of the South Sea that comes and goes in waves, following the tides.

One day I was involved in a conversation with a village head.

'Does the village head here get a ricefield allotment for his position or not?' I asked.

'Of course, he does', he answered, indicating the land around him.

We were standing in front of a house, or more precisely in front of a bamboo-walled shack with a root of thatched palm fronds. Inside the house, there were no walls of any kind. It was just one big room with a sleeping platform made of banana wood on one side, wide enough to sleep five or six. There, the village head, his wife, his older child aged about five and the little one who was still nursing slept, together with my friend and me. In the corner, there was a clay pot for water. In the other corner, there was a homemade earthen cooking oven with three openings. At night, a female goat was tethered inside to a pole of the house, at the foot of the bed. Her two kids were inside but untethered. The house had no bathroom or toilet. We bathed in the underground river that had beautiful clear, cool water, but by heavens, it was far away! If we went there to bathe, leaving at 3:30 pm in the afternoon, we would not get back home again until at least 6.30 pm in the evening.

The earth around the house was hard and full of stones. Around the village head's house, you could see only hills. The name of the area – Gunung Kidul, means southern hills, but it is also called Gunung Sewu – a thousand hills, and you could see why. The hills were not only arid but also weathered by time, so all you could see were huge protruding stones.

'How many hectares is your allotment, Oak?' I asked the village head.

'Oh, you can't measure it. How can hill-people do the measuring? But there are nine hills. Then beyond that are two hills that we own ourselves, he said, pointing them out.

'So, how many quintals [a measure of 100 kilograms] of corn and sweet potato can you produce?'

'Quintal?' he said incredulously. 'I get just two baskets full!'

I was speechless for a moment. I recalled the message on the radio program 'Chatting with Pak Besut', which encouraged people to join the transmigration program.

'Why don't you transmigrate to Lampung?' I asked him.

'Why don't I transmigrate to Lampung?' he repeated my question back to me. 'Yes, people say that Lampung is prosperous. But that is just what people say. But we have no idea what is it really like. But yes, even if the land there is really fertile, is it going to stay like that? If you want to eat, you have to work. That's right, isn't it? And it is the same here. As long as we want to work, we can eat. So there you have it. Why go so far away just to do the same thing? And after all, our ancestors are all buried here. Why go? No. I choose to stay here. As the Javanese saying goes, whether we eat or not, the important thing is to be together.'

Yes, that saying, *mangan ora mangan waton ngumpul*. That is the people of Yogyakarta's motto about life. The first priority is to be together, and only after that, other things, including food and even death. Like the boasting phrase we so often hear in Javanese shadow-puppet performances or *ketoprak*: '*mati bareng dak-lakoni*' – I'm even prepared to die together.

* * *

'I am a transmigrant from Yogya, Pak' the dark-skinned man with the slanted eyes said, waking me from my reverie.

'Really?' I said, 'And how long have you been here?'

'Twenty-six years'.

'Twenty-six years? But I thought that 26 years ago there were not any transmigrants here yet, let alone from Yogya.'

'I was a special class of transmigrant, Pak'.

'Special? What do you mean …?'

'Special, that's all.' He cut me off before I could finish my question. Of course, I knew exactly what he meant. But it was not necessary to state it. Now I did not need to doubt his words. I said to myself. I was even secretly elated. Here, quite by chance, at the very beginning of my trip, I had met up with a 'comrade'. But even so, I must not be naive. Who knows, maybe his 'confession' was just a step towards further play? I had come with a European tourist. And that tourist must have a thick wallet. Even worse, he might be one of the 'cockroach' former prisoner informers. I had not forgotten, and will probably never forget, the names of some of the informers in Savanajaya Village.

'Where in Yogya are you from?' he asked, his opening move.

'Panembahan. The kampung beside the kraton.'

'Oh yes, I know. My football club was also from inside the kraton walls, NKB (Ngudi Kawarasaning Badan).'

'Really? Who was their goalkeeper?' I asked, as my turn to test.

'Unang, wasn't it?' he replied. 'He was actually good at playing forward, but they had a lot of forwards, while good goalkeepers are hard to find. P. Unang S. He was a poet for the daily *Harian Nasional*'s weekly supplement *Remadja Nasional*.'

He was right. I knew that for a fact because my house and the house where the person he called P. Unang S. lived were across from each other. Apart from that, I had been on the editorial committee of *Remadja Nasional*.

He and I were both selected as players for PSIM-B (Persatuan Sepak Bola Indonesia Maratam). Unang was the keeper, I was right wing.

'Who played right wing in the PSIM A team?' I asked, still testing.

'Amir. He was from HW (Hisbul Waton), the Kauman team. He ran as fast as a deer. His passes were long and powerful. But he was not as good as the right wing of the team two before his. No-one has ever been as good … you know … Karto Iwak!'

I laughed.

'What are you laughing about?' Willy asked.

'He's talking about a soccer player from Yogya, a right wing', I said. 'He was actually from West Java, and was famous in the period before the war. His name was actually Kartawa. But people in Yogya don't know how to pronounce the open 'a'. They say 'karto', not 'karta'. And the Javanese language has no single-syllable words, except for interjections, so the 'wa' in his name had no resonance to them. So, this is how it turned into '*iwak*' which actually is Javanese for 'fish'. So his name became Karto Iwak which, if it were Dutch, would be 'Meneer Karto de Vis'.

When the other passengers heard my explanation, they all laughed and smiled. I myself felt calmer. Maybe I still looked strange to them. Because of the clothes I was wearing, the smell of my sweat, and the European woman with the blonde hair who I had 'along with me'. But at least I did not look like a journalist, more like a person skilled at bringing things together in clever ways, *othak-athik-mathuk* as Javanese say. Javanese are incredibly clever at this simplistic 'science' of word-play. There are many pearls of wisdom that are conveyed in this way.

'Where are you getting off?' Willy asked the dark-skinned man.

'At Savanajaya. And you?'

'Also Savanajaya.'

'Do you have family there, or friends, or …?'

'Oh we are just doing the rounds', I said. 'We hear that Savanajaya is the oldest transmigration village on Buru. And people say that it is very prosperous these days. Namlea is really crowded. There's the market, and shops selling all kinds of stuff. No different from Ambon.'

'Where do we get off?' Willy asked.

'Get off with me', he replied. 'At the first bend, we enter the village. My house is just a few steps from there. Please call in. If you want to do the rounds, my son Heru can take you.'

'That is very kind. And what is your name?'

'Purwadi.'

Purwadi! Once again I felt my heart leap with joy. I was grateful for these things that were happening by chance. But what was clear was that chance or not, my 'pilgrimage' was going to be smoother. This was definitely the Purwadi from Savanajaya. He had been in Unit XVI Indrakarya, the unit where the majority of prisoners came from West Java.

From 1972, family groups of Javanese prisoners had been brought in batches to Buru. Purwadi had been one of those who had 'won the lottery'. That is what we called it when prisoners had their wives and children follow them to be 'socialised', as the regime called it, in Savanajaya Village.

Purwadi had been 'released' from Unit XVI and moved to be with his family who had been 'socialised' in Unit IV Savanajaya. About a year prior to this, Unit IV Savanajaya had been emptied of prisoners who were shifted to some of the upper units, and Unit IV Savanajaya was refurbished to be the first prisoner village, using the same name, Savanajaya. The roads were widened from six metres to eight and given fancy names, using the names of heroes, plants and flowers.

The Wai Bini dam was fortified, and the area around it was planted to make a park. The place where the unit made salt near the Sanleko beach was demolished to make a recreation area that was given a fancy English name: Sanleko beach. Needless to say, all this was just face paint, because along with the first group of prisoners' families came a contingent of Indonesian and foreign journalists, as well as visitors from international humanitarian organisations.

Every prisoner who was 'socialised' and grouped with his family was given one three-roomed house with wooden walls, a zinc roof, and an earthen floor; one hectare of wet ricefield and half a hectare of planting land. When the village of Savanajaya was built and the first and second groups of families arrived, I worked as the Coordinator of the Work Unit for Unit XIV Bantalareja, the neighbouring unit to Savanajaya.

Actually, Savanajaya Village was built with labour from all the units. But as far as supplying labour, the work of land clearing, making roads, road widening and upkeep, and even the first clearing of the land for wet ricefields (50 hectares), it was Unit XIV Bantalareja, as the unit that was closest, that bore the brunt of the work. A lot of our workforce and our work hours were occupied in preparing the village, and at the same time, our own unit work quota was non-negotiable. As a result, for a number of months, our work hours were extended from 6 pm at night until 6:30 pm because there were many things that had to be done outside of work hours.

As a result, there was a sharp division among the prisoners in Unit XIV Bantalareja. Or, more precisely, among a minority. That was between the group that was 'left' and those who were 'right' in their attitude towards the government's plan to develop the prisoners' village. The 'pro', meaning those who were prepared to do this, even to make a success of it, and the 'contra', meaning those who wanted it to fail, namely to sabotage it. But the majority, those usually called the 'masses', were like good lambs who always followed the shepherd's stick. Because of this, in this particular situation, and anywhere, the figure of the wise shepherd, who knows the seasons and the weather and is skilled at reading the rays of the lode-star, is always essential for the masses.

* * *

As the work coordinator, I faced a dilemma. There had already been many incidents of 'light' torture imposed on the prisoners, and many times the roll-call bell had loudly tolled its special summons. The prisoners would be gathered in the yard for a session of abuse and threats, along with accusations of sabotaging the government's 'socialisation' plans. But I could not just hurl all of that back, or all of us (except the authorities of course) would be dead. On the other hand, if I just took the abuse, only one group would be safe. Then again, perhaps both would be safe. But I knew that my gamble would not be without consequences. The consequence would be being branded as a 'moderate'.

One night, Samlawi (Where are you now, Bung Sam?) who was known as a champion from Banten, and who I had saved from punishment in the unit, both by the guards and by his fellow prisoners, for homosexual activity, sneaked into my mosquito net.

'Pak', he whispered. I could sense his heart beating fast. 'If you go out to the field to check on the work, do not go alone. And don't let me go far from you.'

'Why?'

'There's a plan to kill you. But don't worry. My friends and I will stay close to you. Don't forget!'

Then he quickly jumped down from my sleeping platform and snuck off into the dark, back to his barracks, or to contact his friends in other barracks. Strange. I did not feel afraid, not even for a moment. What I imagined instead was the painting by Juski Hakim, a painter from the Pelukis Rakyat (People's Artists) group: a painting of Bung Njoto dressed all in white, his clothes crumpled, his eyes still calm and clear, shining from behind his glasses. He was walking determinedly between two lines like a fence of bodyguards from Madura, dressed all in black: baggy long pants, collarless shirts open at the front, red and white striped T-shirts. (Who has that painting by Juski now?)

I could only give a deep sigh. My mind was full of pictures of the prisoners' wives and children. Whether they wanted it themselves or had been coerced and threatened, they were being gathered in the holding barracks in Jakarta and Surabaya, ready to be herded off to Buru. To be turned into political prisoners alongside their husbands. And so wasn't it right that we, who had already been in Buru for some years, now prepared a place of shelter and made it as nice as we could for them? Yes, as nice as possible, even in the worst possible situation!

And so, mindful of those wives and children, whether I had Sam's Banten fighter fences, I was determined to go on. I would accept the consequences. In powerlessness, I could only carry on what had to be carried on. I saw the Savanajaya Village as a *fait accompli* that had to be a success.

* * *

In 1974, for the umpteenth time, the military running the Buru rehabilitation camp unleashed mental terror on the political prisoners. This time, the terror was that all the units had to be 'shaken up', except for the Ancol Unit. The inmates were split up and redistributed. In short, there was a new grouping. There were also two new units created, Unit XIII Giripura and Unit XV Indrapura, which the authorities called Unit Ubinan (ubinan is a land measurement), and sometimes Unit Macan (tiger unit) or Unit Tokoh (leading figures unit). The inhabitants of Unit XIII were political bigshot tigers, while the inmates of Unit XIV were just ordinary tigers. Unit XIII housed many prominent people like Pramoedya Ananta Toer, Rivai Apin, Samanjaya, Tjo Tik Tjoen and Naibaho. But there was also the former primary-school teacher from Cawang Jakarta who, because of his electric shock torture and other torture, had gone crazy, and called himself 'Supardjo P.A.' meaning Supardjo Purworedo Asli (Supardjo from Purworejo) or Supardjo Pikiran Abnormal – Supardjo Crazy Head. Apart from him, I was moved too. I was chosen probably as a logical consequence of my former status in the Asia-Africa Writers Bureau.

I moved from Unit XIV Bantalareja to Unit XV Indrapura. I was freed of my responsibilities as work coordinator, and returned to being just a regular inmate of my new unit. The head of my new barracks was Ahmad Sonjaya, who came from Banten. He had been one of the barracks heads at Unit XVI Indrakarya, where one of the inmates was Purwadi, the man who was now sitting in front of me in the van on Buru twenty years later. Purwadi's wife and children had come to Buru, and because of this he had moved to live in Savanajaya Village, and his connections with his previous unit and with his barracks had remained. The same was true of the other prisoners from other units who had 'won the lottery' like Purwadi. About once a month or so, the barracks would send over a consignment carrying various produce of their own: corn, peanuts, soya beans, vegetable and other things.

* * *

Purwadi's house in Savanajaya Village back then had taken on an extra role. It became the place where Sonjaya's underlings could take a rest in the middle of the day when they returned from working in Sanleko, and secondly, it became part of the chain of secret connections with the Buru locals in the nearby kampung of Marloso (5 kilometres) and Jamlilo (11 kilometres). Not a secret chain in the sense of political affairs and organisation, but in matters of the stomach. The business of survival. Because of this, Purwadi's house became the terminal for the work of the 'ghost *corvée*' and in particular, the devil *corvée* under Ahmad Sonjaya.

As the name implies, the prisoners on this duty carried out their role as ghosts. The ghosts moved in the night, stealthily, using secret codes, going along secret paths to avoid the army patrol. They were like the ghosts who helped Bandung Bandawasa when he built the temple of Prambanan for Dewi Loro Jonggrang, or like the Sangkuriang ghosts when they dug the lake for Dyah Hyang Sumbi at Tangkuban Perahu. The difference was that Bandung Bandawasa and Sangkuriang's ghosts worked for their bosses and their sweethearts, whereas the political prisoner ghosts worked for their fellow prisoners. Those on ghost duty would carry all kinds of produce that were in big demand at the local markets (meaning the traders from Buton), namely sago, soya beans, peanuts, eggs and vegetables, especially green beans.

'Pull over!' Purwadi yelled to the driver. So, the people here stop public transport the same way as they do in Jakarta.

'This is where we get off', he said to us.

I saw him pay the conductor 1,000 rupiah. But Willy and I were asked to pay 1,500 each. We did not protest. Nor did Purwadi look surprised. After all, we were visitors, and one was a lady with white skin.

'That's my house!' Purwadi said, pointing out a house beside the road.

'Here? Didn't it used to be over there further, Pak?' I said

'That's right!' he said, surprised. 'How do you know?'

'He used to be from here', Willy interjected.

'Huh?' yelled Purwadi, stopping dead in his tracks …

Chapter 19

A BIRTHDAY PRESENT FOR MY DAUGHTER

The Javanese say that a child who learns to talk early will usually be slower to learn to walk. And the opposite – that a child who walks early will be slower in learning to speak.

And this is how it was with our daughter. When she was only six months old she could already babble away and say a few short words like *mama, oma, papa, opa, pipis, pup, ma-em* and so forth. But true enough, she did not walk unaided until after she was one, even though she was able to stand when she was only six months old and move around in her playpen. She was so cute. She would roll over from her back to her tummy, then stand up holding the bars of her playpen. She never learnt to crawl properly. This was certainly not because her mummy and daddy knew that as creatures who stand upright on two legs, crawling or creeping on this earth in front of other human beings is something to be frowned upon.

No, that was not the reason our daughter never learnt to crawl. It was because our house was too small. There was no open area large enough for a child to roam around freely. And the tiles on the tiny bit of open floor in our living room, which doubled as our dining room, were too cold for a small child still sensitive to all kinds of things from outside. We lived in a new residential area in Jakarta, in Tebet, which had formerly been an orchard area that was cleared for the Asian Games in 1962. The name of the area – Tebet – is Batawi dialect for

A Birthday Present for My Daughter

'*tebat*', which means 'swamp'. Needless to say, the area was damp and the air was always cold.

But our baby daughter, aged only a few months, could already associate things with sounds that represent them. She would repeat them every day, add new words, and store them all in her vocabulary and memory of the experience. We, her mummy and daddy, not only gained an understanding of a child's *tabula rasa*, but also trusted the Javanese saying, *janma tak kena kinira* – humans cannot be predicted – and that humans are not just adults, but also children, infants even. It is precisely their young age that makes them free of all kinds of self-interest.

So my wife and I together took steps to create a world of symbols, of things, around our daughter. Simple things, of course. In her playpen and on the narrow strip of the floor we would place a few toys, but also pencils or coloured chalk and paper. We closed off the garage that we used for drying the washing and for keeping our seven cats, and I painted it a pale grey. My wife Jitske, who liked to paint, decorated it with a panorama. Trees, shelters, ricefields, mountains and birds flying in the sky, all painted in bright colours to show their simplified shapes. We left the bottom part of the wall empty for our daughter to scribble on, and left coloured chalk for her in a box in the corner.

Sometimes my wife, or I, or the two of us together would help our daughter recognise the drawings and write things. Beside the forms, we would put up sounds, the most common vowels and consonants. When she was only two, our daughter could already read forty two-syllable words; words like o-m-a; o-p-a; m-a-m-a; p-a-p-a; t-i-t-I; a-d-I; o-o-g; o-o-r; s-l-a-p.

One day, Julia came to visit us bringing a small book written by an American specialist of pre-school education. The writer believed that following the ancient theory of *'tabula rasa'*, a child of two was already able to have lessons about the alphabet. Julia and her husband Mas Aam had done this for their son, Adi. We had no doubt at all about what that American writer said, and we became more certain of our own conclusions which were a variant on the saying attributed to the Prophet about the strings of a lyre. The Prophet used the lyre as a metaphor for women, saying the lyre would sing any song depending on the fingers that touched the strings. We saw this as an apt metaphor for children.

* * *

Our daughter's birthday was in a week's time. It was her second birthday. That morning we all went out together taking the blue city bus with the number 91, direction Grogol. My wife was carrying our daughter and a bag full of books as she was going to the place where she worked, a Dutch school at Slipi. I got off in front of the Air Force Headquarters building across the road from the 'Hanuman' statue at Pancoran, Tebet, and changed to a bus heading for Blok M Kebayoran Baru. My wife and I had agreed to buy some Indonesian language books about learning the alphabet. I had the money, five thousand rupiah, in my shirt pocket.

When I got off the bus at the Blok M terminal, I walked over to Gunung Agung bookshop. The bookshop was on a corner of Jalan Panglima Polim which – unless I have lost my sense of direction – was to the south-east of the terminal. Across from the bookshop was a church with a wide yard shaded by some rain trees and bougainvillea. The sign said it was the Effata Church. Back then, the road was not packed with cars and motorbikes like it is today. There were still many becaks and bicycles, and lots of well-dressed people who chose to walk. Because of this, it was not so noisy and unbearably hot.

'Pak Hersri', I heard someone call from the churchyard.

I did not cross the road, but turned. Behind the low stone fence topped with iron grating was a man about my age running as fast as he could towards where I stood on the footpath. Inside the yard, under the shade of the bougainvillea, there was a bench and a round table. Ah, a corner to keep watch, I thought.

'It's Pak Hersri, right?' I heard from behind the fence as he greeted me. His round eyes had not changed. Only his expression was more restless. He looked thinner. His face was browned by the hot sun of Jakarta. His thin moustache was untidy.

'Bang Yasmin!' I said.

Yasmin Sudiro. He had been a cellmate of mine for months in Salemba, at first in F Block and then in I Block. I had been the person in charge of our 'food distribution' group then, and he had been the one who would divide up any food that was delivered to any of the seven people in our group. For the whole time that we had that group, he himself never once received any food parcel from his family. But he was skilled at making labels for the food-parcel containers out of coloured thread that he unravelled from all kinds of old rags. He was able to earn things from this from the other prisoners who ordered labels from him; palm sugar, tobacco, tea and sometimes even a clove cigarette. He made me a round label the size of the circumference of a bowl, with a picture of the profile of Gatutkaca, the hero of Pringgadani who is strong, resolute and reserved. It was a fabulous label.

We had been separated when my turn to go to Buru came before his. He had cried and hugged me tight when I said goodbye at the gate of Block I. We had been separated for a while at Buru when I was in Unit XIV Bantalareja and he was in Unit XVI Indrakarya. Later, for some reason we never knew, there had been a transfer of prisoners between the blocks. Some of the prisoners from Unit XIV were taken to Unit XVI, and the same number were sent the other way. Yasmin was one of those who was transferred to our unit.

When he came back from Buru, with the assistance of Domine M., a former political prisoner, he was given work at that church. Back then there were some charity foundations that were very active in assisting the political prisoners and their families. There were Muslim, Catholic and Protestant organisations as well as general humanitarian ones. At certain times, the foundations would announce workplace opportunities. It might be as a cook, a sweeper, a nightguard, a messenger of other kinds of 'low' jobs.

'And what about you, Bung Yusmin?'

'There are three of us taking turns working here as nightguards. Me, Panjul and Praptono. We all used to work felling sago at Wai Tui. It was only you, Pak Hersi, who did not join us', he said, laughing. I laughed too.

He was right. When Unit XIV Bantalareja was under the Unit Commander First Lieutenant Yusin Zainal who was known for his greed (but tell me, where is there a Unit Commander who is not greedy!) I was appointed as head of the sago-felling work team, which was made up of sixty people. That meant six people from each of the ten barracks were commissioned to work in the sago swamp, the total of sixty divided into twenty groups (which we called *kole*) of three workers each. Yusmin Sudiro, Suparno Panjul and Supraptono were one of those groups. Yusmin was a skilled sago-presser. Panjul and Partono were strong sago-fellers. Partono, in particular, was clever at guessing which sago tree was 'full' and ready to be felled. In our

A Birthday Present for My Daughter

first years at Buru, we would only fell trees that we thought would produce at least 30 tumang. If we thought the tree had less than that, we would leave it until it was more mature. The three of them were able to fell, scour and work on three-quarters of a sago tree five metres long in just one day.

When I was in Salemba, too, I had also shared the same cell block for some time with Panjul and Partono. The two of them were also clever with handicraft. Panjul could make pipes out of coconut shells. Partono could make acupuncture needles out of aluminium spoons. Yusmin, as I said above, was clever at making labels or weaving bags out of plastic. The three of them all came from Madiun, and were primary school or junior high-school drop-outs who had tried to make their way in the big city of Jakarta in the 1960s. They had worked at the pots and pans factory in Cawang, and became members of the union for workers of small industry and construction (SBIRBA, Serikat Buruh Industri Ringan dan Bangunan). They had been picked up during Operation Kalong in early 1966, accused of being members of a labour union that was recruited for the G30S at Lubang Buaya.

'How much do you earn a month?' I asked him.

'Fifteen thousand, Pak', he answered.

'Fifteen?' I said, in an angry tone. I could feel my throat constricting. So little, I thought to myself. At that time, the pretty Miss Fy was receiving a salary of forty thousand rupiah a month as a secretary in the editorial section of *Kompas*, and Bung Kastur Kr, who was administrative staff at our translator's bureau, Inkultra, received thirty thousand rupiah a month. The salary of a household servant in a middle-class home in Tebet was around three to three-and-a-half thousand rupiah a month.

'It's better than being unemployed', he answered, sensing my anger. 'And we also get a quota of rice. It's fine. As long as we get some rice, we're happy.'

'How many kilos of rice do you get a month?'

'Twenty-five. And many of the men working in the office don't pick up their quotas, so they give it to us.'

'Why don't they want it?'

'It smells musty, Pak. Why would they want it?'

I did not go to Gunung Agung bookshop. I got totally involved in retracing old footsteps and entering Bung Yasmun's new ones. It was around midday when we left the churchyard. I stopped by a telephone booth to call my wife. She would get extremely anxious if I was late home and did not tell her where I was. If I was late home, she would carry our daughter in a shawl and wait at the end of the alleyway where the van would stop. She would become anxious and start imagining the worst. Maybe I had been arrested again, or had been terrorised by someone who had done a hit and run?

Bung Ysumin and I walked to Kampung Pela where he lived with his wife. I stole a glance at his feet. He was wearing cheap plastic thongs like we used to wear on Buru. My eyes and heart looked closely and all spoke of the burden of poverty that hung about him, but I also heard his acceptance in facing that heavy burden. The five-thousand rupiah note in my shirt pocket began to trouble me. I suddenly felt embarrassed to go into the bookshop, let alone to spend a third of what Yusman earned in a month on a book. A birthday present for a two-year-old. But on the other hand, I was also embarrassed to meet a friend who shared the same fate and to act like some philanthropist.

I asked Bung Yusman to turn back and come with me into a shop. Not a bookshop, of course. With the five thousand rupiah I bought some things for him: a shirt, sandals, sugar, coffee, and cigarettes. The money left over I forced into his pocket. Yes. The feeling of pity of a person wanting to do good did indeed win out. It was the spirit of overflowing love for a fellow human, but probably devoid of any calculation of being of a similar class.

When I got home, I told my wife everything.

'Tomorrow go back to the church', she said, giving me two five-thousand rupiah notes.

'And look for a book?'

'No. Give this to your other two friends. What were their names?' My wife found it difficult to remember and pronounce Javanese names.

'And the book for our daughter's present?'

'I will make her a book myself. And you can make her a recording. You can sing and tell a story. After all, she will only go to sleep when you sing her a lullaby, and tell her stories of the mouse deer, Kancil.'

I was quiet. I looked at my wife's face. Her eyes were shining and clear. Sincere.

'That coconut shell pipe and the photos of Buru in the cupboard are my most precious gifts to her. Give them to her later on, when she is older …'

And I looked again into my wife's eyes. She was smiling. And I was the one who could not stop the tears streaming from my eyes.

ABOUT THE AUTHOR

Hersri Setiawan (1936) is a writer, journalist and translator. He studied in Yogyakarta at Gadjah Mada University and the Academy of Film and Dramatic Arts. As a student he became active in the arts and culture and in 1958 joined the left-wing cultural organisation LEKRA (Institute of People's Culture). Between 1961 and 1965, Hersri was Indonesia's permanent representative of the Asia-Africa Writers' Bureau in Colombo, Sri Lanka. Following the events of 1965, Hersri was detained without trial for nine years, seven of which were on the island of Buru. After his release, he continued writing about his own experiences and recording the oral histories of other former prisoners as well as exiled members of the Indonesian Left. Many of these writings have been published in Indonesian after the fall of the Suharto regime in 1998. Today, Hersri lives and works in Yogyakarta, Indonesia.

ABOUT THE TRANSLATOR

Jennifer Lindsay, an honorary Associate Professor in the School of Culture, History and Language at the Australian National University, has lived in Indonesia on and off for some thirty years. She now spends most of her time translating and divides her time between Indonesia and Australia.

ABOUT THE HERB FEITH TRANSLATION SERIES

The Herb Feith Translation Series publishes high-quality non-fiction manuscripts not previously available in English, which enhance scholarship and teaching about Indonesia. Published by the Herb Feith Foundation in conjunction with Monash University, the books can be purchased as paperbacks, and are also available online for free download. For more information and a list of titles please visit https://publishing.monash.edu/series/herb-feith.html.